Fodor's EXPLORING

costa rica

FODOR'S TRAVEL PUBLICATIONS

NEW YORK • TORONTO • LONDON • SYDNEY • AUCKLAND

WWW.FODORS.COM

Copyright © Automobile Association Developments Limited 2005, 2008 (registered office: Fanum House, Basing View, Basingstoke, Hampshire, RG21 4EA. Registered number: 1878835).

Published in the United States by Fodor's Travel, a division of Random House, Inc., and simultaneously in Canada by Random House of Canada Limited, Toronto. Published in the United Kingdom by AA Publishing.

Fodor's and Fodor's Exploring are registered trademarks of Random House, Inc.

ISBN: 978-1-4000-1862-8

Fifth Edition

Fodor's Exploring Costa Rica

Author: **Fiona Dunlop**
Revision Verifier: **Nicholas Gill**
Cartography: **The Automobile Association**
Revision Editor: **Apostrophe S Limited**
Cover Design: **Tigist Getachew, Fabrizio La Rocca**
Front Cover Silhouette: **Schafer & Hill/Stone/Getty Images**
Front Cover Top Photograph: **AA Photo Library**

A03259

Printed and bound in Italy by Printer Trento srl.
10 9 8 7 6 5 4 3 2

How to use this book

ORGANIZATION

Costa Rica Is, Costa Rica Was

Discusses aspects of life and culture in contemporary Costa Rica and explores significant periods in its history.

A–Z

Breaks down the country into regional chapters, and covers places to visit, including walks and drives. Within this section fall the Focus On articles, which consider a variety of subjects in greater detail.

Travel Facts

Contains the strictly practical information vital for a successful trip.

Hotels and Restaurants

Lists recommended establishments throughout Costa Rica, giving a brief summary of their attractions.

KEY TO ADMISSION CHARGES

Standard admission charges are categorized in this book as follows:

Inexpensive: Under $6
Moderate: $6–$12
Expensive: Over $12

ABOUT THE RATINGS

Most places described in this book have been given a separate rating. These are as follows:

▶▶▶   Do not miss

▶▶   Highly recommended

▶   Worth seeing

MAP REFERENCES

To help you locate a particular place on a map, every main entry in this book has been given a map reference, such as 176B3. The first number (176) indicates the page on which the map can be found, the letter (B) and the second number (3) pinpoint the square in which the main entry is located. The maps on the inside front cover and inside back cover are referred to as IFC and IBC respectively.

Contents

Fiona Dunlop has a taste for the tropics, especially for developing countries. Before her career in journalism she was involved in the worlds of fashion and art. For this guide Fiona braved the perils of jungle-driving, tropical torrents and active volcanoes to present an insight into Costa Rica's people, places and practicalities. Other books she has written in the AA Explorer series are *India*, *Vietnam*, *Mexico* and *Paris*.

Top left: Península de Osa
Top right: heliconia

My Costa Rica

As the light faded and the jungle chorus moved into gear, water started seeping into the van and the engine cut off. This was Costa Rica, in the depths of the Península de Osa; we'd tried to ford one river too many. Half an hour earlier, an uninspiring-looking man had appeared, wading through the river, machete tucked into his belt, cigarette stuck firmly to his bottom lip, hat low over his brow. Two Western women facing a Tico gold digger in the middle of nowhere... "You'll need a tractor," he stated laconically after surveying the van, which sat entrenched in the riverbed. He then wished us luck and strolled off. Meanwhile, unknown to us, our enterprising driver had borrowed a bicycle from a Guaymí Indian settlement and found just what was needed at a distant farm. Our trauma ended in the glare of tractor headlights as we bounced back onto the pot-holed road.

Such encounters with the unexpected are the norm in Costa Rica, but so is survival. Ticos—Costa Ricans—are always at the ready. Equally open are the expatriates involved in eco-tourism ventures, often motivated by idealism and a taste for tropical nature. Less clear cut is the nonchalant Talamancan style on the Caribbean coast. After a bridge collapsed in Puerto Viejo, nobody quite knew where, when or how the next bus would arrive... Meanwhile, my tight, Western-style schedule was shrieking, but Talamanca was not responding. The bus did eventually materialize, and I made it to my next appointment after a quick sprint down the beach to catch it.

Kayaking at sunset on mercurial Pacific waves, sleeping (or not) to the background booms of Volcán Arenal, diving under a waterfall in Corcovado after an insect-infested trek, being winched 36.5 vertiginous meters (120ft) onto a jungle observation platform, having the intricacies of rain forest ecosystems explained by a botanist, sharing a drink and tall stories with a San José con man, or *finally* spotting the elusive residential sloth of a town square: researching *Explorer Costa Rica* certainly kept all my senses alive.
So, buen viaje y pura vida!
Fiona Dunlop

Costa Rica Is

A biodiversity of inspiring richness is squeezed into this tiny country of 50,800sq km (19,600sq miles), offering an intoxicating cocktail of nature that has now been opened up to tourism. Volcanoes, rivers, rain forest, cloud forest, beaches and two oceans are all in the mix, with an often minimal infrastructure that makes access part of the adventure.

Costa Rica's top generator of foreign revenue is now tourism. But, fear not, the industry is still in its infancy. Travel to Costa Rica and you are offered the extremes, from cosseted guided tours and comfortable luxury hotels to treks through the wilds and beds in basic huts. According to the Department of Statistics at the Costa Rican Tourism Institute (ICT), nearly 1.7 million in 2005 to visit the birthplace of the term *ecotourism*, ready to bird-watch, wrestle with sailfish, snorkel around coral reefs, surf, trek up the cold slopes of Chirripó, pump adrenalin while whitewater rafting, watch a nesting turtle or slap mosquitoes in the jungles of the south. The one thing these diverse activities all have in common, which is essential to appreciate if you visit Costa Rica, is nature.

NATIONAL PARKS This farsighted nation first took formal measures to protect its natural assets in 1955,

when a 2km (1.2-mile) band around every volcanic crater was declared a national park. Foreigners have always played a significant role in Costa Rica's environmental issues (for better or worse). It was a Swedish naturalist who instigated the first nature reserve, at Cabo Blanco, in 1963, then an American biologist who lobbied for Tortuguero's turtle nesting grounds, in 1975. Today, Costa Rica's National Conservation Areas System (SINAC) covers more than 161 areas—national parks, reserves and refuges—comprising roughly 25.6 percent of the national territory.

However, in 1994, park entrance fees for foreigners were suddenly hiked from a ridiculously low 50 cents to an unrealistically high $13.50, so spotlighting the ecotourism issue in dramatic fashion. On the one hand, parks need to be protected from tourism damage and have their infrastructures improved; on the other, they need paying visitors. Balancing these conflicting demands, a compromise was reached: since May 2002 the entrance fee for all national parks was set, and remains, at between $4 and $10 for foreign visitors, depending on which park. Ticos pay $1 to $2.

RURAL PLEASURES Not all Costa Rica's delights lie within the boundaries of its protected areas. Oceans, beaches of white sand, bucolic valleys, open pastures, torrential rivers, tropical vegetation, wildlife and, not least, charming people, are the norm. Roads

Lower left and above: Exceptionally rich wildlife draws many visitors to Costa Rica—despite the tropical downpours. Right: Buggies are a fun option for those wishing to explore the rough backroads

may be appalling but small planes can be used. Add to these attractions a high consciousness of ecotourism issues reflected in carefully planned, small-scale lodges, private nature reserves and biological research stations, and you have a compelling mix. The only deterrent is cost. Many operators have used the eco-bandwagon to hike prices to unacceptable levels, with services that do not match, but the current surfeit of hotels and tour agencies should restore the balance.

WHERE TO GO Costa Rica's small size allows you to zigzag between beach, jungle and mountains, all in one day and despite the atrocious roads. Although it is targeted for increasing beach development, Guanacaste still offers the best in beach facilities as well as extensive parks and reserves. In contrast, the Caribbean coast has a low-key, laid-back atmosphere, boosted by an intriguing local culture—and frequent downpours.

Head north to witness Volcán Arenal spitting fire, experience cloud forests or take a boat trip along the Sarapiquí, then veer east to Tortuguero's Amazon-style waterways or fish at Barra del Colorado. Don't miss Costa Rica's most beautiful beaches at Manuel Antonio; to escape the crowds, go south to where Costa Rica's highest peaks loom and densest rain forests flourish. In this region, Dominical, the Península de Osa, and adjacent Golfo Dulce provide endless wildlife, rain forest and water-sports options through small enterprises whose owners' pioneering enthusiasm is perhaps the most promising sign for Costa Rica's future.

Elections are fiestas in Costa Rica, but political awareness is high, and so is pride in democratic and pacifist traditions. This has not, however, shielded the country from the economic ills of the rest of the world, nor can it prevent social tensions. Economic conditions attached to international loans also irritate the independent spirit of the Ticos, as Costa Ricans call themselves.

In 1949, Costa Rica became "the country with no army." Since the army was abolished, this has been the nation's hallmark, a tradition reinforced by Costa Rica's recurring role as mediator in Central American conflicts. International recognition of this came in 1987 when President Oscar Arias was presented with the Nobel Peace Prize. Yet no system is perfect. Socio-economic problems are mounting despite Costa Rica's moral stance on warfare.

❑ Costa Rica's relaxed attitude toward arms is best illustrated by a 1995 General Auditor's report. This revealed that more than 1,000 weapons, including a bazooka and four cannon, were missing, presumed stolen, from the National Arsenal and the Public Security Ministry. ❑

IDEALS AND REALITY The new constitution of 1949 abolished the army and aimed to eradicate police corruption by allowing senior officers four-year terms only. This move has produced short-term corruption among police chiefs. Nor is it true to say that Costa Rica is a country without arms. Khaki-clad *guardia civil* (police) manning road-blocks near the Panamanian and Nicaraguan borders brandish sub-machine guns, and armed civilian assaults from San José to Limón sporadically interrupt the tourists' idyll. Once a haven of peace and quiet, Costa Rica is now confronting the interlinked problems of arms and drug trafficking.

AUSTERITY After several decades of progress aided by loans from the World Bank, the Inter-American Development Bank and International Monetary Fund, often amounting to more than $350 million per year, Costa Rica experienced and has since recovered from a recession in the early 1990s. With an economy dependent primarily on aid from, and exports to, the United States, Costa Rica weathered the worldwide economic downturn of the late

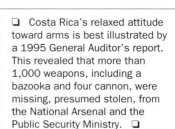

1990s. The Intel Corporation's decision to open a $500 million manufacturing facility in Costa Rica in 1997 lent the economy a huge boost instantly becoming the single most dominant element in the country's economic life. Aside from Intel, NAFTA and globalization in general have created diverse problems in Central America (less so in Costa Rica where tourism is strong), as traditional exports such as coffee, bananas, and pineapples have been in part replaced by textiles and other products as subject to projectionist measures in the US in spite of NAFTA. Global capital flows more freely into Costa Rica bringing greater opportunity, but also, potentially, more foreign control of resources. A proposed Central American Free Trade Agreement (CAFTA) came about in 2003 including five Central American countries. The issue has been met with wide scale protest across Central America, including Costa Rica, which is the last country yet to ratify.

NUMBERS One of Costa Rica's problems is its population. The increase from about 400,000 inhabitants, in the 1930s, to over 4.1 million in 2005 has created problems, from unemployment to financing the extensive welfare

Opposite top: election fever. Above: Oscar Arias receives his Nobel Peace Prize in 1987. Right: "Yanquis out of Iraq" demonstration in San José

system and dealing with squatters (who can claim land by proving they have farmed it). North Americans and Europeans pour in to retire or set up hotels and restaurants. A cheap workforce from Nicaragua makes law enforcement difficult, as many immigrant workers are undocumented. Yet Costa Rican tolerance prevails; in the

❏ Presidency runs in the family. Up to 1970, 75 percent of Costa Rica's presidents were descended from three families of original settlers. President José María Figueres (in office 1994–98) of the Partido de Liberación Nacional (PLN) is the son of Don Pepe, who ignited the 1948 Civil War, while his PUSC predecessor, Rafael Angel Calderón, is the son of Don Pepe's arch-rival. ❏

early 1990s thousands of Nicaraguans were given the right to free medical care and public schooling. Today this altruistic attitude is being tested. Although the official figures range from 130,000 to 225,000, some reports suggest that more than a million Nicaraguans now live in Costa Rica, most of them illegally. Thousands of Panamanians, Salvadorans and Colombians fleeing political or social problems have moved to Costa Rica in recent years. The country remains a beacon of stability and prosperity in Central America.

Predominantly of Spanish descent, the population of Costa Rica has been injected with numerous other nationalities over the years and encompasses three important groups: the Afro-Caribbeans, the Chinese and the indigenous people. This makes it difficult to define the "typical" Costa Rican character.

14

Tico, the self-appointed national nickname, derives from the Costa Rican habit of forming diminutives—a habit that, for example, transforms *momento* ("moment") into *momentico* ("little moment"). Ticos (or Ticas for women) are predominantly direct descendants of Spanish settlers, who first arrived in the 16th century but came in far greater numbers in the early 19th century to grow coffee on free land. *Mestizos* (people of mixed Spanish and Indian descent) are seen particularly in Guanacaste, while indigenous people remain virtually invisible in their reserves. Since the 1870s, Costa Rica has also absorbed Chinese, Italians, Afro-Caribbeans and smaller numbers of German, English, French and Lebanese traders. Today the population is diversifying yet again with a notable influx of *gringos* and *gringas* (foreigners, but especially

Anglo-Americans) following in the footsteps of the Quakers of Monteverde (see panel on page 77).

❏ Costa Rica's inhabitants have Central America's highest literacy rate (96 percent) and life expectancy (74.4 years for men, 79.8 for women). The official religion is Roman Catholicism; more than 76.3 percent of Ticos are Catholic. ❏

THE LIE OF THE LAND The Central Valley still holds some 60 percent of the estimated total population of over 4.1 million, with 36 percent living in San José's metropolitan sprawl. Move out to the edges of Costa Rica—to Guanacaste in the north, Limón in the east or to the southern zone—and you come to the least populated, most impoverished areas. Indian tribes are concentrated in often inaccessible mountain reserves, while in contrast the Afro-Caribbean and Chinese populations are highly visible, particularly in Limón. Guanacaste presents yet another picture, as many of the inhabitants are *mestizo* descendants of Chorotega Indians, with a more outgoing character and a history of close links to Nicaragua. In general, Ticos are friendly, courteous and often discreet,

with a sense of their distinctness from the rest of Latin America. Tolerance and fierce national pride are their overriding features.

JAMAICA'S LEGACY Before the 1880s, a small community of Afro-Caribbeans had for decades been fishing and turtle-hunting off the Talamanca coast, between seasonal work in Nicaragua or Panama (see pages 138–139). Then, suddenly, this population was boosted by 10,000 Jamaican workers brought in by Minor Keith to build the Atlantic Railway (see page 132). Many chose to settle in Costa Rica, working on the banana plantations or their own small farms but proudly maintaining their Jamaican English language, Protestantism and rich traditions. Until 1949 they had no rights, nor were they allowed outside their isolated coastal region, but today they are full Tico citizens, forming 3 percent of the population.

CHINESE Before Keith turned to the Caribbean for workers, he had tried out 1,000 Chinese, who, although "addicted to work," suffered greatly from the climate and tropical diseases. Despite this they soon began to run small grocery stores and restaurants, establish strong community groups, and sponsor the immigration of relatives from China. Some have intermarried with Ticos, but Chinese identity

remains strong, and solidarity is always a priority. Hundreds of Chinese restaurants and shops are scattered across the country.

INDIGENOUS GROUPS High in the Talamanca Mountains and deep in the jungle of the south are the last descendants of Costa Rica's original inhabitants, now numbering approximately 60,000 (see pages 158–159). Visitors who do not make a specific effort to visit their reserves could be quite unaware of the indigenous peoples' existence although ecotourism and its attendant cultural awareness has made visiting indigenous reserves quite popular, and, as a result, many groups are also reviving their craft-making talents as well as their traditional customs.

15

Indian, Spanish, Talamancan—some Costa Rican faces. The people of the Talamancan coast (right) are strongly Caribbean in spirit

Few Central or South American countries can rival Costa Rica for the sheer quantity and range of plants and animals found within its boundaries. For the visitor who is interested in wildlife, the relative ease with which many habitats can be explored is a wonderful bonus.

16

Sandwiched between Nicaragua to the north and Panama to the south, Costa Rica forms part of the land bridge between the Americas, and contains flora and fauna from both continents. By American standards it is a tiny country, an isthmus barely more than 145km (90 miles) wide in places and only 290km (180 miles) long. What it lacks in size, however, it more than makes up for in altitudinal range. Between the Pacific west coast and the Caribbean east coast, the land rises to a central spine more than 3,000m (9,800ft) high. This continental divide runs the length of the country.

PARADISE FOR NATURALISTS
Without its altitudinal range and the juxtaposition of two oceans, a tropical country the size of Costa Rica would have rather uniform vegetation. As it is, the country's altitude has had a profound influence on the climate and, in particular, the temperature and rainfall. This climatic variation ensures

that almost all types of tropical habitat exist within the country's borders, with the added advantage that many can be visited in a single day. From the coasts, with their mixture of sandy beaches, coral reefs, mangrove forests and dry tropical forests, the land rises through rain forests and cleared agricultural land to cloud forests, cloaked in mist for much of the day. At the highest altitudes there are even small areas of *paramo*, a kind of bleak plateau landscape associated with South America. The one habitat that you might expect at this latitude, and do not find, is true desert.

WEALTH OF WILDLIFE The diversity of Costa Rica's habitats is reflected in the wealth and range of its wildlife. Around 9,000 plant species (just under 5 percent of the total world plant list) have been found here, and a staggering 1,200 of these are orchids. Insect life abounds, ranging from army and leaf-cutter ants, mantids,

❑ Humming-birds are referred to collectively as *gurrion*. For certain species, hovering is essential since the nectar-producing flowers upon which they feed can be exploited only from the air. Many plants have these tiny birds as sole pollinators, and some have even evolved flower shapes to suit the bill shape of a particular species. Male humming-birds are often highly territorial and have feathers of bright hues. In some species, the plumage has a startling iridescence in certain lights. ❑

and katydids to stunning blue morpho butterflies and giant hawk moths. Tropical mammals such as sloths and monkeys are common and birdlife is prolific, with more than 800 species. Of these, 600 or so are resident, the rest migrating visitors. Like other Central American countries, Costa Rica is very important for migrant breeding birds from North America. Each autumn, countless millions head south for the winter, the vast majority following the course of the Central American isthmus. More than 50 species of humming-bird alone have been recorded in Costa Rica. Wherever you go, from urban gardens in San José to the cloud forests of Monteverde, you will come across these amazing birds, whose best-known trait is the ability to hover in mid-air (see box).

17

Watch for beetles bigger than small mammals—and for (clockwise from bottom left) the rufous-tailed humming-bird, processionary caterpillars, the cayman and the spider monkey

CORRIDORS FOR LIFE Having the right climate and terrain for tropical habitats and wildlife is not enough these days. Many other countries in the region have lost, or at least degraded, important areas for wildlife through commercial exploitation or simply the pressure of a growing human population. In this respect, Costa Rica has fared surprisingly well. Although it has experienced its fair share of forest clearance in lowland regions for agriculture and dwellings, and although logging and the persistent use of pesticides are still a problem, something like 12 percent of the total land area is

now set aside as national parks and 25.6 percent as protected areas of some sort. These areas are important in their own right, and a new awareness of the need to preserve land corridors between prime habitat sites is developing. This is essential for a genetic mix to occur, and perhaps more significantly because many of the resident tropical bird species are altitudinal migrants. They change altitude according to season and are reluctant to cross cleared land when they travel.

Paradoxes abound in this country, which is regarded as a pioneering environmental force in Latin America. Much of Costa Rica's natural forest has disappeared, and even the label "conservation" often conceals commercial aims. Yet most Ticos recognize that long-term prosperity lies in protecting the environment.

18

Few countries can claim such a high environmental consciousness as Costa Rica. No fewer than 450 environmental organizations keep their watchful eyes on both the public and private sectors, while the government itself preaches the merits of sustainable development—that is, investing in long-term, non-destructive projects that benefit the population. Private reserves, aimed at ecotourism or biological research, spring up yearly, national parks and reserves cover more than 25.6 percent of the territory and future projects include the *Paseo Pantera*, a protected corridor linking other protected areas throughout Central America. But the picture is not entirely rosy. Large companies, often multinationals, are carving up rain forest or dumping noxious chemicals, and buoyant property and tourist industries are spawning developments that violate conservation laws.

Pesticide spraying of bananas—a major environmental problem

BLACK SPOTS Since the 1950s forest cover has been reduced from more than 70 percent to about 23 percent of Costa Rica. Guanacaste, in the northwest, was one of the first regions to suffer when forest was cleared for cattle-raising on huge haciendas. Fast-growing grasses imported and planted to feed cattle turned out to be ecological opportunists, overwhelming the native flora and throwing the ecosystem out of balance. Environmental groups are also warily monitoring Guanacaste's hotel developments, such as the Papagayo mega-resort. The tropical rain forests of Sarapiquí and Osa have long been preferred by logging companies for their precious hardwoods, while much of Talamanca's lowland forest disappeared in the 20th century to make way for banana plantations.

❑ Apart from their ecological shortcomings (fertilizers, loss of topsoil leading to sedimentation in rivers and eventually coral reefs), monocultures such as cacao, bananas and the more recent oil palms are highly vulnerable to parasites. These have already destroyed the source of income of thousands of Talamancans who depended on cacao, and prompted United Fruit Company's transfer of operations from Talamanca to Osa in the 1930s. ❑

ABUSE Even when land is protected by government decree, its problems are far from over. Shortage of funds is a perennial difficulty that engenders massive abuse. Some

17 percent of national park land is still privately owned, rising to 46 percent at the popular Manuel Antonio Park, and the limited number of guards leaves space for poachers, illegal loggers and squatters.

Nor does Costa Rica's diminutive size help. A proposed road link between the Pacific and the Atlantic coasts would almost inevitably pass through a Talamancan indigenous reserve, a wild region also targeted by mining companies, a hydroelectric project and an oil pipeline.

Northern Costa Rica's landscapes show the ravages of logging. Meanwhile, sawmills flourish

HOPE FOR THE FUTURE Fortunately, environmental watchdogs raise the alarm when companies are found to contaminate rivers, when a hotel's waste treatment is inadequate, or when a foreign-owned paper-manufacturing giant proposes to build a chip mill and dock in an ecologically vulnerable zone. In 2000, locally organized environmental watchdog and indigenous groups went to court and successfully (if temporarily) put a halt to plans for new dams on the Sarapiqui River

and exploratory oil drilling off the Caribbean coast. The drilling ban was reaffirmed in 2002 on the federal level. Between Costa Rican laws and other vigilance, investors must watch their step—and, as a result, many choose to bypass Costa Rica for more malleable systems elsewhere.

Meanwhile, the country is seen as an asylum by idealists and those wanting to start afresh. The economy needs more than idealism, however. At Berlin's 1995 Climate Change Summit (the follow-up to Rio's Earth Summit in 1992), President Figueres and the USA proposed that industrialized countries should pay for their pollution by financing energy conversion projects (notably reafforestation) in developing countries. However, Costa Rica's pioneering voice went unheard and the proposal was shelved. The battle between short-term commercial interests and long-term survival is far from over.

Two of the world's most popular products, coffee and bananas, form the backbone of Costa Rica's economy, together representing more than 80 percent of the country's agricultural exports. Blanketing the slopes of the Central Valley are row upon row of lustrous green coffee bushes, while in the coastal lowlands the view is of plantations of banana palms.

For more than a century and a half, Costa Rican coffee has been recognized as among the finest in the world, but it is by no means a native Tico product. Arabica seeds were brought by the Spanish from Africa and the Middle East via Cuba in the early 1800s, when free land and seedlings were offered to anyone willing to cultivate the new plant. The natural nurturing qualities of the Central Valley's cool climate and fertile volcanic soil soon repaid the hard work. Coffee bushes bore fruit so easily that by the mid-1840s coffee had become the country's main export, transported on muleback to Puntarenas and then to Chile and Europe. This was the time of the rise of the coffee barons, a new class with a new prosperity. Then, in 1878, along came bananas.

> ❏ An English sea merchant, William Le Lacheur, was partly responsible for the meteoric rise of the coffee industry. In 1843 he docked at Puntarenas looking for a cargo to fill his empty ship on its return from North and Central America to England. That year's surplus coffee production soon filled his hold—but he had no money to pay for it. The trusting Ticos gave him credit, and two years later were repaid. From then on, they never looked back. Coffee was launched on the European market. ❏

NOT COMPLETELY BANANAS Although bananas overtook coffee in economic importance in the early 20th century and today account for more than twice as much revenue (one-third of total exports), the history and reality of their plantations is less glorious. It was the completion of the Atlantic Railway in 1890 (see page 132) and the founding of an American company, United Fruit, that propelled this fruit to importance in the Costa Rican economy.

The exploitation of immigrant workers and independent planters

Arabica coffee prefers rain and fertile volcanic soil and thrives at altitudes of 900 to 2,000m (3,000 to 6,500ft)

is well documented, and banana plantations continue to have a destructive effect on the environment, through pesticide spraying, soil erosion and the chemical-impregnated protective plastic bags that pollute rivers and land—a negative side effect that is not shared by "cleaner" coffee plantations. The living conditions of banana workers have improved—wages exceed the minimum legal amount by 25 percent, and they enjoy extensive social benefits—but they also suffer from pesticide poisoning.

After a brief dalliance with oil palm plantations on the Pacific coast, businesses such as the Standard Fruit Company, Chiquita and Dole are now expanding their banana plantations as well as controlling overseas shipment, marketing and pricing for the 57 percent of plantations owned by Ticos. Conservation groups, ever alert, have recently devised a label to identify banana plantations and companies that have cleaned up their act to meet certain social and environmental standards—it says "Rainforest Alliance Certified."

A CUP OF COSTA? Costa Rica's best coffee is said to be from the Central Valley, although Cartago, near San José and San Isidro in the Central Valley are strong regional contenders in the stakes. Ticos claim that of the world's 1,200 varieties of coffee bean, theirs make coffee that "tastes as it smells." One of the country's most beautiful sights occurs when plants are in bloom, producing a fragrant white haze (engagingly called "snow"). Today, planters are reverting to the former system of interspersing coffee bushes with taller plants for shade, often *poro* trees, whose deep roots prevent erosion and attract insects away from the plants.

Harvesting takes place from December to February, when the reddest berries are hand-picked, loaded into baskets and then into sacks, and taken to a receiver who pays the coffee pickers. The next stage is at a mill, where washing, sun-drying, filtering and separating are carried out before the final roasting. Decaffeinated coffee is processed in Germany, by steaming, although the best is low in caffeine already.

Plantains—the banana's useful cousin

21

Tico cuisine follows the contours and elevations of the country's varied terrain. From Pacific lobster to Monteverde cheese, Guanacaste tamales and Caribbean "rundown," the menu changes radically. But two dishes crop up again and again—casado and gallo pinto. Develop a taste for these and you won't go hungry.

Keeping the body firing on all cylinders is not a problem in Costa Rica. Roadside *sodas* (small family-run restaurants) abound, offering the full gamut of the day's sustenance, from breakfast through *bocas* or *bocadillos* (snacks and first courses), which accompany drinks, to the main meal. These simple eating places are the stalwarts of Tico rural society, but visitors seeking more sophisticated fare should head for luxury hotels, which usually take full advantage of the cornucopia of produce that Costa Rica's fertile valleys, pastures and oceans nurture.

RICE? BEANS? Apart from an enticing range of tropical fruit, vegetables and ultra-fresh seafood, Costa Rica offers endless variants on

Kitchens in sodas *may be basic, but the ingredients are always fresh*

❏ Typical Tico vegetables include: plantains, longer and thicker than bananas and only edible when cooked; yucca tubers, also known as cassava or manioc and used for centuries by the Indians; *palmito*, palm heart; and *chayote*, a pear-shaped vegetable whose taste resembles squash. ❏

the rice-and-beans theme, the staple diet of Latin America. The classic *casado* (literally meaning "married man") offers a perfect nutritional balance of rice, black beans, meat or fish, and carrot and cabbage salad, all topped with a fried plantain. A budget alternative on *soda* menus is *arroz con pollo* or *gambas* (fried rice with chicken or prawns). *Gallo pinto*, the substantial national breakfast, consists of rice and black beans seasoned with onions and peppers, accompanied by fried eggs and sour cream, and mopped up with a corn tortilla. Start the day with this and you will feel fit to climb the slopes of Chirripó.

Olla de carne, a beef stew or soup made with potatoes, carrots, *chayote* (vegetable pear), yucca and plantain, is sometimes on the menu, as is *sopa negra*, a reincarnation of black beans in soup form.

22

Rice fields near the Río Tempisque

SWEET TOOTH Ticos are renowned for their love of sugary drinks and dishes, a taste shared by the Afro-Caribbeans, who acquired numerous cake recipes from the English. *Tapa dulce*, a local brown sugar sold in solid form, sweetens *tres leches*, a Nicaraguan import consisting of a rich cake containing whipped cream, condensed milk and evaporated milk. Dieters should abstain, but need not despair—Ticos also whip up an excellent *ensalada de frutas* (fresh fruit salad) with seasonal tropical fruits. *Cajeta* (fudge) is ubiquitous, even better as *cajeta de coco* (coconut fudge), and in mountain regions, *natilla*, a bowl of thick sour cream, is the energy giver. Sugar is poured into *refrescos*, natural or bottled fruit drinks, while sugarcane is distilled into *guaro*, the national, potent alcoholic drink which will finish off any meal—and anyone.

23

Another filling soup is *sopa de mondongo*, which is made from tripe and vegetables. A common side dish is *patacones*, fried mashed plantains eaten with a liberal sprinkling of salt. First courses include delicious *ceviche*, raw fish marinated in lemon juice with parsley and onions. *Empanadas* are spicy meat pies.

CARIBBEAN GOODIES A distinctive, tasty cuisine has been developed by the Afro-Caribbeans, who over the centuries have combined typical Caribbean ingredients with elements reminiscent of their days of enslavement to the English. The main ingredient here is the coconut, its milk used to bind any number of ingredients, whether rice and beans or the popular *rondon*, literally "rundown," consisting of fish or meat with yams, plantains, breadfruit, peppers and spices. Grated coconut's flaky goodness is used in countless desserts and cakes. The spongy yellow fruit akee, a plant native to Africa and brought to the Caribbean by the English, is boiled to produce something akin to scrambled eggs, then sautéed with salted cod. *Patti* (similar to the Tico *empanada*), a spicy meat pie, resembles a large turnover.

Refrescos and ices cannot beat a fresh coconut

It is not just for its mountain pastures and political neutrality that Costa Rica is often called the Switzerland of Latin America. The lure of tax-free investment and the less-than-transparent banking systems have combined with Costa Rica's geographical position to attract financial dealers on all scales.

By the 1970s Costa Rica's capital, San José, claimed the highest concentration of foreigners in Central America after Panama. Pleasant living conditions and tolerance had for a long time attracted political refugees from more radical Latin American regimes. In addition to this, Costa Rican law permits foreign ownership of property with no restrictions, and, until the regulations were changed, rights to duty-free goods drew retired people from North America. Along with such respectable folk came shadier citizens, including drug-traffickers, who took advantage of Costa Rica's easy system and its private "offshore" banks.

STAGING POST Costa Rica's strategic position makes it a perfect staging post for drug consignments *en route* from Colombia to the United States or Europe. On the

The trade in Colombian cocaine (top) takes advantage of Costa Rica's liberal banking laws

Caribbean coast this has produced social problems and a proliferation of drug-related crimes. In fact, according to the Drug Control Police (*Tico Times*, April 2004), while land-based drug-trafficking through Costa Rica has actually declined in recent years, the amount staying in the country and offered for sale to Costa Ricans has increased, as has the abuse of marijuana, cocaine and ecstasy, which are plentiful and cheap.

A headline case in 2004 involved a San José based investment company called The Brothers Villalobos and its money exchange company, Ofinter, S.A. "The Brothers" offered annual returns to investors of 30 percent or more in the mid-1990's and hundreds of North Americans and Europeans living in Costa Rica bought into it. In 2002, the assets were frozen by the government in a dispute over unpaid taxes and drug connections, which proved true. One of the brothers was eventually jailed for 2 years and the other disappeared and was never found, along with the expat's investments.

24

Costa
Rica Was

The distant past of Costa Rica is still a matter of conjecture, but a picture is gradually emerging of agrarian societies steeped in ritual, who developed highly sophisticated craft techniques. Their strategic geographical location on the land bridge between Mesoamerica and South America was to shape their culture.

26

The mysteries of Costa Rica's pre-Columbian inhabitants have been significantly researched since the late 20th century, although some excavations started in 1861. This lack of research, combined with the absence of reliable records by *conquistadores*, means that the picture is nebulous. Even the names of the original tribes have been lost, replaced by Spanish identifications that probably derived from the names of local *caciques* (chiefs). As a result, archeologists resort to a geographical definition, breaking the country down into three main indigenous regions: Greater Nicoya (Guanacaste), the Atlantic watershed (Talamanca), and the southern Pacific zone (Térraba and Península de Osa). Each developed its own craft forms and trade contacts, in effect making pre-Columbian Costa Rica a cultural crossroads for the "high" civilizations of Mesoamerica to the north and the Andes to the south.

> ❏ Mesoamerica was a vast multicultural zone extending from central Mexico down through Guatemala, Belize, western Honduras and El Salvador. Over the centuries, this area was home to major civilizations such as the Olmecs, Teotihuacan, Zapotecs, Mayas and Aztecs. ❏

Nicoya. All peoples continued to gather wild fruits, fish and hunt monkeys, tapirs and armadillos with bows and arrows. By AD500, ranked societies had become established, with political and religious leaders in each community.

EARLY DAYS
Nomadic inhabitants roamed the region from about 20,000BC, but not until around 1000BC did small settlements take shape, marked by agriculture and the creation of ceramic pots. Root crops and *pejibaye* (palm fruit) were cultivated, later joined by corn and cacao (cocoa), both Mesoamerican imports. Cocoa beans were also used as currency among the Indians of

GROWING SOPHISTICATION Jade-carving skills can be traced back to around 500BC. By AD700, jade was replaced for mortuary work by gold. The origins of metal-lurgy are typical of Costa Rica's frontier role: gold techniques came from South America and copper techniques from Mesoamerica, together leading to the creation of the alloy tumbaga. The Diquís of the southern Pacific zone became masters of metalcraft, producing thousands of zoomorphic ornaments from gold nuggets found in local rivers. More perplexing is the source of jade: none has ever been found in Costa Rica, yet Greater Nicoya and the Atlantic watershed have yielded thousands of exquisitely carved pieces. This stone could have been brought directly by the Olmecs or by the Mayas, or traded through intermediaries. Olmec influence has also been traced in "baby-face" sculptures that possibly followed the same route.

Pre-Columbian artefacts can be seen in San José's National and Jade museums

LIFESTYLES There were two main linguistic groups: Nahuat was spoken by the Chorotegas of Guanacaste, who are thought to have emigrated around AD900 from southern Mexico, while the older Chibcha language was shared by ethnic groups of southern Costa Rica, Panama and Colombia. These were not peace-loving people. Tribal wars were fought to acquire slaves for human sacrifices or to hunt heads for trophies, and many excavated tombs have revealed that slaves were killed to accompany their masters into the afterworld, along with offerings of elaborate vases, gold ornaments or semiprecious stones. Warrior cults and fertility rites appear to have held an important role, symbolized by countless sculptures and phallic images, while *chicha* (alcohol) drinking bouts and the ritual use of *coca* (cocaine) were both common.

ENIGMA By the time Columbus disembarked, Guanacaste's sheltered bays and the Tempisque Valley nurtured extensive settlements producing highly sophisticated polychrome ceramics. In the Talamanca Mountains the impressive city of Guayabo had flourished until about 1400, when it was mysteriously abandoned. Meanwhile, the Diquis in their fortified villages of the south had mastered the art of weaving fine cotton cloth as well as the technology for their perfect stone spheres— perhaps the most enigmatic emblems of early Costa Rican history.

Compared with adjoining Nicaragua and Panama, this tiny but inhospitable corner of Central America proved difficult to conquer. From the day Christopher Columbus stepped onto Costa Rican soil, it was to take 60 years of death, disease and destruction for a permanent Spanish colony to be founded.

28

One fine day in 1502 Christopher Columbus—Cristobal Colón in Spanish—anchored off Puerto Limón to repair his storm-damaged ships and restore the spirits of his exhausted men. This was the Italian navigator's fourth voyage across the Atlantic in search of a passage to the fabled riches of Asia, and to the growing list of territories that he had acquired for the Spanish Crown he now added Costa Rica (the Rich Coast) de Veragua. Veragua was the Indian name for the Panamanian coast. It was called "rich" allegedly because of the dazzling gold ornaments worn by the Indians who greeted Columbus's expedition and who unknowingly fanned the blaze of the Spanish lust for ingots.

A 16th-century portrayal of Columbus

from the Indians foiled the *conquistadores'* ambitions again and again. In 1522 a second expedition led by Gil Gonzalez Davila succeeded in reaching Nicoya on foot from Panama, carrying out mass baptisms, amassing gold, and enslaving hundreds of Indians in the process. Frustrations grew, as did Indian attacks and avaricious in-fighting between the *conquistadores* themselves, and it was not until 1562 that Juan Vásquez de Coronado succeeded where the others had failed. Recognizing the potential of the Central Valley, he moved a nascent settlement up to the cooler air and fertile, volcanic soil of Cartago.

> ❏ "On Sunday, Sept. 25th towards midday, we dropped anchor in an islet named Quiribiri off a coastal town named Cariay, which were the best people, country, and places that we had so far discovered; this was because the high land was full of rivers, with abundant tall trees..." From *Life of the Admiral, Don Cristobal Colón* by his son, Hernando Colón. ❏

HARDSHIP Dense jungle, rugged mountains, tropical diseases, extreme climatic conditions, food shortages and, not least, aggressive resistance

SLAVERY In contrast to previous leaders, Coronado was relatively respectful of the Indians and soon managed to gain the confidence of certain chiefs, and to make allies by siding with one tribe against another. *Encomienda* slavery had been officially abolished in 1542 thanks to various enlightened clergymen, but a replacement system called *repartimiento* allowed forced work of one week per month. Coronado's successor, Perafán de Rivera, succumbed to the arguments of struggling settlers and in 1569 bent the rules to permit slavery again. However, one of the

problems the colonizers faced was a lack of people to enslave. Where were the Indians?

DISEASE The near-destruction of the indigenous population had begun in waves, in some cases before any physical contact with the *conquistadores* had been established. It was caused by European illnesses against which the local population had no resistance: influenza, measles, smallpox, typhoid and the bubonic plague. Terrible epidemics took place in 1519, then again in 1545–48, reducing an already small Indian population to next to nothing. No reliable figures exist for the number of Indians at the time of the Conquest—estimates vary from 27,000 to 500,000—but what is certain is that within a century of Columbus's disembarkation, the tiny surviving indigenous population had sunk into oppression.

Below: St-Blas, Nicoya, founded in 1522
Right: Indians were shipped off to the mines in South America

❑ The Spanish *encomienda* system lies at the basis of many unresolved socio-political problems in Central America, especially Guatemala and Mexico—where, for example, it led to the 1994 Zapatistas' rebellion in Chiapas. This system allowed early colonizers to enslave large numbers of Indians. Although it was later outlawed, it had made thousands destitute, landless and chained by debt to their masters. ❑

29

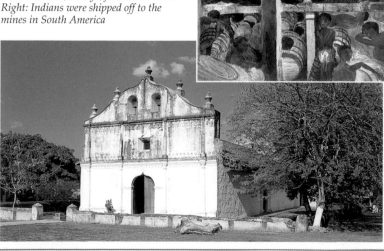

For most of the 17th century Costa Rica foundered in poverty, its lack of progress caused partly by its remoteness from central power and partly by its difficult terrain. Two centuries went by before the colony finally raised its head from ploughing fields and envisaged real development.

Colonial Costa Rica was far from dynamic. The gold that had so inspired Columbus had been exhausted, and manpower was severely limited as the Indians had perished from disease or enslavement, or fled to the mountains, their fine artistry reduced to distant memories. In their place came poor Spanish immigrants from Cataluña, Galicia, and Andalusia, who settled for the most part on isolated farms in the Central Valley, eking out an existence by subsistence farming.

BACKWATER The government of this newly subjugated colony was in distant Guatemala, from where the Spanish colonial governor ruled over El Salvador, Nicaragua and Costa Rica, leaving Panama under the Spanish Colombian yoke. This meant that Costa Rica was a poor cousin at the end of a long line, three months on horseback from the "capital," with even its bishop based in Nicaragua. Once the Indian tombs had been looted (by royal decree of Carlos V, in 1540), Costa Rica held no interest for the Spanish Crown, and the struggling farmers were left to their own limited resources. By the early 1700s, settlers were so poor that they had to revert to the old currency of the cocoa bean.

SOCIAL SYSTEM Much has been written about how this period was also the key to the Tico character, producing self-reliant homesteaders with no caste system of powerful *hacienda* owners like those of Guatemala or Mexico. *Mestizos* (descendants of Spaniards intermarried with Indians) are said not to

have existed, and yet recent research has shown that the lack of Spanish women led early soldiers and settlers to take Indian women as mistresses, producing generations of mixed-race descendants. At the same time, traditional Indian hierarchies were disrupted by the subservient role imposed by the white men. This subjugation was emphasized in 1747 when the Indian resettlement policy relocated hundreds from the remote Talamanca Mountains to the Central Valley in order to provide a desperately needed workforce.

PIRATES If life went on in relatively bucolic fashion in the fertile valleys of central Costa Rica, such was not the case over on the Caribbean coast. This became prey to swashbuckling pirates and privateers of the Spanish Main: French and Dutch buccaneers, but above all the English—Morgan, Mansfield and Owen. By the late 17th century, the English had found faithful allies in the Miskito Indians of the coasts of Honduras and Nicaragua, whose looting targets included the extensive cacao plantations that had been developed

> ❏ The Miskitos' fidelity to their early English allies created an unsettling threat to Spanish supremacy in the Caribbean for almost two centuries. In 1783 England finally gave up the Central American shores in return for receiving Gibraltar, but local Miskitos continued to reject Spanish colonization and prefer the English language. ❏

Following in Drake's footsteps, Henry Morgan (c1636–88; portrayed below left) was one of many buccaneers to lead expeditions from Europe to Central America in pursuit of Spanish merchantmen

in Limón. Raids were so successful that by 1779 the Miskitos were able to demand tribute from Costa Rica, a tradition that continued until 1841. A black market also flourished between the pirates and settlers.

GROWTH Costa Rica was gradually changing. Three new towns were founded—Heredia (1706), San José (1737) and Alajuela (1782)—which joined the tiny capital of Cartago, virtually wiped out by an eruption of Irazú in 1723, but soon rebuilt. During the same period tobacco was developing as a commercial crop and, in a vain attempt to stimulate the ailing colony, Spain gave Costa Rica exclusive rights to cultivate the crop in her colonies. This met with limited success, but luckily a new product on the horizon was to propel this backwater colony to the forefront of Central America. In 1808 free land was offered as an incentive to anyone who would grow a new import from Cuba—coffee.

Costa Rica must be one of the few countries to have remained ignorant of its new state of independence for a full month, and to have achieved independence without even aspiring to it. For several decades the fledgling nation veered between democracy and military coups, on the climb to its economic zenith.

In October 1821 news came by special mule-courier from Guatemala that the Spanish Crown had relinquished control over Mexico and its Central American empire. Suddenly Costa Rica found itself propelled into a situation it had never envisaged, one that had been brought about by the more politically motivated and oppressed populations of the north.

CONFUSION Although the leaders of the four main towns rapidly agreed on a constitution (based on the Spanish one of 1812), confusion reigned. Two routes were open: total independence, or adhesion to the newly declared Mexican empire of General Iturbide. A split soon appeared between San José's and Alajuela's supporters of independence on the one hand and, on the other, the more conservative inhabitants of Heredia and Cartago. The independence movement won the day in typically small-scale Tico fashion, in a battle that left 20 dead. More democratically, the inhabitants of Guanacaste chose by referendum to join Costa Rica rather than Nicaragua.

BRAULIO CARRILLO In their first try at democracy, Costa Ricans elected as head of state a modest schoolteacher, and became part of the short-lived federal republic of five Central American states. Government became more structured in 1833 with the election of the authoritarian Braulio Carrillo, a San José lawyer with despotic leanings. The burgeoning coffee plantations were by then creating a prosperous middle class, but prosperity had side effects such as prostitution, gambling and

theft. Braulio Carrillo stepped in with a strong hand, built new roads and ports, repaid national debts, introduced civil reforms and, in 1837, moved the capital to San José. But he went a step too far and, after reclaiming power through a military coup in 1842, found himself deposed and exiled by a general with the coffee barons' backing.

NATIONAL THREAT The next significant episode in Costa Rica's embryonic history took place under President Juan Rafael Mora, an astute representative of the coffee oligarchy who is perceived today as a hero, although his 10-year rule ended abruptly, like that of others before and after him, in front of a firing squad.

❏ William Walker (*above*), a Tennessee goldminer, adventurer and hack journalist, had already considered Mexico's Baja California as a base for his infamous "ideal" state, where slavery would be institutionalized. His Nicaraguan incursion was sanctioned by the US President and a group of American industrialists. ❏

32

Mora's legendary status stems from his swift rebuttal of the first threat to Costa Rica's national sovereignty.

In June 1855, William Walker took control of Nicaragua, from where he aimed to implement his Central American territory of slavery, as well as constructing a canal linking the Atlantic and the Pacific. With 300 filibusters (adventurers), he advanced into Costa Rica as far as what is today Parque Nacional Santa Rosa and prepared an attack on San José. President Mora rapidly organized a motley army, including many farmers and traders, which, after dislodging Walker and his men, achieved its final victory at Rivas, in Nicaragua. Here a heroic drummer boy, Juan Santamaría, set fire to the invaders' hideout, losing his life in the process.

Walker's ambitions ended with his life in 1860 in Honduras, the same year as the overconfident Mora was executed for an attempted *coup d'état*.

PROSPERITY By 1889, when Costa Rica's new constitution was drafted and four-yearly democratic elections were implemented (women and Afro-Caribbeans, however, could not vote), the nation was enjoying a new-found prosperity. European ideas, cosmopolitan lifestyles, a university (1844), free elementary education (1869), a rejection of Church domination (the Bishop was temporarily expelled in 1884), a major railway under construction and the potential profits of the new crop—bananas—all added to the confidence of a burgeoning nation.

33

Coffee (top) came before banana planta-tions (right), which were first introduced by the builder of the Atlantic Railway

As Costa Rica's fortunes increased, so did social divisions and ambitions. The 20th century has been a period of tumultuous politics, a roller-coaster economy and, despite difficulties, important social reforms, culminating in civil war, a new constitution and a reborn country.

In 1890, the long-awaited Atlantic Railway was completed, 19 years after the contract was signed. More than 4,000 imported workers had died building it, and 324,000ha (800,600 acres) of trackside land had been given to its constructor, an American named Minor Keith. After the trains started running, Keith concentrated on building up the United Fruit Company, an economic force that was to transform the country economically, ecologically and socially. By 1913, the Talamanca plantations were producing 11 million bunches of bananas annually, and Costa Rica was the world's top exporter. Then came banana disease and World War I, a double blow to production.

POLARIZATION As the republic prospered, its interests became increasingly polarized between the conservatism of the plantation owners and the reforms demanded by a growing workforce, backed by intellectuals as well as the Church. In 1917 the democratic tradition was interrupted by Federico Tinoco Granados who imposed himself as dictator, but in 1919 he was toppled by a popular movement spear-headed by the extraordinary character Jorge Volio Jiménez, a former Catholic priest who was later made a general. For more than a decade Volio campaigned for social improvements, even leading Nicaraguan revolutionaries in battle, and in 1923 he founded the Reformist Party, which advocated extensive agrarian and social reforms. However, his vitriolic attacks on Costa Rica's ruling classes finally earned him psychiatric internment in Belgium.

RISING TENSION From that point on, reformist aims could not be ignored. Further advances came in 1931, when an intellectual follower of Volio, Manuel Mora, formed the Costa Rican Communist Party. This helped to organize strikes on the plantations and to legalize unions, and later supported President Rafael Angel Calderón Guardia, elected in 1940. Calderón's momentous presidency coincided with the foundering of the national economy, precipitated by the 1930s' world depression and the outbreak of World War II. After declaring war on Germany and Japan, Calderón unwisely confiscated property owned by Germans (often longstanding immigrants and well positioned within the nation's economic élite), a move that sparked off xenophobic riots. He also implemented social reforms. Having antagonized both the upper classes and the conservatives, he allied himself with the Church, so adding the intellectuals to his adversaries. After rigging the elections of 1944, Calderón's party annulled the opposition victory in 1948. Tension and distrust reigned. Then along came

❏ Figueres worked in the US but returned to Costa Rica in the 1920s to establish a community farm (*La Lucha sin Fin*, "The Endless Struggle"). His outspoken criticism of Calderón's administration resulted in exile to Mexico in 1942–44. Inspired by revolutionary idealism, he concluded that an armed uprising was the only solution to his nation's woes. After his victory he was twice elected President, in 1953–57 and 1970–74. He died in 1990. ❏

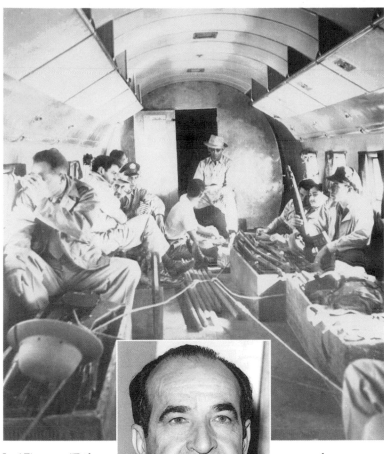

José Figueres, "Father of the Nation," known as Don Pepe.

CIVIL WAR In March 1948, Figueres launched a well-planned offensive from his farm near Cerro La Muerte, to which arms had been flown in from Guatemala. Forty days of civil war, which left 2,000 dead, culminated in the overthrow of Calderón's disciple, President Picado, and a triumphant procession through San José. For the next 18 months, Figueres wiped the slate clean with radical, often unpopular measures. He reformed the corrupt and inefficient public administration, expanded Calderón's social reforms, nationalized banks and abolished the army. Not least, women and Afro-Caribbeans were given the vote, and the latter were at last given citizenship. Don Pepe's 1949 Constitution provided the foundation for a unique pacifist democracy, and his party, the Partido de Liberación Nacional (PLN), is a major force in Costa Rica today.

National symbols of resistance: above left, statue of Juan Santamaría in Alajuela. Above: government troops are flown into action, 1948, and inset: Don Pepe

A-Z Guanacaste

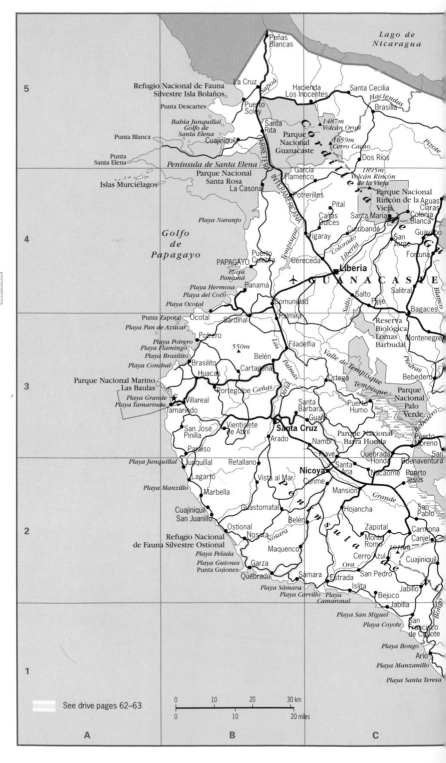

Guanacaste

CRUISING THE GULF

The Golfo de Nicoya is dotted with little islands, many of which are protected as biological reserves (Isla Pájaros, Islas Negritos, Isla Guayabo), while others such as the Islas Tortugas have become popular and often overcrowded day-trip destinations. The best way to see these islands is by boat tours, which can be arranged at Tambor, Montezuma, or Bahía Gigante, or directly with the tour company in San José. Alternatively, paddle out there in a sea kayak (see panel on page 55).

Pages 36–37: late afternoon sun illuminates the contours of volcanic Rincón de la Vieja Below: the resort of Playa Flamingo in Guanacaste

39

The unmistakable Guanacaste tree gives welcome shade in a tinder-dry landscape

GUANACASTE TREE

In English and Spanish this majestic tree (*Enterolobium cyclocarpum*) is also known as the elephant's ear, monkey ear or mulatto ear. Often growing in complete isolation, it is easily identifiable by its thick grey trunk, with branches spreading umbrella-style in a strikingly symmetrical fashion, providing generous shade for cattle and people. Even more curious are its seed pods. These huge, ear-shaped pods (up to 10cm/4in wide) dangle from the tree in the dry season and are preferred snacks for cattle. Guanacaste wood is used for making furniture and boats, and the bark for tannin, soap and medicine.

GUANACASTE Vast plains of savannah, rolling hills, superb beaches and towering volcanoes form the north-western corner of Costa Rica, most of which belongs to the province of Guanacaste. Known for its proud cowboys, glorious sunsets, huge cattle ranches and oven-like temperatures, this once remote region is evolving fast. The transformation of Daniel Oduber Airport in Liberia into an international airport (served by five US carriers) has given extra impetus to developments west of the provincial capital. Elsewhere, this sparsely inhabited region, home to only 7 percent of the population, offers wide-scale development by many foreign institutions that will soon transform the region into one of the premier resorts in Central America.

INTO THE HEART This section of the book includes the entire Península de Nicoya and the national parks of the striking Cordillera de Guanacaste (a mountain range that creates a northeastern barrier), but it excludes the Laguna de Arenal, more logically inclu-ded in The North (see page 72). There are three main entry points to the region, two of which are off the Inter-american Highway: first, the new Taiwan Friendship Bridge speeds traffic directly into the heart of the peninsula; second, some 64km (40 miles) farther north, the regional capital, Liberia, the gateway

to the far north, volcanoes and burgeoning beach resorts; the third access route is by sea, from Puntarenas to Playa Naranjo, Paquera and Montezuma in the south.

INDEPENDENT-MINDED Guanacaste's indigenous people were joined, probably in about AD900, by a major new influx, the Chorotegas from southern Mexico. Many of today's inhabitants are *mestizo* descendants, with deep-toned complexions and dark wavy hair, although this Indian group suffered more than any other from colonial slavery. In the 15th century the Isla Chira in the Golfo de Nicoya was a buzzing marketplace trading Nicoya pottery with the Aztecs; earlier still, the Chorotegas had traded with Mayas and Zapotecs. Countless jade, gold and ceramic artefacts showing a high level of artistry have been unearthed in the peninsula. Under Spanish rule, Guanacaste found itself tossed between Nicaragua and Costa Rica (both part of the Spanish Captaincy General of Guatemala). After independence in 1821, the Guanacastecos chose Costa Rica by referendum, but they maintain their independent streak, preserving their own flag and displaying signs inscribed *orgullosamente Guanacasteco* (proud to be Guanacastecan). This determined cast of character has also helped them fight off repeated invasions from Nicaragua over the years.

INTO THE OVEN Craft traditions continue in the kilns of Guaitíl, but the tropical dry forest that once clad the peninsula has been mercilessly shorn, though reforestation efforts are underway. African grass now blankets the plains and hillsides, providing sustenance for thousands of Brahma cattle but creating ecological and climatic complications. When it's dry in Guanacaste, it's very dry indeed: rivers become waterless, animals head for the mountains and tourists for the breezy beaches. Fortunately, large tracts of land are now protected, above all the three adjacent national parks (Guanacaste, Rincón de la Vieja and Santa Rosa) which, with some smaller spots, form the Área de Conservación Guanacaste, to the benefit of local people and wildlife alike.

TO THE BEACH
Leisure pursuits are well catered to along the coastline, where Guanacaste's beaches offer some of the best fishing and water sports in Costa Rica, coupled with some remarkably designed, often isolated hotels. Several golf courses have opened in recent years. Swimming is not always safe (see panel, page 55), but areas such as the Bahía de Culebra (Papagayo and Playa Hermosa), Playa Conchal, Playa Tamarindo, Playa Flamingo, Playa Sámara, Playa Tambor and Montezuma all have sheltered beaches. Getting around the peninsula can be a problem although, with careful planning, travel by bus is easy and inexpensive. However, unless you choose to fly directly into a beach resort from San José or Liberia, the most convenient form of transport is a rental car.

41

Now home to the Paradisus Playa Conchal, one of Costa Rica's largest beachfront resorts, Playa Conchal fortunately still possesses a quiet beauty, with sheltered waters safe for swimming

POTS

In pre-Columbian days, much-prized Chorotega pottery from Guanacaste was traded with the Aztecs. During Spanish occupation the craft died out, possibly because of the pagan images and symbols used for decoration, but the tradition was revived so successfully in the 20th century that many new pieces are indistinguishable from early artefacts. They are still handmade, almost always by women in this traditionally matriarchal culture, and are painted only with white, black and ocher pigments from the nearby mountains. After drying in the sun for a day and before firing, the objects are rubbed with a special stone dipped in water to produce a natural sheen.

A Guaitíl potter works local clay in a huge pestle

▶ Cañas
39D3

This small agricultural town in the hot plains of Guanacaste on the Interamerican Highway, is useful only for some budget hotels, but several kilometres to the north are three organizations worth investigating. At Km marker 193 on the Interamerican Highway, Safaris Corobicí (tel/fax: 669-6191, www.nicoya.com) organizes half-day tours boating down the gentle Río Corobicí, with plenty of potential for bird- and wildlife-watching and swimming, or longer trips into the estuaries of Palo Verde, again with a strong likelihood of bird sightings. Close by is **Las Pumas▶** (tel/fax: 669-6044, www.geocities.com/laspumas2000 *Open* daily 8–5. *Admission free*, donations welcome), a private rehabilitation sanctuary for wild cats run by associates of the late Lily Hagnauer, who died in 2001. Here, too, is **Hacienda La Pacífica▶▶** (tel: 669-6050, fax: 669 6055, pacifica@racsa.co.cr), an interesting model of sustainable development that combines agriculture, forestry, conservation and tourism. Its dry tropical forest offers horseback-riding, hiking and fantastic bird-watching (225 species spotted so far), particularly along the banks of the Corobicí, with howler monkeys as common companions. A small museum and library, an organic farm, a cattle ranch, a tilapia (fish) farm and a restaurant complete La Pacífica's attractions.

▶▶▶ Guaitíl
38C3

Guanacaste's pottery-making hub lies in scenic pasturelands east of Santa Cruz. This tiny village is composed of 85 houses, nearly all devoted to making pots, urns, vases or zoomorphic whistles whose design and technique date from pre-Columbian times. Luis Sing (tel: 839-1659) showcases Guaitíl pottery in his Nicoya shop, while in Guaitíl individual stands front the numerous family workshops. Wander round, talk to the potters and watch clay creations being crafted, dried, then put into igloo-shaped kilns before they are hand-painted with natural pigments to produce the traditional polychrome designs. Farther on, the even smaller village of San Vicente produces pottery that is marginally more intricate in form and painting, displayed at the co-operative showroom on the main road.

▶▶ Juntas
39D3

This picturesque old mining town (also called Las Juntas de Abangares) offers some surprises—namely decorative, harmonious and unspoiled old houses, hand-paved streets, lush vegetation and a landmark statue commemorating gold miners in the main square. From 1884 to 1931 Juntas was a hub for gold miners who flocked here from all over the world in search of a fortune. Mining still goes on nearby, and visitors can

make an interesting side trip to ecomuseum **Las Minas de Abangares** northeast of Juntas on a little-used rough road to Tilarán. The museum preserves old mining equipment, displayed beside photos and models (tel: 662-0544. *Open daily 9–5. Admission: inexpensive*). Its rural riverside location and shady access road offer plenty of bird-watching, and across a suspension bridge lies the nature reserve of Aguas Claras. Ask about the local hot springs as well.

▶ La Cruz
38B5

Guanacaste's last outpost before the Nicaraguan border is a sleepy, hot, rather ramshackle town just west of the freshly repaved Interamerican Highway, in an area that has only recently opened up to tourists. It makes a good base for exploring the beaches of northern Guanacaste. Road checks are common owing to the proximity of the Nicaraguan border, so always carry your passport.

Arriving from the south, turn left at the filling station to reach the main square, before continuing uphill to a windy lookout point, El Mirador. This offers breathtaking vistas (spectacular at sunset) over windy Bahía Salinas and the wildlife refuge of Isla Bolaños, as well as the fishing community of Puerto Soley 5.5km (3.5 miles) away down at the water's edge. This is where boats can be rented to take you near to the 240ha (590-acre) island refuge. Two new resorts now occupy swathes of the formerly pristine beach. For exquisite protected waters and deserted white sand, drive south from the resorts to **Playa Rajada▶▶**, just beyond the remote village of Jobo, or to **Playa Jobo▶** on the tip of the peninsula. It is also possible to reach Bahía Junquillal (part of the Área de Conservación Guanacaste, see page 41) by cutting south across the headland along a rough dirt road.

Frame-houses line the few streets of La Cruz, near the Nicaraguan border

ISLA BOLAÑOS
This windswept little island rising 79m (260ft) out of the magnificent Bahía Salinas was declared a wildlife refuge in 1981 in order to protect its nesting colonies of brown pelicans, American oystercatchers and magnificent frigate birds. The latter build their nests in the frangipani and alfaje trees that make up much of the island's dry tropical forest. Other species that can be spotted are magpie jays and black vultures. Landing boats on the island is not allowed.

PUERTAS DEL SOL
Common features of Liberia's traditional adobe houses are the *puertas del sol* ("doorways of the sun"), diagonal doorways that let both morning and afternoon sun into north-facing corner houses. Terracotta-tiled roofs are also common, but enter any of the more elaborate mansions on Calle Central and you are plunged into pure 19th-century colonial style. Grandiose rooms with high ceilings are sometimes decorated with cherubim-enhanced murals, while kitchen quarters are relegated to the rear beside a court-yard used for drying grain.

A remnant of Liberia's golden age in one of Calle Central's 19th-century houses

▶ **Liberia**   38C4

The historic capital of Guanacaste, founded in 1869, is currently seeing increased prosperity from tourism generated by the international status of the nearby Daniel Oduber Airport. Liberia is built on a grid system, but finding your way around is made tricky by the lack of street signs. Thanks to its position on the Interamerican Highway, it has a straggle of hotels, bars and restaurants. Often dubbed the "White City," it is renowned for its old adobe houses constructed from the white volcanic soil of Rincón de la Vieja: some lovely examples remain in **Calle Central▶▶**, which runs south off the main square. Many have been restored, and owners leave their front doors wide open to allow visitors to peek inside. Back on the main square, follow Avenida Central (which becomes Avenida Julio 25) to its eastern end to reach **La Agonía▶▶**, a simple 19th-century adobe church that replaced a 1769 chapel. The bare, raftered interior functions partly as a museum, with displays of religious statuary. It is usually open after midday.

Cultura The helpful local tourist office (tel: 665-0135. *Open* Mon–Sat 9–5, Sun 1–4) is at the Casa de Cultura, a 19th-century adobe house signposted from the main square. It doubles as the small **Museo del Sabañero▶**, which pays tribute to Guanacaste's great cowboy tradition with displays of saddles, costumes and other related objects. The tourist office can advise on local tour agencies that organize day-trips to the nearby national parks and volcanoes, or you can set off on a hired mountain bike.

▶▶▶ **Montezuma**   39D1

Costa Rica's original New Age hippy resort has raised its standards and now offers some good lodgings, stylish dining and clean beaches. Its fabulous, isolated location at the bottom of a steep hill at the southern tip of the Península de Nicoya means that road access is slow, though things are changing with the growing tourist influx to Tambor and the explosive growth of the trio of towns strung out along the coast north of Cabo Blanco—Malpaís, Santa Teresa and Manzanillo. Buses to Montezuma meet the Paquera ferry three or more times daily, depending on the season.

The hub Shops, bars, hotels and restaurants are clustered around the main intersection, which borders a small fishing beach to the south (not good for swimming) and, five minutes' walk north past a pretty timber church, a magnificent white beach edged with gentle surf. Money exchange, ticketing, rafting, fishing, scuba-diving, and horseback-riding tours, and full-day trips to Parque Nacional Cabo Blanco can be organized through Cocozuma

Traveller (tel: 642–0911, www.cocozumacr.com), inside El Sano Banano restaurant/bed-and-breakfast. The new Waterfall Canopy Tour (tel: 642-0911) offers 11 viewing platforms over the Montezuma River.

Peace and quiet Follow the main road south from the intersection and around the point to a stretch of small hotels overlooking more beaches, and a river with a 20-minute trail leading to La Catarata (waterfall). Complete peace and quiet can be found by driving some 10km (6 miles) south past sandy coves along a rough road (necessitating four-wheel drive during the wet season) to **Cabuya▶**, a straggling coastal village practically at the entrance to the Cabo Blanco reserve (see page 60). Beyond Cabo Blanco, Malpaís, Santa Teresa and Manzanillo comprise a long beachfront stretch of hotels, *cabinas*, campgrounds and restaurants ranging from cheap to impossibly pricey. This is Costa Rica's hottest new destination and a surfer's paradise.

▶▶ Nicoya   38C2

The crossroads position of this little town makes it useful for changing money or buying necessities. The focal point is the lively Parque Central, dominated by the church of **San Blas▶▶**, founded in 1522, rebuilt in 1644, subsequently damaged by an earthquake, restored, and now a museum (*Open* 8–noon, 2–6. Closed Sun, Wed. *Admission free*). Adjoining it is a shady garden, and bordering the square are several decorative buildings, including a 1930s cinema converted into a café.

ISLA CABUYA
Lying in the ocean just off Cabuya, this strange little island is accessible on foot at low tide. Although uninhabited by the living, Isla Cabuya remains a cemetery for local villagers, a use dating from fishermen's customs in the early 20th century and continued by Cabuya's first settlers in the 1950s. For a few decades, before the Montezuma road was built, it was also the village lifeline, as all ferries from the mainland stopped there to unload supplies and passengers, who would cross to the shore on foot.

45

Bird's-eye view of a stretch of coast near Montezuma

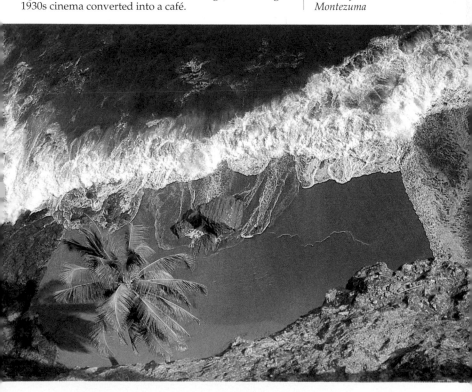

INVENTORY OF SPECIES

Parque Nacional Guanacaste is the site of a 10-year survey (INBITTA) that aims to analyze and list every living species—from the tiniest micro-organism to fungi, birds, insects, mammals and lofty tropical trees—that exists within the Guanacaste Conservation Area. This vast zone was created in 1989 when five adjoining conservation areas (Santa Rosa, Rincón de la Vieja, Guanacaste, Bahía de Junquillal and Isla Bolaños) were amalgamated. It is hoped that analysis of some 300,000 species will provide essential data for medical, agricultural and biotechnological advances.

Papagayo and a blowhole at Nosara

▶▶▶ Nosara
38B2

Understanding the layout of Nosara and its beaches is not easy, but wrong turns only bring you into closer contact with the superb natural surroundings. These forested hills with sweeping views, cliffs, sandy beaches and rich bird life have attracted extensive North American property development, but conservation standards are high and the roads appalling, so scenic beauty survives intact. The rural village of Bocas de Nosara itself, 5km (3 miles) inland, has little to offer. Most visitors arrive from the south via Sámara and Garza, passing the wide sweep of Playa Guiones, an emerging surfing destination, and Playa Pelada, with their several hotels and the popular beachfront Olga's Bar. A short drive northwest is Ostional's nature reserve (see page 58). Most hotels arrange surfing, diving or fishing trips. Anglers can also contact Harbor Reef Lodge in Guiones (tel: 682-0059, www.harborreef.com) or Abusadora Charters in Nosara (tel: 682-0396, fishtalecr@yahoo.com).

▶▶ Papagayo
38B4

Costa Rica's most controversial beach development covers an idyllic peninsula of sheltered coves curling around the beautiful Bahía Culebra. Billions are being invested in the bay and more than 20,000 new hotel rooms are expected to be built in the next decade, making it the largest resort in Central America. Several large resorts have already been built including a successful Four Seasons Resort, and the construction of a large marina is currently underway. Clashes between environmentalists and developers have been frequent; however, the government and ICT, Costa Rica's national tourism authority, are on the side of the developers so the onslaught of big money resorts will continue in Papagayo.

▶ Paquera   39D1

This small town has lightened the heavy ferry traffic from Playa Naranjo, some 24km (15 miles) farther north, with a new service and a smooth new road financed by the large Spanish-owned resort of Barceló Playa Tambor. Car and passenger ferries run five times a day, and some have direct bus connections with Montezuma. The town itself lies a inland. It is a useful place for stocking up on provisions, and offers some places to stay.

▶▶ Parque Nacional Barra Honda   38C3

Open: daily 8–4. Admission: moderate

More than 2,000ha (5,000 acres) of hilly terrain punctuated by limestone peaks are riddled with 42 caves, the main interest of this national park. This area emerged from the sea 60 million years ago, and since then millennia of rain have eroded the calcareous rock and filtered below to create underground waterways, chambers and vaulted ceilings. Spectacular stalactites and stalagmites are at their best in the caves of Terciopelo, Trampa and Santa Ana. The deepest, at 238m (780ft), is Santa Ana. Pozo Hediondo attracts hundreds of bats, and in Nicoya pre-Columbian human bones and artefacts have been found. Outside these caverns is a very hot, tropical dry forest, best appreciated from the look-out point above the caves. Wildlife is scarce, but you may spot a raccoon or coati, coyotes, a flock of orange-fronted parakeets or white-faced monkeys. Park headquarters is reached from Nacaome, 21km (13 miles) east of Nicoya, and two trails lead into the park. Guides are essential for visiting the caves.

▶▶ Parque Nacional Guanacaste   38B5

Open: daily 8–4. Admission: moderate

In 1989, 32,000ha (79,000 acres) of land in northern Guanacaste were declared a national park. Starting on the plain 200m (650ft) above sea level, this area rises 1.5km (1 mile) into the volcanic Guanacaste Mountains and, together with the adjoining Santa Rosa park, provides essential migratory corridors for wildlife, as well as protecting some surviving stands of tropical dry forest. The evolving topography creates a variety of superb landscapes, but access is extremely difficult to the best viewpoints, on Cerro Cacao and Volcán Orosí, where biological research stations are located. Scientists are still identifying the great diversity of more than 3,000 plant species, some 300 bird species, and 5,000 insects, not to mention monkeys, peccaries, tapirs and even jaguars. Park infrastructure remains limited (there are rough dorms at the Cacao station), so it's best to get information from Santa Rosa's ranger stations. Alternatively, head for atmospheric Los Inocentes Lodge (tel: 679-9190, 679-9294, fax: 265-4385, www.losinocenteslodge.com), where horseback tours of the park are organized (see panel).

LOS INOCENTES

This beautifully preserved ranch on the northern boundary of Parque Nacional Guanacaste once belonged to the Viquez family. The two-floor hacienda, built in 1890 of tropical hardwoods, presided over an extensive ranch of some 8,000 cattle. Dairy farming continued under new owners until 1994, but since then the hacienda has been completely turned over to ecotourism, functioning as a hotel and organizing horseback tours of the surrounding pastures and volcanoes. Advance notice is required if you want to ride to the peak of the dormant Orosí volcano—a tough 14-hour trip.

47

Los Inocentes: The raising of Brahma cattle once formed the livelihood of the region

Costa Rica is becoming known as one of the world's top countries for bird-watching, offering an astounding diversity that matches its varied topography. Waterbirds, seabirds, raptors, birds of the cloud forest or of the rain forest: all are present in astonishing numbers.

Above, from left to right: rufous-tailed hummingbird, tricolored heron, blue-gray tanager, golden-collared manakin, green-crowned brilliant, turquoise-browed motmot

48

Right: limpkin

Below: Costa Rica's national bird, the clay-colored robin

NATIONAL BIRD
With such an array of spectacular birds, it is surprising that Costa Rica has chosen as its national bird a rather understated and modest species called the clay-colored robin (*yigüirro*). Visually uninspiring, it rarely even sings, except in April during the breeding season. The fact that this coincides with the onset of the rains, an agricultural high point of the year, is the reason for the robin's status.

Altogether, more than 850 bird species have been identified in Costa Rica (as compared with 800 or so in the whole of North America), a quarter of which are migratory. Many eco-tourism agencies cater almost exclusively to that determined category of people, bird-watchers, whose most precious items of luggage are their binoculars and life lists (their ongoing check-lists). For them, Costa Rica is definitely paradise.

Top ten Priority destinations are the rain-forest area around La Selva, which claims more than 400 species; Monteverde's cloud forest with 400; Chirripó and La Amistad parks with more than 400 (although the full potential of the latter is still unexplored); Parque Nacional Corcovado, claiming in excess of 360; Parque Nacional Braulio Carrillo with 350; the Wilson Botanical Gardens, where ornithologists have recorded 330 species; Tortuguero's waterways, sustaining 309; Palo Verde, with about 300; and the wildlife refuges of Caño Negro and Ostional, each of which has nearly 200 species, mainly waterbirds. Besides these major mainland destinations, several uninhabited Pacific islands are protected as nesting sites. The Isla Bolaños off La Cruz (see panel on page 43) is home to the magnificent frigate bird, while the Gulf of Nicoya's Guayabo, Negritos and Pájaros islands conserve nesting grounds for brown pelicans. Laughing gulls, parrots, brown boobies and white-tipped doves also circulate around here.

Waterbirds The lowland marshes and lagoons of Palo Verde, Caño Negro and Ostional attract countless wildfowl and waders, both migratory and resident, including huge flocks of black-bellied whistling ducks, roseate spoonbills, blue-winged teals, wood storks, cattle egrets, white ibis, black-crowned night herons, neotropic cormorants, and particularly in Caño Negro—permanent colonies of Nicaraguan grackle, a bird endemic to nearby Lake Nicaragua. Another lesser-known area for waterbirds is the delta of the Río Térraba, near Sierpe, where extensive mangrove swamps and tributaries shelter nearly 400

species of forest birds, seabirds and wildfowl. In contrast, along the well-known waterways of Tortuguero, some birds actually wait for snacks from the boatloads of tourists.

High visibility If you spot a male resplendent quetzal on a "joy flight," you will not forget it. Its long, silky green tail-feathers, scarlet belly, yellow bill and iridescent green crew cut are a stunning sight, matching the sonorous, deep-throated calls that fuse into a mellow flow. Also vibrant and very audible is the parrot family, of which 16 species exist in Costa Rica. From tiny green parakeets to spectacular scarlet macaws measuring around 1m (3ft) in length, they screech across the skies, flashing their brilliant plumage. However, this family is the most sought-after for a caged, domestic existence, and once-common scarlet macaws may now number as few as 1,000 in the wild.

Chattering toucans are another typical, highly decorative inhabitant of lowland areas, and Costa Rica's six species are unmistakable, with huge curved bills and bright, contrasting plumage. Flashy kingfishers and purple gallinules, blending turquoise and cobalt-blue plumage, exhibit their hues beside rivers and along the coastline.

Spin-offs If you see an airborne blur near a flower, it will be a humming-bird. More than 50 species of this extensive family live in Costa Rica, playing an important pollinating role as they feed from the nectar of red, orange and yellow flowers. Some Ticos attract the birds to their gardens with flower-shaped feeders filled with sugared water. The extraordinary engineering that makes a humming-bird's wings flutter, rotate, and hum at high speed allows it to hover, move backward and accomplish vertical take-offs.

Also remarkable is the Montezuma oropendola, a weaver of intricate, pendulous nests that festoon tall trees. These nests are also a popular feeding ground for the giant cowbird, and when hung as decoration from the eaves of houses are sometimes recycled as second-hand homes by the olive-backed euphonia (one of 45 species of tanager).

THE EARLY BIRD...
The best time for bird-watching is from dawn until about 9am, when activity slows, then again near dusk as birds return to roost. Night prowlers may see and hear the bare-shanked screech fowl, the mottled owl or the crested owl.

LONG-DISTANCE TRAVELS 49
More than 200 species fly south to escape the cold North American winter. They include warblers, swallows, flycatchers, tanagers, finches, orioles and raptors such as hawks, falcons and eagles. Millions of these migrants cross Costa Rica to reach their wintering quarters in northern South America, and huge numbers of certain species remain within the country for the winter months.

Members of the parrot family range from tiny pygmy parrots to macaws more than 1m (3ft) in length

▶▶▶ Parque Nacional Palo Verde   38C3
Open: daily 8–4. Admission: moderate
Waterbirds are the incentive for exploring 16,000ha (39,500 acres) of scenic, tranquil freshwater and saltwater marshes, lagoons and channels formed by the basin of the Río Tempisque and Río Bebedero. These seasonally flooded areas change dramatically over the year, and during the dry season there are vast concentrations of black-bellied whistling ducks, blue-winged teals, wood storks, herons and roseate spoonbills. Orioles, kites, egrets and ibises are common, particularly in the mangrove forests.

Despite its astonishing ecological diversity (15 habitats), the park is named after the green-barked *palo verde* (horse bean) tree, found in tracts of tropical dry forest. Most visitors enter Palo Verde with a boat tour organized from Cañas, or from the fishing village of Puerto Humo, on the west bank of the Tempisque.

▶▶▶ Parque Nacional Rincón de la Vieja   38C4
Open: daily 8–4. Admission: moderate
The volcanic Cordillera de Guanacaste includes the dramatically beautiful park surrounding Rincón de la Vieja (1,895m/6,220ft), an intermittently active volcano that last erupted in 1991. Access to Sector Las Pailas is hard work along a rough, dusty road via Curubandé, signposted from the Interamerican Highway just north of Liberia. A toll is demanded for crossing private hacienda land, and it takes an hour to cover the 19km (12 miles). From the park entrance, trails lead to cool waterfalls (many rivers flow through the park) or to steaming mud-pots, geysers, hot springs and other volcanic delights. The trail up to the crater of Von Seebach, with views over nearby Rincón de la Vieja, is an arduous 8km (5 miles), but it leads through remarkably diverse landscapes, home to some 257 bird species as well as ocelots, jaguars, sloths and monkeys. The other entry point is at **Santa María**, 24km (15 miles) northeast of Liberia, on the equally bumpy road to Colonia Blanca. Near this entrance you'll find Simbiosis Mud Springs and Spa (tel: 666-8075, www.simbiosis-spa.com) adjoining Hacienda Guachipelín Hotel, a working ranch where you can relax in volcanic springs or mud pools, or indulge in a lavish spa treatment. Both entry routes require four-wheel-drive during the rainy season, but are just passable in high-clearance two-wheel-drive vehicles during the dry season.

One of many trails in and around Parque Nacional Rincón de la Vieja

▶▶▶ Parque Nacional Santa Rosa   38B4
Open: daily 8–4. Admission: moderate
This remarkably hot park preserves more than 48,500ha (120,000 acres) of tropical dry forest and overgrazed pastures hugging the coastline of the Península de Santa Elena, where its purpose is to protect turtle nesting grounds. Easy of access and well structured, Santa Rosa was the site of three historic battles to preserve Costa Rica's independence. The first and most dramatic, in 1856,

is well illustrated by the exhibits at the small museum of **La Casona▶▶**. This restored adobe and timber hacienda displays some wonderful old agricultural and domestic artefacts, 19th-century furniture and old photographs and engravings. From here a short nature trail runs through tropical dry forest, where parrots, snakes and iguanas hide among typical plant specimens. An uphill path leads to a look-out point dominated by the Monumento a Los Heros, a concrete arch dedicated to the victims of Santa Rosa's battles. The park headquarters, canteen and campground lie just west of La Casona.

Dry country Wildlife sightings are more likely during the dry season, when animals emerge in search of water, but as the season progresses, Santa Rosa's aridity is accentuated by the hot dry winds sweeping in from the Pacific. Sightings of jaguars are not unknown, and most visitors should see agoutis and tapirs. Birdlife is rich and varied and includes tinamous and great curassows. Insect life is also prolific and various. For a refreshing contrast, continue 11km (7 miles) south to Witches Rock, the surfers' beach, at Playa Naranjo, if you can—this road is not always passable even with a four-wheel-drive vehicle, so check before setting off. Alternatively, head north via the Interamerican Highway and Cuajiniquil to the idyllic **Bahía Junquillal**, much preferred during the rainy season by four of Costa Rica's turtle species, as well as by brown pelicans and magnificent frigate birds, whose aggressive aerobatics make a striking sight (see panel). The wide 1.6km (1-mile) long beach has two campgrounds.

FRIGATE BIRDS
Magnificent both in name and by nature, these huge sea birds can often be spotted in the Golfo de Santa Elena, around the Isla Bolaños and in the Bahía Junquillal. The combination of an immense wingspan and a light body makes it difficult for the bird to launch itself into the air from a normal standing or running position. For this reason it chooses to land only on high ledges or cliffs, from where it can take off, aided by wind currents, in an ungainly leap. Frigate birds in flight are, however, incredibly aerobatic as they chase and harass other sea birds into relinquishing their last meals. They never rest on the water, and spend the whole day on the wing.

51

A taste of the 19th century at La Casona

FLAMINGO FISH

There are no pink flamingos in the Playa Flamingo area, but the deep blue waters of the Pacific are teeming with vivid life. Fishing may involve wrestling with sailfish, blue and black marlin, amberjack, roosterfish, tuna and some 25 other varieties. Divers may see white-tip reef sharks, grunts, yellowtails, spotted eagle-rays, stingrays, eels, angelfish, octopus, starfish, seahorses and, on a somewhat larger scale, whale sharks measuring up to 9m (13ft), spinner dolphins, pilot whales and false killer whales.

OUT AND ABOUT

One of several in the area, the agency Costa Rica Diving (tel: 654-4148) has an office on the road to Playa Flamingo, from where it organizes reasonably priced diving trips (including deep dives to 30m/100ft) to the Islas Santa Catalina, as well as kayaking, snorkeling, sailing trips and motorcycle rental. For fishing, try Flamingo II Sportfishing (tel/fax: 654-4867, watsonge@racsa.co.cr), or you can sail on the *Shannon* (tel/fax: 654-4536, marflam@marflam.com).

▶▶ Playa Conchal   38B3

A short walk south across a rocky headland from Playa Brasilito brings you to this crescent-shaped beach of golden sand dominated by the crushed seashells of its name (*conchal* means "shell"). With no direct road access, Playa Conchal was for years a secluded hideaway, but a sprawling new low-rise golf resort opened behind the beach in 1996. The resort has a casino and claims to have the "largest swimming pool in Central America."

▶ Playa del Coco   38B4

This is the quintessential Tico family beach resort and a gathering place for the surrounding expat community. Its brash seaside atmosphere comes complete with street vendors, fishing boats unloading their catches, loud open-air bars, garbage on the beach, uninspired food and sandy streets. The seawater itself is far from pristine, and any would-be swimmers should head for cleaner environments immediately south or north. Coco's popularity stems from its being only 34km (21 miles) west of Liberia along a paved road. That said, for those who want some good-natured nightlife and promenading with reasonably priced hotels and *cabinas*, this is where to go.

▶▶ Playa Flamingo   38B3

The status of Guanacaste's one-time"jet-set" beach resort once stemmed mainly from its 60-yacht marina, the first fuel dock for boats sailing south down the Pacific coast after Acapulco in Mexico, but now facilities at Herradura have somewhat eclipsed it. Flamingo also boasts extensive diving and fishing facilities as well as one of the few nightclubs and casinos. Despite this, Flamingo remains small in scale, with a cluster of hotels, apartment blocks and villas clambering around the headland of Punta Salinas. This offers lovely views over the adjacent Isla Plata and more distant volcanic-rock pinnacles of the Islas Santa Catalina, which attract divers. Otherwise, the area is most attractive to boaters requiring the shelter of a marina.

Confusion sometimes arises, as the name Playa Flamingo also refers to the blissful white sweep of Playa Blanca, which lies south of Punta Salinas and is joined to the north by **Playa Potrero▶ ▶**, **Playa La Penca▶ ▶**, and finally the remote **Playa Pan de Azúcar▶ ▶ ▶**, the latter monopolized by the relaxing luxurious Hotel Sugar Beach. This string of fine, sheltered beaches is reached by a twisting unpaved road through pretty hills where you may see a troop of howler monkeys. Facilities are expanding but are still far from overdeveloped.

▶ ▶ ▶ Playa Grande   38B3

Immediately north of the popular Playa Tamarindo lies Playa Grande, preferred for centuries by nesting leatherback turtles and now grandly named the Parque Nacional Marino Las Baulas de Guanacaste. From November to April access to the beach is restricted, free by day but payable at night (*Admission: moderate*). It protects 445ha (1,100 acres) of beach, forest and mangrove swamp full of blue-winged teals, black-bellied whistling ducks, white ibis, cattle egrets, great blue herons and muscovy ducks. Caymans, ctenophores, grey squirrels, howler monkeys and white-faced monkeys are also present. The shadeless sweep of the

beach is popular with surfers and fine for swimming away from the surfing area. Canoeing, sailing, horseback-riding and, in season, nocturnal turtle-watching tours are available through the Hotel Las Tortugas.

▶▶ Playa Hermosa   38B4

This lovely curving beach northeast of Playa del Coco is overlooked by a sprinkling of villas, hotels, *cabinas* and restaurants fronting the beach, and dominated by a major time-share resort complex which scars the hillside at the north end. Activities include kayaking, windsurfing, canoeing and snorkeling in crystalline waters. Beyond the northern point lies **Playa Panamá▶▶▶**, an equally beautiful, once-deserted beach that now has several major trendsetting resorts.

▶ Playa Junquillal   38B2

Halfway between Ostional and Playa Tamarindo, this long, uncrowded beach is backed by dry forest and occupied by a handful of widely dispersed, foreign-owned hotels. Swimming is sometimes dangerous here, but the hotels offer activities—or relaxation by a tranquil pool.

Playa Flamingo's marina has one of the few deep-water moorings on Costa Rica's Pacific coast, but the new marina at Herradura, north of Jaco, has replaced Flamingo as Costa Rica's premier marina. Non-sailors take note: dozens of prettier, quieter beaches can be found minutes away from Flamingo, whether you're making the journey on foot or by car

Wide sands at Playa Sámara fill up on weekends during the dry season, but coconuts can drop at any time—beware!

▶ Playa Naranjo · 39D2

For years this ferry port opposite Puntarenas monopolized all public traffic across the Golfo de Nicoya. But now that Paquera has a rival ferry service and a new bridge spans the Río Tempisque, local hotel owners have had to spruce up their image. A sprawling village without much of a beach (despite its name), Playa Naranjo features a complex by the ferry-side road combining hotel, pool, supermarket, car rental and filling station. A short drive south through beautiful hills brings you to **Bahía Gigante▶▶**, with its island views.

▶▶▶ Playa Ocotal · 38B4

This tiny idyllic cove (less than 1km/0.6 miles long) lies 4km (2.5 miles) south of Playa del Coco in a stunning setting backed by hills of lush forest alive with parrots and monkeys. Tourist infrastructure is growing, but it remains a delightful spot with some excellent places to stay. Great scuba diving is provided by Ocotal Diving (tel: 670-0321, www.ocotaldiving.com), which operates on Hermosa beach, and by Rich Coast Diving (tel: 670-0176, www.richcoastdiving.com). South of the rocky headland is the small, black-sand beach of Bahía Pez Vela, where you'll find the posh hotel of the same name. Indulge yourself with a facial at the new Fusion Natural Spa (tel: 670-0914). Above all, don't miss a meal with a fabulous view from the hilltop hotel, El Ocotal.

▶ **Playa Sámara** 38B2

Seemingly endless off-white sands backed by coconut palms form this 5km (3-mile) long beach, where outlying coral reefs keep the waves gentle. The consequently safe swimming combined with easy road access from Nicoya have made Sámara a popular Tico resort, and its airstrip flies in foreign and Tico owners of some large resort villas. Hotels run the gamut of prices and the beachfront is dotted with breezy open-air restaurants.

Hotels pepper the road east before it swings around to **Playa Carrillo**▶▶, a crescent of palm-fringed beach ending in a forested headland dominated by a luxury Japanese-owned hotel, complete with a nearby airstrip and fishing boats. Otherwise this beach is superbly empty. The surrounding lush jungle continues along a magnificent coastal track (viable only in the dry season with four-wheel-drive) past Playa Camaronal to the extraordinary **Punta Islita**▶▶, where an innovatively designed hotel offers excellent rooms, and the beach is safe for swimming. An easier route, feasible with two-wheel-drive, reaches Islita from the east, passing through tiny villages and crossing undulating valleys on the way.

▶▶▶ **Playa Tamarindo** 38B3

The well-paved road leading into Tamarindo, and its freshly paved main streets, reflect the ongoing "gentrification" of this once dusty town, long preferred by Ticos as a spot for wealthy homes as well as by low-budget North Americans bearing backpacks and surfboards. Today, Tamarindo (and nearby Langosta) are overwhelmed with stylish hotels, *cabinas*, restaurants, shops and real-estate offices, as development fever burns hot.

The 1.5km (1-mile) white-sand beach has rocky platforms, exposed at low tide, and it is edged by coconut palms and tamarind trees. Surfers head to the river mouths north and south of town, or hike north 5km (3 miles) to Playa Grande's better break. Iguana Surf (tel: 653-0148, www.iguanasurf.net) rents surfboards and kayaks and offers estuary mangrove tours. Tamarindo Adventures & High Tide Surf Shop has all of the above plus motorcycles (tel: 653-0108, fax: 653-0640, www.tamarindoadventures. net). Most hotels offer turtle-watching at Playa Grande (see pages 52–53). Night-time social diversions are provided by numerous open-air bars and restaurants, many featuring continental menus. Despite the array of activities, Playa Tamarindo is decidedly relaxed.

▶▶ **Playa Tambor** 39D1

In the middle of the Península de Nicoya's southeast coastline lies **Bahía Ballena**, a magnificent bay backed by deciduous forest. Its beauty has been exploited by a Spanish hotel group whose sprawling, controversial and heavily guarded resort occupies a central position in the surrounding vegetation. It may be popular with package tours but Hotel Barceló's golf course, oversize clubhouse buildings and barracks-like holiday homes are not so understated and are highly visible from the road. The village of Tambor, to the south, has a modest cluster of beach hotels, shops and restaurants catering to every budget. At the bay's southern point is the Restaurant/Bar Bahía Ballena Yacht Club with safe anchorage, satellite TV, a pool table and boat fuel.

ISLAND KAYAKING

The waters around the southeast corner of the Nicoya Peninsula are generously sprinkled with uninhabited islands, the most famous being Islas Tortugas, with pristine, jungle-backed beaches. Boat tours run here from Puntarenas, Tambor and even Montezuma, but the best way to explore these and some 15 other islands is by sea kayak. Outfitters in Bahía Gigante, between Paquera and Playa Naranjo, offer great paddling tours that include Isla Gitana, immediately offshore. This lush private island has rustic *cabinas*, a popular yachters' bar and friendly wildlife.

55

BEWARE THE RIPTIDES

Costa Rica's Pacific beaches are not always what they seem. Riptides can carry even strong swimmers out to watery graves, and there are drownings every year. No signs exist to warn visitors of the dangers, so it is your own responsibility to check on the safety of a beach and its waves. Never swim off a deserted beach without inquiring locally. If caught in a riptide pulling you out to sea, don't struggle pointlessly against it. Instead, swim parallel to the shore to a point where you see breaking waves, which will help you back to the beach.

For more than 100 million years these creatures, whose ancestors once shared the planet with dinosaurs, have been migrating vast distances across oceans to lay their eggs on specific tropical beaches. Costa Rica is the destination of five species of turtle, which cruise in to the same spots on the Caribbean and Pacific coasts every year.

THREATS TO SURVIVAL

Sea turtles are faced with threats that are far more destructive than the taking of eggs, meat and tortoise-shell. Beachfront constructions deprive turtles of safe nesting areas, and in conta-minated waters they may die after ingesting plastic bags, or get trapped in floating debris that stran-gles or drowns them. More turtles die from accidental capture in fishing nets than from all other life threats combined. Sadly, the *Tico Times* reports that, at a recent symposium, scien-tists predicted that the leatherback may be extinct in as few as 10 years. Worldwide numbers have dropped from an estimated 110,000 in 1980 to less than 25,000 in 2007.

56

Baby loggerheads (above) and freshwater turtles (below)

Leatherbacks, greens, hawksbills, loggerheads and Pacific olive ridleys are the five species of sea turtle that for untold generations have nested on the beaches of Costa Rica. Their homing techniques still baffle scientists, but what is certain is that they commute long distance between feeding grounds and nesting grounds, possibly following a specific smell or substance. Tagging by scientists has sketched the turtles' marine path, and a more precise picture is now emerging with the use of satellites. Since 1954, the world's longest ongoing turtle research station, the American-funded and -run Caribbean Conservation Corporation (CCC), at Tortuguero, has pioneered the protection of turtles, and today Costa Rica claims four major conservation sites. Visitors must follow strict regulations and are often accom-panied by former turtle hunters who have become guides.

Giant nomads On the Península de Nicoya, a new national park was created in 1991, at Playa Grande, to protect nesting leatherbacks (*baulas*). This giant of the turtle world measures up to 2.4m (8ft) and weighs around 680kg (1,500lb). Unlike other turtles, it does not have a hard shell but a thick, black, leathery skin—hence its name; nor does it show strong fidelity to a particular nesting site. Solitary female leatherbacks come ashore on the Pacific coast between November and April to dig their huge nests, where they lay about 100 eggs in a laborious nocturnal operation, before covering them with sand and waddling back to sea. After 60–90 days the hatchlings emerge to make their way to the ocean across the treacherous beach, making easy

prey for crabs, seabirds and mammals. Only a tiny percentage survive. The eggs themselves have tradi-tionally been plundered by villagers, although this habit is now changing.

Between February and July, leatherbacks also nest on the Caribbean coast, at Tortuguero and at the Gandoca-Manzanillo Wildlife Refuge. At the latter, regula-tions now limit the number of eggs that villagers may collect, while the rest are hatched in incubators and the young turtles introduced to the sea.

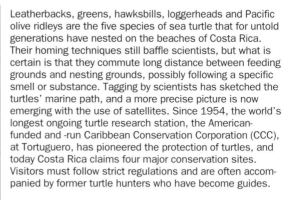

No room on the beach It takes luck to witness nesting leatherbacks, despite their tractor-like tracks, but quite the opposite is the case with Pacific olive ridleys, especially at Ostional and Nancite in Santa Rosa National Park (see pages 50–51). This much smaller species arrives in flotillas of hundreds, and sometimes there is so little room on the 1,000m (1,100yd) beach that latecomers nest by the road. These amazing arrivals, called *arrihadas,* take place every month of the year, but especially from July to December, and last four to eight days. Again, villagers can collect eggs during the first 36 hours, and even the research station is funded by the sale of eggs. Tagging of more than 6,000 Pacific olive ridleys has charted their path north to the United States and south as far as Peru. Ostional is also visited, more rarely, by leatherbacks and greens, making it the second most important sea turtle hatchery in the world.

Vegetarians Research into green turtles is concentrated on the black-sand beaches of Tortuguero, which claims the largest hatchery in the western Caribbean, as well as less frequent visits from leatherbacks, hawksbills and logger-heads. When Dr. Archie Carr started his research in the 1950s, greens were being harvested by locals for their much-prized flesh. Unlike the jellyfish diet of leatherbacks or the sponges devoured by hawksbills—which make them toxic—the seagrass diet of greens makes them particularly tasty. Former turtle hunters are now employed as guides or guards, and the CCC is working to expand the national park across the Nicaraguan border. Greens come to nest between June and November, when they lay 100 to 140 eggs before continuing north to feed off Nicaragua's Miskito Coast, and then disperse throughout the Caribbean.

Hawksbill turtles continue to be hunted illegally for their shells

FLAPPING IN VAIN
"When the crashing wave breaks, they jump onto shore. They turtle along, dragging their shells in a rhythmic centuries-old minuet. They spawn deep in the sand, and when they attempt their return, they are flipped belly up and are left, flapping in vain, rocking back and forth stubbornly on their shells. Turtle in the soup, eggs in the gut of some turtle-bashing drunk. Sure, God made the animals first and then man. If the animals are dying, does the diviner divine who's next?" Abel Pacheco, *Deeper Than Skin* (1972).

▶▶ Refugio Nacional de
Fauna Silvestre Ostional

38B2

Open: daily

Located on the coast southwest of Nicoya, this 248ha (615-acre) wildlife refuge protects the nesting grounds of the small Pacific olive ridley turtle. This species' homing instincts and the limited choice of potential nesting sites bring regular armadas, called *arribadas*, to this spot, above all from July to December during the moon's last quarter, when you will see them arrive, looking like hundreds of floating boulders. Leatherbacks are occasionally seen between November and January, but hawksbill and green turtles are very rare here. A turtle research station, located at the entrance to this black-sand beach refuge, provides information and basic dormitory facilities, and there are a few *cabinas* in the village.

*Top: brown pelican
Above: the magnificent
frigate bird. Pelicans
skim the sea surface,
hunting sardines
and mackerel; frigates
soar high, preying
on baby turtles and
other creatures*

Airborne The coastal wetlands and forest are home to some 190 species of bird, including the brown pelican, frigate bird, royal tern, neotropic cormorant and roseate spoonbill. Walks extend along the seashore for some 18km (11 miles) north to Punta India or south along Playa Nosara to Garza, and at low tide will reveal a wealth of sea urchins, anemones, crabs and small fish trapped in the abundant rock pools. The entire beach has strong currents, so would-be swimmers should take heed of a memorial sign to a young American who drowned in 1992.

▶▶ Refugio Nacional de
Vida Silvestre Curú

39D1

This privately owned wildlife refuge, which is discreetly signposted from the road 6.5km (4 miles) south of Paquera, incorporates a 84ha (208-acre) mixture of pastureland, tropical hill forest, mangrove swamp, and 4.5km (3 miles) of idyllic beaches. It was established in 1933 by the Schutz family, which still runs it, and is named after the indigenous name for the massive Guanacaste tree. The hacienda's varied history well reflects the environmental problems and solutions that Costa Rica is still finding. The initial decision to carry out selective cutting of tropical trees, and to establish pasture and agricultural land, was followed in 1974 by an invasion of squatters, leading to the decision to protect both forest and mangroves and then, in 1983, the fragile marine habitat.

Ongoing activities Curú now has a small research station, used for educational projects. Several basic huts are available for overnight stays, with preference given to students and researchers. Current projects include reafforestation, introduction of natural pest predators in order to eliminate pesticide use, preservation of turtle habitat, and the reintroduction of the spider monkey into the area. You can follow one of the 11 trails of varying difficulty that wind through the refuge, and the fine, white-sand beach is ideal for swimming. Some 226 species of bird, 78 species of mammal and 87 reptile species inhabit the refuge, including domesticated creatures that prowl around the house and research station. Olive Ridley and hawk's-bill turtles nest on the beaches, and the forest is full of howler, capuchin and spider monkeys as well as ocelots, pumas, agoutis, deer, sloths and anteaters.

Visitors should book in advance, even for a day visit (tel: 641-0100/641-0590, www.curuwildliferefuge.com *Admission: moderate*).

▶ Reserva Biológica Lomas Barbudal · 38C3

Open: daily 8–4. Admission: moderate
In 1986 it was decided to protect 2,200ha (5,440 acres) of the dry tropical forest and extensive grasslands in the middle of Guanacaste's hot, dry plains and hills (lomas barbudal means "bearded hills," and refers to the patches of dry forest that still remain). During the wet season Lomas Barbudal visually leaps out from the surrounding deforested savannah, but as the dry season advances it soon assumes a parched appearance.

Some mammals live here, but the reserve's biological importance lies above all in some 250 species of social and solitary bees (including the so-called Africanized or killer bees) and in its numerous moth species. Local communities have been extensively involved in developing and manning the reserve, as explained at a Visitor Center in Bagaces, run by the Amigos de Lomas Barbudal (tel: 671-1290/200-0125). Access to the reserve is from Pijije on the Interamerican Highway, from where a gravel road leads to the park headquarters on the banks of the Río Cabuyo. A welcoming feature here is a freshwater pool.

CHEWING-GUM TREE
The useful evergreen chicle tree reaches heights of about 20m (66ft) and grows in Mexico, Central and South America and the Caribbean. Its sweet brown fruit can be eaten raw, and is made into syrups and preserves throughout the region. And the chewing gum? This is obtained by tapping the tree every two to three years, when it yields up to 73L (19gal) of chicle. The chicle is then transformed into that well-known substance—the plague of streets and bus seats the world over.

59

During the dry season, thirsty trees become natural sculptures all too vulnerable to forest fires

GRINGO NOSE
The gumbo-limbo tree can be seen from Santa Rosa to Cabo Blanco. It attracts a variety of names, whether gumbo-limbo, *indio desnudo* ("naked Indian"), tourist's tree or, even more eloquent, gringo nose. These lyrical descriptions are due to the way its dark-yellow bark peels to reveal a greenish under-bark. This photosynthetic process takes place during the dry season to feed the tree.

►► Reserva Natural Absoluta Cabo Blanco
39D1

Open: Wed–Sun 8–4. Admission: moderate

This is the longest-protected area in Costa Rica. The reserve was instigated in 1963 by a Swedish nature-lover, Olof Wessberg, who was far-sighted enough to recognize the importance of preserving and regenerating the last tracts of tropical rain forest on the peninsula. As a result, the numerous rivers running through the 1,174ha (2,900-acre) reserve are always flowing, unlike those in the rest of this drought-ridden region, a clear environmental lesson. Visitors have been allowed in this "absolute" reserve only since the late 1980s.

Forest trail One 5km (3-mile) trail leads from the park entrance over densely forested hills before descending to Playa Cabo Blanco, opposite Isla Cabo Blanco (a popular nesting site for the brown booby). A second trail offers a 2km (1-mile) loop through the forest. Typical trees are the spiny cedar, gumbo-limbos, mayflowers, chicle trees, Panama woods and lemonwoods. Wildlife includes white-tailed deer, squirrels, tiger cats, howler, spider and white-faced monkeys, plus screeching parakeets. Watch for rat-eating snakes, grass snakes, boa constrictors, vipers and the aptly named coral snakes—the latter can be deadly.

Right: the deadly coral snake
Below: cattle grazing the parched grasslands of the Guanacaste region

▶ Río Tempisque   38C3

This important 160km (100-mile) river has its headwaters high on the slopes of Volcán Orosí in the far north of Guanacaste, from where it flows south through Lomas Barbudal and Palo Verde before emerging into the Golfo de Nicoya. Its once fertile valley attracted prehistoric settlers, and it has long been used for transportation by boat, but sedimentation is now causing the water level to sink quite dramatically, making navigation hazardous. One of the problems is that local farmers build small dams along the Tempisque in order to redirect water for irrigation; another problem is deforestation along its banks, which leads to topsoil deposits. Despite this, Palo Verde, upriver by boat, remains a fabulous destination for bird-watching.

Bridge Visitors to the Nicoya Peninsula's central and southern regions no longer need wait tedious high-season hours to ride the decrepit old Tempisque Ferry, as it has been replaced by a handsome new bridge which opened in early 2003. Named the Taiwan Friendship Bridge, the $26 million, 780m (853yd) span was paid for in full by the government of Taiwan. Look for the turn off the Interamerican Highway about 19km (12 miles) south of Cañas.

▶ Santa Cruz   38B3

Santa Cruz is Guanacaste's burgeoning university and cultural hub. It hosts numerous festivals but for visitors serves mainly as the gateway for Playas Tamarindo, Grande and Junquillal. Along its hand-paved streets, decorative old clapboard houses stand next to less appealing concrete low-rises, many of which have filled in a large section of the central area that was devastated by fire in 1993. Most hotels are in or near the Plaza de Los Mangos, west of which lies the Parque Central, dominated by a weathered pink clock tower, all that is left of a colonial church destroyed by an earthquake and now over-shadowed by a modern church. Three blocks farther west is the **Coope Tortilla▶▶▶**, an astonishing barnlike building where a 12-woman co-operative dishes up some 500 low-cost meals a day to hungry locals and visitors seated at long wooden tables. One man is employed to fuel the external tortilla ovens. The bustling atmosphere of blackened pots bubbling on wood-burning stoves is hard to beat, and you're unlikely to find a less expensive, more authentic meal anywhere.

▶ Volcán Miravalles   39D4

The highest peak in the Guanacaste Mountains rises over 2,012m (6,601ft) out of the hot savannah north of Bagaces. Although it is dormant, this volcano contains natural heat reserves that since 1994 have been exploited to produce geothermal energy, regarded as a more consistent source of energy than hydroelectric power (the latter formerly produced 85 percent of Costa Rica's energy needs). Las Hornillas (tel: 839-9769, www.lashornillas.com) offers tours to the summit and horseback riding in the private reserve where encounters with toucans, monkeys, or even wildcats are possible. The full day tour also adds hanging bridges, La Escondida waterfall, and bathing in bubbling, therapeutic mud pots similar to those at Rincón de la Vieja.

61

BULLS
Not all those cattle you see scattered over the pastures of Guanacaste are destined for the dinner plate. Bullfighting is still a popular tradition throughout northern Costa Rica, and bullrings are a common, often precarious-looking, municipal fixture. However, in true pacific Tico fashion, bullfighters do not aim to kill the bulls. Quite the contrary, it is often the *montador* (climber) who gets hurt in his macho attempts to clamber onto the bucking bull's back and seize its horns.

ROADS GOOD AND BAD
Complaints about Costa Rica's brain-rattling, pothole-scarred roads are legion, but there is a downside to smooth paving. All over Guanacaste, improved roads have brought bigger, more expensive hotels, golf courses, and housing developments for wealthy foreigners. As with many other regions, when tiresome, time-consuming access routes are made fast and easy, quaint little towns, alluring beaches, and even jungles, can change beyond recognition.

Drive

Península de Nicoya

See map on pages 38–39

Allow a long day for this circuit through the peninsula's heart, taking in the main towns and pottery workshops and ending at some stunning beaches. It can be covered in a sturdy two-wheel-drive vehicle. A detour to the Parque Nacional Barra Honda is possible.

Start at **Playa Tamarindo** and from there drive through Villareal to the intersection at Huacas. Bear right and continue through open pastures with hills rising on both sides of the road and, in the dry season, splashes of yellow corteza trees. White Brahma cattle loiter in the rare shade provided by Guanacaste trees, or are herded by cowboys on horseback as the road winds through tiny villages and past isolated farms. If the road is blocked by a *sabañero* and his herd, don't expect him to move it: the local habit is to weave your way slowly through the seemingly unconcerned cattle. About 19km (12 miles) farther on, reach the crossroads at Belén. Turn right here

toward Santa Cruz, entering a flatter rural landscape. Stop at **Santa Cruz►** to sample an early Guanacaste lunch at the **Coope Tortilla►►►** (see page 61).

Leave the town on the main road from the Plaza de Los Mangos and, shortly after crossing the Río San Juan, take a left turn toward Santa Bárbara. Grasslands, low hills in the background, clumps of green flowering trees, and royal palms contribute to the beauty of this route. After 10km (6 miles, beyond Santa Bárbara), reach **Guaitíl►►►** (see page 42). Visit the pottery workshops here, then continue to the hamlet of **San Vicente** to compare the techniques and imagination of the pottery. From here the bumpy gravel road winds through more villages, with the limestone hills of the **Parque Nacional Barra Honda►►** (see page 47) gradually coming into view. Tracts of forest may include quamwoods, wild cotton and lemon woods. At Piave, along the turning to Nacaome, a detour can be made to the park, but the road needs a four-wheel-drive vehicle. Otherwise, to visit the park, continue 2km (1 mile) to the main road, turn left, and then drive 11km (7 miles) to a left turn where there is a sign for the park (another 5km/3 miles). It is possible to continue by circling back to Nicoya, but time will be short and you may have to spend the night in Nicoya.

Stock up on inexpensive fruit in Nicoya

For those who have not made the detour to the park, the picturesque main route finally leads into **Nicoya**▶▶ (see page 45), where decorative fretwork buildings, often shrouded in bougainvillea, surround the town's historic church (it also functions as a museum). There is no shortage of *sodas* for refreshment, and the shady garden adjoining the church is a pleasant place to recover from the bone-shaking road. Leave Nicoya's main square by driving downhill from its southeastern corner: this is the main road south that leads through Curimé and eventually reaches Playa Sámara, 34km (21 miles) south. Continue for some 29km (18 miles), twisting through shorn hills dotted with palms, and past cattle and fields of melon and watermelon. After the neat village of Belén (a different one!), the

Sorting the tomato crop. Coffee, bananas and other export crops aside, Costa Rican agriculture is primarily small-scale and local

road climbs to overlook a magnificent wide valley edged with handsomely contoured hills. Mustachioed cowboys, traditional thatched buildings and sprouting fences (see panel on page 81) are common sights in this area. Some 5km (3 miles) before Sámara turn right on a bumpy road to Barco Quebrada, which necessitates fording some shallow rivers.

Next stop is **Garza**, a pretty village straggling along a rocky cove that offers good swimming, bars, restaurants and some places to stay. The drive can end here, or continue to the beaches and hills of **Nosara**▶▶▶ (see page 46).

The North

▶▶▶ REGION HIGHLIGHTS

Previous pages: horses provide the only means of transport in the rugged mountains on Laguna de Arenal's southern banks

THE NORTH Unfolding northward from the natural mountainous barrier of the Cordillera Central and the Cordillera de Tilarán is a patchwork of landscapes encapsulating Costa Rica's incredible natural riches as much as its environmental woes. Volcanoes, waterfalls, mineral springs, rushing rivers, marshes, cloud forest, rain forest and rolling cattle pastures combine to create this concentrated topographical diversity. Towns remain small in scale, and points of interest are well scattered over a network of rough roads, so this is certainly a region where a car is advisable. Watch out in the rainy season, when many roads become impassable, and make sure your clothing is adaptable to rapid changes in temperature. The northern region is also home to a handful of Costa Rica's pioneering eco-lodges, whose isolated

ENFORCED MYOPIA

"Go up and down mountains. Touch clouds and shiver with cold. Sometimes waterfalls thunder, at other times wide rivers flow with clear and resonant waters, occasionally currents so deep that you can barely see the bottom from the top of a narrow bridge studded with crosses in memory of accidents. Coming down, you always arrive at a meeting of bridge and river; going up, you always run into mist for miles of enforced myopia." Carmen Naranjo, *Believe It or Not* (1991).

locations make unusual demands on even the most well-seasoned visitors. Try the tractor ride to Rara Avis or a riverbank stay at Selva Verde, near La Selva.

HOT SPOTS On the shores of Laguna de Arenal, water sports, fishing and horseback-riding vie with the attractions of the fierce Volcán Arenal, most comfortably, if riskily, observed while enjoying a natural water massage at the hot springs of Tabacón (said by some to lie in a highly vulnerable position on the volcano's flank). Some visitors home in on Fortuna de San Carlos, while serious bird-watchers head for the rain forest of La Selva or the wetlands of Caño Negro. Boats from Puerto Viejo de Sarapiquí chug northeast along the Nicaraguan border and eventually into the Amazon-style waterways of Barra del Colorado and

RESPLENDENT QUETZAL

Both sacred (for the Maya) and elusive, the resplendent quetzal (pictured on page 173) lives all year round in the high-altitude cloud forests of Central America, from southern Mexico to Panama. Today its numbers are decreasing alarmingly owing to the destruction of its natural habitat. The nesting season—March to May—offers the best chance of sightings, when male and female can be seen swapping shifts for incubating the eggs. Nests are built in the hollows of dead trees. The brilliantly hued male's long green tail feathers are spectacular, especially in flight, and are at their best in the spring.

Self-sufficient homesteads are a Tico tradition in the lush hills north of Monteverde

Tortuguero (see pages 133 and 142–143 respectively), another bird-watchers' paradise. These boat tours are best organized through agencies in San José. One of the world's largest volcanic craters, Poás, is easily accessible from San José but the northern trail's popular destination is the cool hill country of Monteverde and Santa Elena, where cloud-forest reserves offer flashes of the resplendent quetzal, as well as endless hiking possibilities. Monteverde is no longer quite the idyllic retreat it was, and is often crowded in high season. Yet, by offering visitors educational slide shows, lectures and other diversions, and hiking in alternative, nearby reserves such as Santa Elena, Monteverde's managers have managed to establish successful "crowd control"—a model of ecotourism in a fragile environment.

ECO-ENLIGHTENMENT It is in this region that you can learn how the rain forest functions as the planet's lungs, a complex, sophisticated interactive system. There is no shortage of information or experts, and private environmental initiatives are mushrooming, particularly around the Limón highway, as it cuts through the Parque Nacional Braulio Carrillo, and in the hills around Monteverde. Though great swathes of the northern lowlands and foothills have been logged and/or given over to agriculture or cattle grazing, much of the rolling green terrain remains unchanged. Today, the people of the Sarapiquí are organized, and determined to put a halt to over-development. *Campesinos* (farmers) on horseback, farms hidden in lush valleys, and tiny villages with their *sodas*, *pulperías* and central squares, give an equally authentic picture of rural Costa Rica.

▶ Bosque Eterno de los Niños   66B2

The Bosque Eterno de los Niños (Children's Eternal Forest) has, since 1988, acquired and protected more than 22,000ha (54,000 acres) of cloud forest.

Children from 30 countries finance conservation, international environmental education, reafforestation and the establishment of biological research stations. Local communities are closely involved through school projects or by adopting farming methods that are compatible with conservation. Problems such as fires, poaching, logging and squatters remain, and the number of forest guards is insufficient to patrol such an area, but the managing group inspires confidence for the future.

A small section of the forest, **Bajo del Tigre▶** (see page 77), lies in Monteverde itself, but more interesting are the trails surrounding **San Gerardo▶▶**, an isolated research station situated near Santa Elena. The scenic landscapes reveal the region's fantastic biodiversity. Horses are available for trekking. Contact the Monteverde Conservation League in Monteverde (tel: 645-5003/5305, fax: 645-5104, www.acmcr.org) for information.

▶▶▶ Catarata La Paz   67D1

A luxury hotel combined with a first-class nature tour is not a new idea in Costa Rica, but Waterfall Gardens (tel: 225-0643, fax: 225-1082, www.waterfallgardens.com *Open* daily 8.30–5.30. *Admission: expensive*) is the best. The five spectacular waterfalls and gardens are breathtaking, and trails and platforms have been sited to maximize views and photo opportunities. Butterfly and humming-bird gardens are also in place, with horseback-riding and trout fishing to come. The Welcome Center has a shop and dining areas.

▶ Ciudad Quesada (San Carlos)   66C2

A humid gateway to the north, often known by its former name of San Carlos, Ciudad Quesada lies at the foot of the Cordillera Central. It is an important sugarcane, citrus fruits and cattle area, and its cattle fair in early April is one of Costa Rica's largest.

The town is of limited interest, but the main square has a crafts co-operative, a vegetable market, and a casino (in the Hotel La Central). Local *talabarterias* (saddlemakers) are known for their finely crafted leather saddles. A small tourist office, Catuzon, (tel: 460–1822. *Open* weekdays 8.30–11.30, 1.30–5) is located at the southern entrance. Occidental El Tucano, a luxury hotel built on hot springs, is just outside town.

INFANT INITIATIVE

At the origin of the Bosque Eterno de los Niños was a group of Swedish children who, concerned by the demise of the rain forest, raised money which they sent to the Monteverde Conservation League. From that point the project took off, and schoolchildren from Britain, the United States, Germany and Japan were soon actively working to raise funds. Its educational work continues in informative newsletters, which juxtapose serious articles with pages designed for young children.

69

Much pride is taken in a cowboy's accessories, the best being from Ciudad Quesada

HELICONIAS

Although the name heliconia derives from Mt. Helicon, the Greek mythological home of the Muses, these decorative flowers are native to Latin America and some islands of the Pacific. They develop in secondary forest in humid lowland tropics or higher up in the cloud forest, and are pollinated by humming-birds. Flat, two-dimensional leaves grow vertically on long stalks, and the plants are easily mistaken for their close cousin, the banana palm. From the stalk the vivid flower branch emerges, usually bright red, yellow or pink. Some 50 flowers blossom on each inflorescence, lasting anything from a few days to months before they die and rot away.

Walk or drive 5km (3 miles) from La Fortuna, then take a 15-minute hike on a steep, at times slippery, trail to reach La Fortuna waterfall

▶ Fortuna de San Carlos (La Fortuna)　　66B2

Fierce, fiery and deadly, Volcán Arenal looms over La Fortuna, spitting incandescent fireballs and floods of molten lava. Drawn by the volcano, visitors flock here, and the town buzzes with guides and tour agents offering trips on horseback, by Jeep or by boat to the volcano (day or night), myriad volcanic hot springs, the Venado Caves, Caño Negro or Río Frío. One tour company, Desafío (see below) even offer tours of a local Maleku indigenous reserve where a shaman demonstrates the uses of medicinal herbs. Commercial sharks abound and prices vary, but reliable service is provided by Sunset Tours (tel: 479–9585, fax 479–9800, www.sunsettourcr.com), by the Rancho Cascada Restaurant on the town square, or by Desafío Adventure Company (tel: 479-9464, fax: 479-9463 www.desafiocostarica.com), a block away behind the church. Hikers can explore the lower slopes rising toward Arenal, or head southwest to the **Catarata Río Fortuna▶▶▶**, a magnificent waterfall thundering down to a jungle pool. The access road winds uphill past isolated farms and agricultural land before penetrating forest where jaguars are said to roam. Take a cooling swim, or scramble around behind the waterfall for a dramatically different perspective.

▶ Guácimo and Guápiles　　67E1

The interest of these two towns, 11km (7 miles) apart, lies in their surroundings. Banana companies have transformed much of the character of the region, but it is attracting an increasing number of conservation-inspired projects, all on or just off the Limón highway. Number one is **EARTH (Escuela de Agricultura de la Región Tropical Humedo)▶▶** (tel: 713-0000, fax: 713-0001, www.earth.ac.cr), which lies at Pocora, immediately southeast of Guácimo. Since 1990, students from all over Latin America have come here to take university courses in sustainable tropical agriculture, and trails through a private rain-forest reserve are open to tour groups and independent visitors. Situated opposite, the **Hotel Rio Palmas▶** (tel: 760-0330, fax: 760-0296, riopalma@racsa.co.cr) has developed a 2½-hour trail through its own reserve, with river, waterfall and heliconia garden.

Gardens Closer to Guápiles, accessible by a 5km (3-mile) gravel road from a turn-off at the Soda Buenos Aires, is the family-run **Jardín Botánico Las Cusingas▶▶** (tel: 710-2652. *Open* daily 7–4. *Admission: moderate*). This project preserves a tract of secondary rain forest (with a two-hour trail) beside an experimental garden for medicinal plants, and is developing an educational station for adults and children. More commercial in spirit is **Costa Flores▶** (tel/fax: 228-3571. *Open* weekdays. *Admission: expensive*, guided tour), Costa Rica's largest tropical flower farm, 15km (9 miles) east of Guápiles.

Part of the garden has been landscaped next to a restaurant, and the entire area attracts humming-birds and butterflies. The 12,000ha (29,600-acre) Parque Nacional Barbilla (accessible by four-wheel-drive only) lies south of Guácimo. Dedicated in 1997, it protects the northeast flank of the Talamanca Mountains. Facilities are limited.

Rain forest Reached from a short track leading north from the Río Corinto, is the **Centro Ecológico Morpho▶** (tel: 221-9132, fax: 257-2273), a rain-forest reserve that organizes environment-related workshops (medicinal-plant science and guide training, for example), with a small lodge, tents and trails for visitors. Children will enjoy the Frog Trail. The region's crowning attraction is the **Rain Forest Aerial Tram▶▶▶** (tel: 257-5961, fax: 257-6053, www.rainforesttram.com *Open* daily 6–3.30. *Admission: very expensive*), an extraordinary enterprise that opened in 1994. The open cable-cars float visitors above the jungle canopy along a 3km (2-mile) route that takes about 1½ hours. Observation stops can be made on request to the accompanying guide, but this is not a zoo, so do not expect to see wildlife swinging along beside you. Bird-watchers should aim for the very early morning; otherwise, afternoons are less crowded but booking is always advisable. Access by tractor down from the highway is followed by a short trail that leads to the unobtrusive information point and restaurant.

The Rain Forest Aerial Tram

DR. PERRY
The inventor of the jungle cable car is Dr. Donald Perry, an imaginative California professor of tropical biology who, since 1974, has been developing various methods of exploring the fascinating world of Costa Rica's forests. Adapting mountain-climbing techniques, he started with a rope web system strung over the jungle canopy, continued at Rara Avis with an automated web, which included observation platforms, and in 1992 started the ambitious aerial tram project. Installation logistics were mind-boggling, but in October 1994 the aerial tram finally opened.

RAIN FOREST PALMS

One of the most characteristic plants found in the subcanopy (9 to 24m/29 to 79ft) of primary rain forest is the palm, and at La Selva, 32 species have so far been identified. The most common is the *Welfia georgii*, distinguishable by its brilliant-orange young leaves and its long, serpentine growths that spread over the forest floor. The seeds of this palm are much appreciated by monkeys, agoutis and other mammals, which in their turn attract the hungry bushmaster viper. Another common rain-forest palm is the *Socratea exorrhiza*, recognizable by its triangular web of spiny roots.

►► Laguna de Arenal   66A2

This mirrorlike expanse, reflecting Volcán Arenal (see page 83) at its eastern end and skimmed by windsurfers at its western end, is Central America's largest artificial lake. In 1973 an existing lake was enlarged by flooding the original town of Arenal, and this is now a hub for water sports (windsurfing above all), fishing (rainbow bass), and horseback-riding. A paved but frequently washed out road runs from the volcano, along the northern banks, to curve eventually around the windier western end, where it cuts south to Tilarán (see page 81). Places to stay are scattered up slopes beside the road, nearly all with fabulous vistas across the water to the Cordillera de Tilarán. The wild southern banks are most easily accessible on horseback.

Mineral soak The **Tabacón Resort►** (tel: 519–1900, fax: 519–1940, www.tabacon.com *Open* daily 10–10. *Admission: expensive*), 11km (7 miles) west of La Fortuna, is a spa built to take advantage of Arenal's thermal springs. Five pools, a restaurant, Jacuzzis, massages, landscaped gardens, and a pricey, over-size new hotel across and up the road, are part of the package. Less expensive are the Baldi Termae (tel: 479-9652, www.balditermae.com *Open* daily 10-10. *Admission:* moderate) with 10 thermal pools at varying temperatures and a spa, at the base of the volcano closer to La Fortuna. Southeast of Nuevo Arenal (a budget stop) along a killer stretch of road is the **Jardín Botánico Arenal (Arenal Botanical Garden)►►►** (tel: 694-4305, fax: 694-4086, www.junglegold.com *Open* daily 9–5. *Admission: inexpensive*). This small, beautifully landscaped garden offers a serpentarium and a butterfly sanctuary, together with a fantastic array of more than 1,000 varieties of native and exotic plants, alive with butterflies and humming-birds. Along the same road are the **Arenal Hanging Bridges** (tel/fax: 479-9686, www.hangingbridges.com *Open* daily 7–4. *Admission: expensive*), a private forest reserve with 3km (2 miles) of trails, six hanging bridges and eight fixed bridges.

La Selva's network of bridges and trails contains several habitats, ranging from pasture to tropical wet forest

►►► La Selva   67D2

This OTS (Organization for Tropical Studies) station reigns over 1,600ha (3,950 acres) of protected rain forest adjoining Parque Nacional Braulio Carrillo. An average annual rainfall of more than 381cm (150in) combines with 62 percent primary rain forest to make it one of the top four places in the world for rain-forest research.

American and Costa Rican scientists flock here to study the remarkable biodiversity, which includes more than half (in excess of 400) of Costa Rica's bird species. Tapirs, jaguars, sloths, coatis and howler monkeys are among the

113 mammal species that lurk in the shadows of this spectacular reserve, while butterflies, amphibians and reptiles add to the abundance. Some 50km (31 miles) of well-marked trails cross the humid forest, and are best followed with an informative guide, but as this is primarily a scientific and educational establishment, access for non-specialist visitors is restricted. Reservations, even for a day visit, must be made well in advance through the OTS office in San José (tel: 524–0607, fax: 524–0608, www.ots.duke.edu *Admission: expensive*). Access is from the main road south of Puerto Viejo along an unmarked road heading west from a bus stop.

▶ Los Chiles 66B4

A straight, flat road slices through northern Costa Rica to the Nicaraguan border at Los Chiles, a dilapidated town that serves as a base for touring the wetlands of Caño Negro (see page 80) or for crossing into Nicaragua. This sparsely populated area is characterized by orange groves, sugar-cane plantations and sawmills piled high with gigantic logs. Los Chiles itself has some quaint clapboard houses but lodgings are limited. Most visitors come on day-trips arranged in La Fortuna. Locally, tours can be arranged through Servicios Turísticos Colibri (tel: 399-8607), while San Carlos Sportfishing (tel: 395-5053, www.nicaraguafishing.com) runs fishing tours on the Río San Juan.

IT'S THE CICADAS
"There is a voiceless murmur at first, brilliant, then vibrant, that grows, stuck to the earth. There are thousands of voices. Myriads of screeches. It isn't the sound of the trees or the rivers, it isn't human voices. It's the cicadas. Their voices grow under the green, in the dust, in the gardens. They move the leaves, stir the river, build forever and ever, as if they were never going to end, maddening, in waves surging from the ground, fanning down from the houses, forever and ever and ever..." Yolanda Oreamuno, *The Spirit of My Land*.

73

Open-sided boats with sun-and-rain canopy protection depart from Los Chiles down the Río Frío to Caño Negro. Visitors are advised to bring insect repellent—the mosquitoes are voracious!

The medicinal secrets of tropical plants have still to be extensively explored by scientists, but for centuries indigenous people, Afro-Caribbeans and descendants of the Spaniards alike have relied on them. Every Costa Rican market has vendors of folk remedies, and herbal medicines are now gaining a hold on visitors seeking an alternative to antibiotics.

74

GO TO NO DOCTOR

In the words of Mr Selvyn Bryant of Old Harbour, transcribed by Paula Palmer in her folk history of Talamanca's Afro-Caribbeans, *What Happen:* "One time machete cut these three finger, all three right to the bone. Go to no doctor. Just get the cocoa and scrape it on there, tie it up. Machete chop off this finger too, when I was a boy, and I wave it till this end piece practically come off, and my mother take it and just clamp it on back and get cocoa and bandage it up. Go to no doctor."

ONGOING TRADITION

Herbal medicine is by no means dying out in Costa Rica. In 1981 an international congress on medicinal plants took place in San José, and delegates were taken to Bribrí and Puerto Viejo to investigate traditional cures used by *curanderos* (healers). Since then, concern about diminishing knowledge among indigenous communities has led to a series of workshops among the Talamanca and Guaymi populations, so that they could share their knowledge and renew confidence in natural medicine.

Ironically, in a country that boasts a highly developed public health service, with more than 85 percent of homes covered by local health care and a life expectancy of 73-plus years (just behind North America's 76 years and well ahead of all other Central American states), folk remedies still play a major role in daily life. Talamanca Indians, Afro-Caribbeans, and the Ticos of the capital are all well acquainted with the medicinal uses of plants and fruits. Stinging nettles, cocoa pods, coconuts, manioc, knotgrass, mango leaves, passion fruit, aloe, ginger, custard apples, pineapples, leaves of the breadfruit tree, sap of the tallow tree—all of these, and hundreds of others, may be brewed into teas, made into solutions or applied directly to wounds.

Mystical application Plant cures are traditionally used by Costa Rica's Indian population in mystical rituals performed by a *awapa orjawa* (shaman), a crucial spiritual role inherited through the male line. Armed with an *ulu* (a balsa-wood stick painted with images of the god Sibu and mythological plants and animals) and wearing a pouch around his neck containing magic stones to detect illness or pain, he launches into ritual chants before administering the appropriate remedy. Ceremonies take place only at night. Every Talamanca Indian acquires an intimate knowledge of the use of plants for everyday problems: ulcers are cured with a preparation of leaves from the *frailecillo* (cassava marble), colic with an infusion of white mustard leaves, arthritis and hair loss with a preparation of leaves from the guarumo and quina trees. An extract of the cycad plant treats snake bites, as does the juice of no fewer than 18 lemons, drunk at six intervals of 10 minutes.

Tie it up The Afro-Caribbean population of Limón is particularly resilient (with a genetic resistance to the tropical killer malaria) and shares medicinal knowledge with local Indians. General good health means that medicinal care is most commonly needed only for childbirth, snake bites or accidents such as machete cuts. Midwives and snake doctors were once the most respected members of a Talamanca Afro-Caribbean community, the latter working in a semi-mystical fashion similar to that of the Indian shaman. For machete cuts the common remedy was simply to apply a peeled green cacao pod. The sticky inner cacao flesh was bandaged to the wound and left there until it healed.

Brew it up Tico market bristles with bunches of leaves, vines, roots and cactus leaves, all classified for their respective treatments. For facial inflammations, try an infusion made from a fragrant river valley shrub, queen-of-the-night (whose genus *Datura* is a source of antidotes for certain pesticide poisonings). For allergies apply the squeezed sap of papaya leaves; for intestinal worms take a morning draught of coconut and pineapple juice; for diarrhoea choose from manioc, the boiled young leaves of the guava tree, or passion fruit; for arthritis boil the root and top of the sulfur plant or use a preparation of ripe plantains; for coughs and bronchitis make an infusion of oregano; for insect bites apply a solution made from the leaves of the natural blue...the treatments and ingredients are endless.

Certain plants have multiple uses. An infusion of the aloe vera cactus relieves bronchitis, diabetes and colitis, and the gelatinous leaves are used externally for burns, rashes and dry skin—something the cosmetics industry appreciates too. The geranium, brewed into a tea, is said to help sore throats, hysteria and menstrual disorders. And for a really fortifying energy kick, some Ticos drink an infusion of *culantro de coyote* (spirit weed).

LEAF OF LIFE
The seemingly miraculous *hoja de aire* (the leaf of life, air plant or miracle plant) whose leaves have the ability to grow after being separated from the plant, is said to cure coughs and colds.

75

Gnarled roots and bundles of leaves hardly seem inspiring, but curanderos *(healers) know their hidden properties*

GETTING THERE
Several companies now
have cut the time for the
trip between Monteverde
and La Fortuna by a combination of jeeps and a boat
across Lago Arenal with
stunning views of Volcán
Arenal and the lake. The
trip takes about three
hours, down from more
than five. Contact Eagle
Tours (tel: 479-9091,
www.eagletours.net) for
more information.

▶▶▶ **Monteverde** 66A2

Monteverde is famous for two things: firstly its cloud-forest reserve, and secondly a farming community founded by American Quakers in the 1950s. The combination makes it one of Costa Rica's top tourist destinations. The road there is slowly being paved, possibly making day trips from San José an option, although you could easily spend a week here.

Pastoral straggle The village straggles some distance along a ridge between Santa Elena and the reserve, so you have to hike or taxi between points of interest, but the cool climate, fragrant pine trees and lovely views make walking very pleasant. Numerous conservation projects, ecologically minded hotels and a constant influx of students and volunteers contribute to the earnest and "alternative" atmosphere. From January to mid-February, the mood changes somewhat, with a festival of classical, jazz and Latin music.

Forest The priority destination is the **Reserva Biológica del Bosque Nuboso de Monteverde (Monteverde Cloud Forest Reserve)**▶▶ (tel: 645-5122, fax: 645-5034, www.cct.or.cr *Open* daily 7–4; earlier entrance possible. *Admission: expensive*), a 10,100ha (24,960-acre) private reserve owned by the Tropical Science Center of San José. It has well-marked trails and a fantastic array of wildlife, including jaguars, ocelots, bellbirds and the resplendent quetzal, as well as (possibly) the golden toad, once found only

Monteverde's cloud forest supports more than 500 butterfly species

here and now feared extinct. Nevertheless, some visitors go home disappointed, if they get in at all—numbers are restricted and bookings are essential in the high season. It takes forethought to ensure that your visit lives up to expectations. A good time to go is between February and April, when bird-watching and weather are at their best. From the Visitor Center, with its humming-bird feeders, follow one of the many trails that enable you to spend the entire day alone. Howler monkeys and quetzals are fairly easy to see overhead. Other forest dwellers are more secretive—stand still and violet sabre-wing humming-birds may come and investigate you, and antbirds and trogons will emerge from the undergrowth. Start early in the morning: by early afternoon, cloud and mist have often descended. Follow the main trail up to the Continental Divide and watch the clouds flow eerily over the ridge itself.

Other places to visit There is plenty of wildlife, even around some of the hotels and boarding houses. In the grounds of Pensión Flor Mar, run by Quaker bird enthusiasts, you may see emerald toucanets, brown jays and masked tityras—even, perhaps, a two-toed sloth. A short distance downhill from the main reserve is **Reserva Sendero Tranquilo** (tel: 645-5010, elsap@sol.racsa.co.cr *Open* daily. *Admission: expensive*), a small private reserve and farm offering personalized cloud-forest tours. At the intersection with the main road stands a Monteverde landmark that has nothing to do with the wildlife—**La Lechería**. This cheese factory (tel: 645-5029, tour information: 645-7090. *Open* tours 9am and 2pm. *Admission: moderate*) is a model of high-technology but environmentally responsible production. At the heart of the village, next to the central grocery co-operative, is **CASEM** (tel: 645-5190, casem.cr@yahoo.com), a women's co-operative selling souvenirs and craft items. Just opposite are **Meg's Stables** (tel: 645-5052), with horseback tours to local look-out points, and, next door, **Stella's Bakery** (tel: 645-5560), a coffee shop selling American cakes.

Education From here, the rural road winds past a river to another cluster of activity, including the offices of the **Monteverde Conservation League▶▶** (tel: 645-5003, fax: 645-5104, www.acmonteverde.com). The league publishes information on environmental issues, especially its main project, the Bosque Eterno de los Niños (see page 69), and the **Bajo del Tigre▶** trail (*Admission: inexpensive*) through secondary and tertiary forest (downhill from the cheese factory and good for bird-watching). Signposted from the main road near here is **Monteverde Butterfly Garden▶▶▶** (tel: 645-5512, www.best.com/~mariposa *Open* daily 9.30–4. *Admission: inexpensive*, guided tour) with more than 40 species of local butterfly. You can tour the tree canopy via a network of platforms with Sky Trek or, the gentler version, Sky Walk (tel: 645-5238, fax: 645-5796, skywalk@sol.racsa.co.cr *Admission: expensive*), or walk or tour the canopy hanging in a harness from cables with Selvatura (tel: 645-5929, fax: 645-5822, www.selvatura.com *Admission: expensive*).

THE QUAKERS
Monteverde's founding fathers were a group of 44 Quakers from Alabama, who in 1951 rejected their country's draft policy and decided to join their destiny with that of newly pacifist Costa Rica. The pleasant climate and fertile, inexpensive land of Monteverde were ideal for their agricultural pursuits. Having bought about 1,580ha (3,900 acres), they set about creating pastures and developing dairy farming, the results of which are visible at today's cheese factory. Their Friends' meeting-house and school are located along the road to the reserve, but most Quakers prefer to avoid the tourist-oriented town and stay well away on their farms.

77

On the rough and rutted road to Monteverde

Boat trips from Puerto Viejo di Sarapiquí give views of monkeys, caymans and countless birds

► ► **Parque Nacional Braulio Carrillo**   67D1

Open: daily 8–4. Admission: moderate

Less than 30 minutes' drive from San José, the main highway to Limón cuts through this magnificent park, which is too often admired only from the comfort of a vehicle. Rugged mountain peaks, primary forest, dormant volcanoes, thundering waterfalls, deep canyons and semi-permanent cloud and/or rain combine to create a unique environment of 4,400ha (10,900 acres). There are three entrances with facilities, information points and trails: two on the highway and a third on the slopes of Volcán Barva, along a rough road from Sacramento, only passable during the dry season. A five-hour trek here (with potential sightings of quetzals along the way) brings you through volcanic landscapes to the crater lake of Danta.

Wild variety Braulio Carrillo has extraordinary diversity. Where it abuts the reserve of La Selva (see pages 72–73), the low altitude of 200m (650ft) nurtures hot and humid rain forest, in contrast to the cool, cloudy southern section (around the highway), which rises from 1,500 to 2,000m (4,900 to 6,500ft), culminating at 2,906m (9,534ft) on the summit of Volcán Barva. These more accessible highland areas are clad in oaks, mountain cypresses, cedars, magnolias, mosses and the distinctive gunnera, or "poor man's umbrella." Birdlife is correspondingly rich, including the three-wattled bellbird, king vulture, solitary eagle and resplendent quetzal, while mammals include coyotes, agoutis and wildcats. A short walk along one of the trails should provide views of owls, butterflies, squirrels, cuckoos and flycatchers. Watch the ground for huge red-legged tarantulas, and be prepared for rain and cool temperatures (see also page 71 for the nearby Rain Forest Aerial Tram).

DOWN BY THE RIVERSIDE
The new Centro Neotrópico Sarapiquís (tel: 761-1004, fax: 761-1415, www. sarapiquis.org *Open* daily. *Admission: moderate to expensive*) is a riverside lodge in a pocket of virgin rain forest, which incorporates a natural history museum, an on-site archeological dig and a botanical garden. The private 300ha (740-acre) Tirimbina Biological Reserve lies directly across the river.

►► Parque Nacional Volcán Poás 66C1

Open: daily 8–3.30. Admission: moderate

The spectacular crater of Poás slips elusively from view as clouds drift across this stark, powerful landscape. Park authorities have even felt obliged to post warnings that visitors may not see the crater at all, but the 648ha (1,600-acre) park always offers easy trails through cloud and dwarf forest, and some 79 bird species. This is the most visited national park, and includes a museum, cafeteria, auditorium and gift shop, from which a short path leads to the crowded look-out point. Here, if you are lucky, you will gaze out over the 3km (2-mile) crater, its lake and steaming fumaroles backed by a cone of slag. Visualize the *azufreros* (sulfur collectors) who, as recently as the 1950s, transported the yellow mineral on foot to sell to medicine-makers. Poás's second crater lake, Laguna Botos, is located along a short trail to the south. The self-guiding La Escalonia trail leads through the cloud forest, rich in bromeliads, lichen and mosses. Birds that you might encounter include the mountain robin, brown jay and scintillant humming-bird. Measuring a mere 6.5cm (2.5in) from bill to tail, this may be the second-smallest bird in the world. Plenty of insects here are considerably larger.

► Puerto Viejo de Sarapiquí 67D2

This nondescript riverside town is the starting point for river trips down the jungle-edged **Río Sarapiquí►►** to the Río San Juan, which forms the Nicaraguan border. From here boats can continue east through the swamps of Barra del Colorado to enter the waterways of Tortuguero. Organized tours from San José are the cheapest, but boats can be hired from the dock at hourly rates. *El muelle* (the dock) is located at the eastern end of a dirt-road straggle of budget hotels and restaurants. Vast banana and pineapple plantations have eaten up much of the virgin rain forest of this humid region, leaving only a few pockets, notably at La Selva (see pages 72–73) and Rara Avis (see page 80), and Centro Neotrópico Sarapiquís (see panel page 78).

BOOM!

Poás was active in the 19th century and erupted in 1889, but it was in 1910 that this volcano really left its mark. A major eruption resulted in a cloud mushrooming some 3km (2 miles) above, and left a gigantic hole measuring more than 8km (5 miles) across. One hour later an estimated 650,000 tonnes of volcanic debris started showering the Central Valley. Constant rumbling and violent emissions of burning rock culminated in the next major eruption in 1953, which 10 years later led to the formation of the lake. Occasional geyser eruptions continue, and between 1989 and 1991 gas emissions led to acid rain damaging surrounding coffee and strawberry plantations, as well as aggravating asthmatic conditions. It erupted for several days in March 2006, after 12 years of inactivity, and again that September and October. The eruptions were relatively minor and contained within the crater.

A rare cloudless and steamless view of Poás Volcano, thought now to be coming out of an active phase

ARROW-POISON FROGS

Of the 160 or so amphibian species that lurk in Costa Rica's more watery environments, the arrow-poison frogs (*Dendrobates spp*) are the most toxic. These tiny, gaudy frogs, ranging in palette from bright red with black dots to fluorescent green with black markings, have long been caught by the Indians for their poisonous skin secretions, which were used for soaking arrow-tips prior to hunting. When the toxin penetrates the bloodstream by arrow or through an open wound, it causes neuromuscular contractions that can lead to paralysis and death. Researchers have identified nearly 300 alkaloid compounds secreted by arrow-poison frogs, including analgesics 200 times more powerful than morphine.

Innocuous-looking perhaps, but the arrow-poison frog's toxin can be fatal

►► Rara Avis 67D2

One of Costa Rica's most remote and renowned ecotourism projects was founded in 1983 by a biologist and former manager of La Selva, Amos Bien, to explore economic alternatives to logging the rain forest. The 1,295ha (3,200-acre) private reserve bordering Braulio Carrillo and La Selva provides a clear demonstration of the benefits of conservation, with related projects such as studies of the harvesting of ornamental and medicinal plants, a butterfly research farm and a rain forest nursery garden.

Access to this pioneering project is, come rain or shine, by a strenuous four- or five-hour tractor ride from Las Horquetas, a village 18km (11 miles) south of Puerto Viejo. The demanding journey offers an explicit picture of the transition from desolate, logged cattle ranches into dense, rich virgin rain forest. This, too, is where Donald Perry first developed his AWCE (Automated Web for Canopy Exploration) in 1987, a precursor to the more sophisticated aerial tram (see panel on page 71). A variety of primitive yet expensive places to stay are available, and booking is essential (tel: 764-1111, fax: 764-1114, www.rara-avis.com).

►► Refugio Nacional de Vida Silvestre Caño Negro 66A3

This increasingly popular wildlife refuge in the far north of Costa Rica encompasses 10,000ha (24,700 acres) of lowland swamp crossed by the Río Frío before it drains into the Lago Caño Negro. During the dry season the area is reduced to small lagoons and channels, but nothing deters the creatures that inhabit these wetlands—the cattle egrets, roseate spoonbills, white ibis, wood storks, black-bellied whistling ducks and neotropic cormorants (it shelters Costa Rica's largest colony of the cormorants). The surrounding grasslands, marsh and forest are home to several monkey species, sloths, otters and a few wildcats, while caymans and 30 species of freshwater fish profit from the rivers. The best way to visit is by organized tour from La Fortuna (see page 70) or from Los Chiles (see page 73).

►► Santa Elena 66A2

Northwest of Monteverde, Santa Elena offers a budget alternative and is reached by equally rough roads. The attraction here is the **Reserva Santa Elena**►►► (tel/fax: 645-5390, www.monteverdeinfo.com/reserve *Open* daily 7–4. *Admission: inexpensive*). This locally managed conservation project, opened in 1992, offers 8km (5 miles) of trails through 310ha (770 acres) of cloud forest. This land is 83 percent exuberant primary forest, rich in dripping epiphytes, vines and mosses; pumas, howler monkeys and quetzals also inhabit the reserve. Less visited than Monteverde's cloud-forest reserve, yet with the same flora and fauna and equally well-organized (with rubber boots, rain ponchos and guides for rent), Santa Elena's reserve is an attractive alternative. It lies about 5km (3 miles) northeast of town along a bumpy track.

Whisked away The heart of Santa Elena town is the main crossroads, around which are the bus terminal, some reasonable hotels, restaurants, a bookshop, a bank and tourist information at the Albergue Santa Elena. Horseback tours around this beautiful region are offered by Sabine's

Smiling Horses (tel: 645-6894, www.smilinghorses.com The more adventurous Canopy Tours (tel/fax: 291-4465, www.canopytour.com) winches visitors in harnesses 40m (130ft) up through the trees to observation platforms. The system has expanded to include "Sky Trek" and "Sky Walk," a network of seven platforms connected by rope (see Monteverde, page 77). Also in Santa Elena is a small snake farm, the **Serpentario▶** (tel: 645-5238. *Open* Mon–Sun 9–8. *Admission: inexpensive*); the Bat Jungle (tel: 645-5052. *Open* Mon-Sun 9-8 *Admission*: inexpensive); and an Orchid Garden (tel: 645-5510. *Open* Mon-Sun 8-4 *Admission*: inexpensive).

▶ Tilarán   66A2

There is little scenic or other interest in this small, windy town just south of Laguna de Arenal. It nevertheless makes a useful stop-over for bus passengers and provides reasonably priced hotels and restaurants. People are friendly and arrangements can be made here for fishing trips, water sports or tours to Volcán Arenal. South from here is a stunning though rough drive along a road that winds through rolling pastures and dairy-farming communities to Santa Elena and Monteverde—allow at least two hours to cover the 32km (20 miles); a bus plies the route regularly as well.

LIVING FENCES
The pastures of Costa Rica are often bordered by living fences. These sprouting wooden pickets are actually living branches planted in the soil. Once the posts have been planted they grow for decades, occasionally requiring pruning, and providing a pleasantly leafy barrier. Only a handful of tree species are suitable; most farmers use a dense, local wood, and swear by specific, well-timed methods to ensure growth. Branches should be cut only during the waning phase of the moon in March, and are then "cured" for three days or so by placing them on an incline, before the final planting.

81

CROSSING THE BORDER
Historically, Nicaragua and Costa Rica have had tense relations, and never more so than during the 1980s when Oliver North's operation supplied arms to the Contras from northern Costa Rica. Nonetheless, in the mid-1990s the two nations established a new pedestrians-only border crossing at Los Chiles. As of this writing, US, UK, Canadian, French and German citizens can cross into Nicaragua without a visa, although Costa Ricans do need one. Exit visas cost 200 colone; Nicaragua charges $10 for a tourist card. Servitur in Los Chiles (tel: 471-1055) offers tours into Nicaragua. Check with the ICT or a local agency before planning to cross, as relations between the two nations remain strained.

A hole in your shoe? On-the-spot repairs at Tilarán

Constant cloud is the easily definable characteristic of Costa Rica's extensive cloud forest, which starts at altitudes of around 1,500m (4,900ft). This is where rain forest becomes a seemingly paradoxical world of abundant tropical plants flourishing in cloud, rain and cool temperatures.

TAPIRS

Of the 100 or so mammal species found in cloud forests, Baird's tapir was once numerous. This particular species can be found from southern Mexico to northern South America, where it hides in thickets and swamps during the day, emerging only at night. They are much sought after by hunters for their meat, and this, combined with their intolerance of man's presence and sensitivity to habitat disturbance, is leading to their gradual disappearance.

82

Hot lips (top) flourishes in the mist and drizzle of the Parque Nacional Braulio Carrillo

The low cloud of Costa Rican cloud forest is produced by moisture-laden trade winds blowing in across the Atlantic and over the Continental Divide, where it cloaks the forested mountains in a veil of mist, drizzle and rain. As a result, these dripping forests and their numerous waterfalls and streams are an essential watershed for drier areas at lower altitudes. The Monteverde area is the most renowned of Costa Rica's cloud forests, but this same ecosystem continues down the spine of the country and can be explored near San Ramón (Los Angeles Cloud Forest), in valleys around Cerro La Muerte and at the national parks of Braulio Carrillo, Tapantí, Chirripó and La Amistad.

Flora and fauna The sheltered tracts of evergreen forest are thick with ferns, palms, epiphytes, mosses and lichen, while at higher altitudes oaks with gnarled roots and buttress trunks take over, before vegetation finally dwindles into wind-sculpted dwarf forest on exposed ridges (making in total about 2,500 species of plants). Insect life is astonishingly varied, and resplendent quetzals, three-wattled bellbirds (making their loud, unmistakable "bong" call high in the canopy), clay-colored robins (Costa Rica's national bird), wrens, humming-birds, flycatchers, woodpeckers, trogons, owls and hawks are all among the 400 or so species of birds.

Hot lips Among the begonias, heliconias, monsteras and philodendrons of the lower layer are "hot lips" (*Cephaelis elata*), named after their large red leaves. The roots contain chemicals used in pharmaceutical products, while the flowers, blooming most of the year, attract humming-birds and butterflies. Butterflies are another of the cloud forest's vibrant inhabitants: about 500 species hover and flit through the undergrowth in search of their host plants, and often play a crucial pollinating role.

►►► Volcán Arenal 66B2

This near-perfect 1,633m (5,358ft) volcanic cone rises majestically out of the lush pastures and forest at the eastern end of Laguna de Arenal. Intermittent rumbling, explosions and nocturnal fire-spitting are the mesmerizing features that draw visitors to its base by day and night. Cloud often obscures the summit, but when lava-flows cascade, incandescent rocks fly and Arenal roars, few that see it forget it. Its flanks have been declared a national park (*Open* daily 10–4. *Admission: moderate*), but the nocturnal light show can be witnessed equally well from outside the boundary. Continually active and evolving in form since 1968, Arenal is extremely dangerous; nobody should venture onto its slopes. Any appearance of a lull in activity is deceptive: this is an erupting volcano, and in recent years several imprudent hikers have died of gas emissions or burns.

Arenal, a natural light show. The most violent eruption in 30 years occurred in August 2000. It resulted in two deaths and a major evacuation of the area

Blanket of fire Lively but ancient, Arenal is 2 to 3 million years old. No records exist of eruptions during the Spanish colonial period, but mineral samples suggest that it was booming between 1200 and 1500. Records of crater activity started in 1937. Then, 31 years later, Arenal moved into its current phase, which began with tremors followed by an eruption on 29 July, 1968, that killed 87 people. The town of Pueblo Nuevo was eradicated, large tracts of farmland and forest were destroyed and 600ha (1,480 acres) were blanketed in molten lava before the colossus entered a quiet phase of hot gas and ash emissions. Fumaroles soon appeared in the newly formed craters, and a lava flow started advancing toward the Tabacón river valley at the rate of 10 to 30m (11 to 33yd) a day. Today, vegetation has reappeared among the boulders and solidified lava, but vulcanologists consider the Tabacón area particularly vulnerable to hot avalanches.

Night views Night tours are arranged from La Fortuna and even from San José, but visitors with their own transport can drive to a good viewpoint on Arenal's western side, which offers the best sight of the inferno-like activity. Drive to the park entrance, then branch right along a rough track that leads to several hotels and the Arenal Volcano Observatory, a residential observation station open to vulcanologists and visitors.

SEISMIC MYSTERIES
Major zones of seismic activity follow the boundaries of the tectonic plates making up the earth's rigid surface layer. Costa Rica's volcanoes are at the fragile meeting of the Caribbean Plate and the Cocos Plate in the Pacific. This string of volcanoes continues south through the Andes and north through Mexico, making for a particularly volatile area.

Drive

Cloud forest, rain forest, volcano and plain

See map on pages 66–67

This drive through an extraordinary variety of landscapes and climates will necessitate an overnight stay. The shorter, alternative route can be done in a strenuous day (five or six hours' driving in a four-wheel-drive vehicle), but it is in any case better to spend a night on the way in order to explore.

Before setting off, make sure that your clothing is designed for rapidly changing climatic extremes.

If starting from San José, head out on the highway to Limón, which for more than 65km (40 miles) presents an unusually well-maintained surface. Enjoy it while it lasts. While winding through the semi-permanent drizzle of **Parque Nacional Braulio Carrillo**▶▶, turn into one of the stopping places, the better to admire dramatic vistas over the cloud forest. Clouds permitting, you may see parrots flying over the tree canopy or birds of prey soaring over the ridge. Just before a tunnel beneath the 2,047m (6,716ft) peak of Cerro Hondura is a toll booth (inexpensive) and soon after it the road crosses a bridge over the Río Sucio. You can pull in after the bridge and walk down a path to the river for a close view of the strange meeting of a clearwater current with a yellow, sulfurous stream straight from Volcán Irazú. Soon after, you pass the entrance to the **Rain Forest Aerial Tram**▶▶▶ (see page 71) on the right, though the actual structure is invisible from the highway. This entire mountainous area offers fantastic views over dense virgin rain forest, while the

Left: cattle ranch in the Póas region

roadside is thick with "poor man's umbrella" (gunnera) and palms.

Between here and Guápiles are numerous private ecological projects (see pages 70–71): watch closely for signs if you decide to visit any of them. About 24km (15 miles) beyond the Zurquí tunnel, at Santa Clara, take a left turn that cuts straight through an extensive, flat and much hotter plain of palm-heart and pineapple plantations and cattle ranches. All of this was once clad in dense rain forest, well exemplified farther north by the lush research grounds of **La Selva**▶▶▶ (see pages 72–73; advance booking necessary). After 42km (26 miles) from the Santa Clara turn, the straight road arrives at **Puerto Viejo de Sarapiquí**▶ (see page 79), worth a stop to take a leisurely boat trip along the **Río Sarapiquí**▶▶ in search of crocodiles, howler monkeys and exotic birds. Police road checks are common around here, as many Nicaraguan immigrants use the river to enter Costa Rica illegally.

From Puerto Viejo, continue west, stopping for wholesome Tico food at Restaurant Jacaré, about 5km (3 miles) from Puerto Viejo on the left, or at Chilamate to look at the botanic garden, birds and butterfly enclosure of Selva Verde Lodge. Near here you will see a roadside pottery vendor: the pots in traditional Guanacastecan style are brought from Guaitíl and prices are reasonable. At La Virgen is an alternative food and/or kayaking stop at Rancho Leona on the banks of the Sarapiquí River. From here the road starts twisting wildly. For the long route, turn right at San Miguel, then again at Anguas Zarcas. Bear left at the fork toward Muelle, then follow the signs into La Fortuna. Spend a night here, or in one of the hotels on the road to Arenal, and appreciate the awesome sight of

Volcán Arenal▶▶▶ (see page 83). Next day, take the road through Chachagua, Ciudad Quesada and Zarcero back to San José.

For the shorter route, stay on the road from La Virgen and, instead of turning right at San Miguel, continue on through the villages of Ujarrás and Cariblanco, taking in the increasingly spectacular mountain scenery. Soon after Cinchona, you will see Catarata La Paz: this thundering waterfall, now accessible on foot from above via the tourist destination of **Catarata La Paz**▶▶▶ (see page 69), is fed by a river that cascades straight down from **Volcán Poás**▶▶ (see page 79). Continue south through pine forest and rolling hills of strawberry and coffee plantations until a fork in the road offers the choice of returning to San José via Alajuela or Heredia.

85

Wildlife comes in all guises

The Center

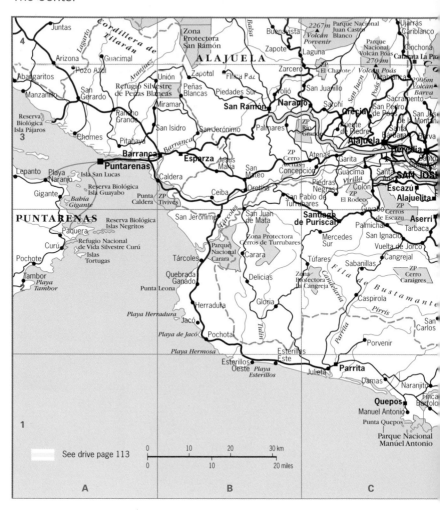

See drive page 113

0	10	20	30 km
0		10	20 miles

THE CENTER This section covers an area spilling over from the Central Valley, north to the mountain towns of Sarchí and Zarcero, south to the magnificent Cerro La Muerte, east to Turrialba and west to the corresponding shores of the Pacific. All places mentioned can be reached on day-trips from San José if necessary. The Central Valley (or, more correctly, plateau) is the heart of Costa Rica's economic life, where some 60 percent of the population is concentrated, attracted by the extreme fertility of the volcanic soil and a comfortable spring-like climate. Twisting roads are common currency as they negotiate sharp changes in altitude, and landscapes take on epic proportions. Coffee plantations are still the most common sight on the cultivated slopes, with sugar-cane, corn and dairy farms following closely behind.

Previous pages: all roads lead to San José, the forward-looking capital of Costa Rica

ON THE ROAD TO SAN JOSÉ At the heart of the valley lies the capital, San José, which, whatever your itinerary, you will see more than once. All roads and most flights lead there, and it long ago outstripped its urban rivals, Cartago,

89

Alajuela and Heredia. Although not the most visually inspiring of cities, it nevertheless makes a friendly, lively place to spend a few days between trips, and its museums provide an important cultural introduction to the country. The only rival town in terms of infrastructure and interest is Heredia, a mere 20 minutes from the capital by car, and known as "the city of flowers" or "the city of culture." For those wary of San José's errant muggers, impossible traffic and pollution, Heredia makes a pleasant enough base with a distinctive character owing to the presence of a large university. All towns in this region have suffered from earthquakes and volcanic eruptions, and evidence of colonial history is thus conspicuous by its absence. Amends are made by the relaxed, rural atmosphere of the region's small communities, such as Barva, Atenas, Santa Ana, Zarcero and even the burgeoning international community of Escazú, another viable alternative to staying in San José as it is well supplied with bed-and-breakfasts and some more luxurious hotels.

So far this iguana has avoided the cooking pot

LUMINOUS FROGS CROAKING

"In the wide valley below, the lights of the city sparkled, a myriad of tiny luminous frogs croaking in the pool of darkness. Here and there in the distance, patches of light could be seen, some weaker, others stronger. They all indicated the positions of towns on the *meseta*, as if clusters of stars had fallen from the constellations above. More than 40 years ago there'd been fewer luminous frogs. San José wasn't as spread out then, and most people in the villages were without electricity..." Fabian Dobles, *El Targua* (1984).

UNDER THE GIANT MANGO TREES

"...It was easy to see that nobody felt like working on such a hot afternoon. In the Parque Central, without a doubt, under the giant mango trees, policemen, the druggist, shoeshine boys, a few students, and numerous beggars fanning the flies away with their open, bony hands would be resting like animals in a zoo. Meanwhile the cantinas would be deserted, because the drunks preferred to doze on the lawn of the Parque Juan Santamaría..." Fernando Duran Ayanegui, *Monday* (1988).

SEDUCTIVE WILDS Head out into the wilds and it is a different story. Thrill-seekers can choose between white-water rafting on the Río Pacuare, bungee-jumping near Grecia, mountain-biking in Tapantí, horseback-riding or any number of water sports on the coast. But much of the enjoyment can be more passive. When the still-active volcano, Volcán Irazú, is not showering its spectacular slopes with ash—as it does sporadically—you can peer vertiginously into the crater, whose desolate landscape has been said by visiting astronaut Neil Armstrong to resemble the surface of the moon. Alternatively, head off to explore the national archeological site of Guayabo, concealed in a rich rain-forest setting.

Compare the magical Orosí Valley, unfolding seductively, with the brooding valleys of cloud forest around Cerro La Muerte, where the resplendent quetzal resides. Take the beautiful route through Orotina to the Carara national park and watch scarlet macaws roosting at dusk, or hike through dense rain forest nearby to see a thundering waterfall. If you have four-wheel-drive, explore the backroads off the *costanera* (coast road), where tiny villages with stunning ocean views rise into the foothills of the central mountains.

STAR TURN You may encounter a brasher atmosphere in the coastal towns of Puntarenas, Quepos (both of which have embraced tourism as a new source of prosperity following the demise of their ports) or the once tackiest of Costa Rican resorts, Jacó, now home to numerous high end hotels on Punta Leona including the design-conscious Villa Caletas hotel and several major development projects. Between these main towns are some reasonable beaches, most offering some form of lodging and either good surfing or good swimming. Playa Hermosa, for example, has emerged as a top surfing destination, while Herradura now contains Costa Rica's finest marina. Ultimately, however, nothing can beat Costa Rica's most popular national park and beaches, at Manuel Antonio. Conservationists are anxiously monitorin developments here, as this tiny reserve and its stunning surroundings are becoming engulfed by tourist facilities and crowds, with the environment suffering as a result. Manuel Antonio's future development may serve as a measure of Costa Rica's real dedication to the environmentally responsible tourism it espouses.

GETAWAY For those really wanting to escape the crowds, this central region is not the most recommended, as the proximity of major points of interest to San José makes them easy targets for tour groups and domestic tourism. Compared with other parts of the country, roads, public transport and communications are excellent, and road signs are mostly easy to follow. Isolated and less visited exceptions do exist, however, and there are some outstanding lodges hidden away in mountain retreats or on the coast. Environmental projects are not absent and are generally wildlife-oriented, whether concerned with butterflies, crocodiles, iguanas or scarlet macaws. Of particular significance is Turrialba's CATIE, one of the world's leaders in agronomical research.

► **Alajuela**   *88C3*

This provincial capital was founded in 1782 with the name of Villa Hermosa, but its distance of only 19km (11 miles) from San José has always left it on the sidelines, and life here is decidedly unhurried. Today, the population of 55,000 enjoys a peaceful existence in and around the verdant Parque Central, where the dense mango trees are said to house a sloth or two. Alajuela's warmer climate (it is 200m/650ft lower than the capital) attracts city dwellers for a stroll, while the proximity of the airport, barely 3km (2 miles) southeast, brings a few tourists to its limited hotels. Every April the town springs to life for Costa Rica's most ambitious cultural festival, and in July a craft fair is held under the name of the Fiesta de Los Mangos.

The only permanent point of interest is the **Museo Juan Santamaría►** (Avenida Central/Calle 2, tel: 441-4775, fax: 441-6926, www.museojuansntamaria.go.cr *Open* Tue–Sun 10–6. *Admission free*). This focuses on the 1856 battle in which an Alajuela-born drummer boy, Juan Santamaría, torched the hideout of William Walker's filibusters (see pages 32–33) . The exhibits give a haphazard background. A statue of the hero stands in the Parque Juan Santamaría, two blocks south of the Parque Central.

An owl butterfly exhibits its silken finery at the Butterfly Farm near Alajuela

91

Out of town At Garita, about 11km (9 miles) west of Alajuela, is **Zoo-Ave►** (tel: 433-8989, fax: 433-9140, www.zooave.org *Open* daily 9–5. *Admission: moderate*). Along with the rescue and rehabilitation of injured and orphaned birds, this 2ha (5-acre) bird zoo features 116 Costa Rican species and rare imported birds. You can sharpen your natural history knowledge at the **Butterfly Farm►►** at Guácima, near San Antonio de Belén (tel: 438-0400, www.butterflyfarm.co.cr *Open* daily 8.30–5, last tour at 3. *Admission: expensive*), the world's second largest exporter of butterfly pupae. This farm offers a choice of two-hour guided tours and can arrange hotel pick-ups from San José.

Alajuela's popularity has waned in the face of San José's socio-cultural life (below)

LA NEGRITA

Miracles have been associated with this statue ever since its discovery in 1635 in the forest that once grew on this site. The legend goes that, after the statue was found by a young girl, it was installed by a priest in the local parish church. Twice it disappeared to return to the forest, only staying put once a basilica had been built on the spot. Even the spring water from behind the church is said to have curative powers, another good reason to attract thousands of pilgrims— some of whom complete their journey on their knees—every 2 August.

► Atenas 88C3

High in the hills west of San José lies what residents and the *National Geographic* claim to be the town with one of the best climates in the world. This region of rolling coffee plantations can be taken in by a short detour if you are driving to the Pacific via Orotina. Atenas itself features wonderful fruits, a pretty church, and the nearby Central American School of Animal Husbandry, where the Agro-Eco Tourism Project teaches visitors about dairy operations, iguana farming, butterflies, crocodiles and reafforestation (tel: 455-1000, fax: 446-8000, info@ecag.ac.cr *Admission: expensive*).

► Cartago 89D2

Costa Rica's former capital of Cartago dates from 1563 but was officially replaced at independence by San José in 1823. Sadly, most of its colonial past has disappeared in the rubble of major earthquakes, thanks to Volcán Irazú, which looms nearby. In testimony to Cartago's former glory are the roofless arches of **Las Ruinas►►►**, which rise beside the Parque Central. The original church, erected in 1575, was destroyed by an earthquake in 1841 and another quake in 1910 left only the present ruins, which were closed indefinitely in 2004. The walls now enclose a pretty graveyard splashed with bougainvillea. The old bell is suspended over the central arch. Flanking the southern side of the square are some decorative clapboard houses with fretwork eaves and interior archways.

Six blocks east of this rise the massive walls and white cupolas of the vaguely neo-Byzantine **Basilica de Nuestra Señora de los Angeles►►**, dedicated to the Virgin Mary, Costa Rica's patron saint. Demure angels enhance the façade topped by a victorious Archangel Michael, while the interior has rich wood panels, heavily decorated pillars, tiles and stained glass. The national importance of this 1926 basilica, which replaced an earlier structure destroyed in the earthquake, focuses on one statue, that of "La Negrita," a term of endearment referring to the Virgin Mary. Don't miss her shrine, packed with offerings: abandoned crutches, artificial eyes and legs, and other items testifying to her miraculous healing powers. At almost any time of day you can see pilgrims crawling down the church's central aisle, an unusual sight in this generally secular country.

Las Ruinas, Cartago

Right: Cartago's basilica, ornate home of La Negrita

89E2

Escazú combines rural pursuits with services for wealthy Tico and foreign residents

BEFORE THE INTERAMERICAN

It was only in the 1920s that a cart trail was first laid over the Talamanca Mountains. Before that, farmers from the fertile southern valleys had to accomplish excruciating journeys on foot, herding pigs and loaded down with 50kg (110lb) packs of blackberries, rice or corn to trade at San José's market. Often barefoot and wearing little more than a thin shirt and trousers, they negotiated the Cerro La Muerte pass in bitterly cold and permanently wet conditions.

▶▶▶ Cerro La Muerte (Death Hill)

This 3,500m (11,480ft) pass is where the Interamerican Highway reaches its highest point in Costa Rica. Temperatures plunge, the air thins and the road often disappears behind thick banks of fog or rain. The name was earned when farmers used to trudge across on foot, and today the well-paved road to the pass is dotted with white crosses that mark fatal accidents. The *páramo*-type vegetation (see page 160) that cloaks the highest points of Cerro La Muerte makes for fascinating, if eerie, exploration. Even at this altitude, humming-birds can still be found, as can rufous-collared sparrows and jays. The vegetation itself is stunning, the subtle shades of green and strikingly architectural foliage being worthy of any garden designer.

Quetzal valley If you are approaching the pass on the beautiful stretch from Cartago, a scenic detour can be made by turning off just after Empalme to Jardín and **Santa María de Dota**▶▶, then returning to the Interamerican Highway via Copey, known for its trout restaurant. About 10km (6 miles) south of here, at marker 80, lies the blissful "quetzal valley" of **San Gerardo de Dota**▶▶▶, reached by a twisting road descending to the west. This cool, tranquil valley, crossed by the trout-rich Río Savegre, offers exceptional hiking through cloud forest as well as a chance of spotting a resplendent quetzal (March to May is the best time). Several hotels cater to bird-watching and trout-consuming visitors. At marker 89 on the Interamerican Highway is a restaurant, Las Torres, opposite which a dirt road leads up to a cluster of radio masts. This peak has breathtaking views across mountains and valleys, west to the Pacific beaches and, on exceptionally clear days, east to the Caribbean.

▶▶ Escazú   88C3

Escazú is virtually joined to San José by a sprawl of chic western suburbs. Witches were once said to proliferate here, but craftspeople and an international community seem to have replaced them. Easy access (15 minutes' drive and frequent buses though traffic may slow progress), cooler temperatures, luxuriant vegetation and wide views make it a popular haven for wealthier Josefinos and expatriates. Clay-colored robins (the national bird) are common in gardens here, as are rufous-tailed humming-birds, great kiskadees (a bird that calls its name), and Montezuma oropendolas.

Escazú's main square is dominated by a church flanked by old adobe houses. Elsewhere new shopping malls, hotels and modern houses are in bizarre contrast with the rural scenes of cows and ox carts along the main road winding up to San Antonio de Escazú. From San Antonio there is a steep 700m (2,300ft) climb to the mirador of Pico Blanco.

▶ Esterillos   88B1

The seemingly endless palm-fringed beach of Esterillos lies in a flat, featureless region of plantations southeast of Jacó and is reached by three main turnings off the coastal road. Esterillos Oeste (West) leads to a breezy section of the beach and the posh new Xandari Pacifico Spa and Resort. The currents here are dangerous but there are budget hotels. Esterillos Este (East) takes you to a similarly unspectacular beach with the advantages of a slow descent to the sea and safe swimming. The small community has a handful of mid-range hotels, and there are hikes to nearby rain-forest waterfalls. A third, unnamed turning farther east leads to campsites and other mid-range hotels.

▶▶ Grecia   88C3

Halfway between Alajuela and the crafts town of Sarchí lies Grecia, a well-maintained hill town that is dependent on the surrounding coffee, sugar-cane and pineapple plantations. Its verdant square is dominated by the twin-spired church of Las Mercedes. Constructed in 1958 from bolted metal plates, the church's impressive vaulted interior features a lavish all-marble altar. The town is also home to a small regional museum (tel: 494-6767. *Open* Mon–Fri 1–5).

Nearby, 1.5km (1-mile) down the Alajuela road, is the World of Snakes (tel: 494-3700, www.snakes-costarica.com *Open* Mon–Sun 8–4. *Admission: expensive*).

95

The powerful spires of Las Mercedes in Grecia

CARARA CROCS

American crocodiles have hardly changed in the past 200 million years. They reach lengths of 3 to 6m (10 to 20ft) and may live 60 to 100 years. Their eggs are buried in the sandy banks of a river, where the shell absorbs moisture to help the embryo develop. Survival of these embryonic crocodiles generally averages only 2 percent, but at the Parque Nacional Carara (see page 109) it has been estimated that barely 0.5 percent actually develop. Local sharpshooters and egg-trampling cattle are partly to blame, but river pollution and fertilizers also create havoc.

Heredia's Basilica depicts St. Matthew in one of its new windows

▶▶▶ Heredia 88C3

Of all Costa Rica's provincial towns, Heredia is perhaps the one with most character and interest, although this aspect is, as yet, little exploited and you certainly would not believe it from the outskirts. Founded in 1706, Heredia pre-dates both San José and Alajuela, and today much of its population of 43,000 is connected with Costa Rica's second-largest university, whose campus lies east of the central area, injecting the town with youthful dynamism. Spanish-style tiled roofs, adobe houses and stately stone buildings are plentiful, while the higher, northern slopes of the town command sweeping views across San José, the valley and distant mountains. A new high-speed train service was announced in early 2007 that will link commuters to the capital in under 20 minutes.

Faith and fun At the middle of the grid of streets stands the impressive Basilica de la Immaculada Concepción (1797), whose deteriorating façade belies a completely renovated interior with pristine stained-glass windows and church bells from Peru. An unusually squat, solid design (sometimes classed as "seismic baroque") has helped the church withstand the earthquakes that have toppled most of its contemporaries. A domed side chapel with a separate entrance from the adjoining garden is a place of constant prayer. Equally intense promenading takes place on Sundays under the huge centennial trees outside, around the focus of live bands playing in the white kiosk.

Military imagination Opposite the church and its garden, on the north side of the Parque Central, stands an elaborate stone post office, dating from 1915, next to the colonial-style Palacio Municipal. However, the curious jewel in Heredia's architectural crown is a military fort, El Fortín, built by the eccentric President Alfredo Gonzalez Flores early in the 20th century. His bizarre approach to military strategy produced a beehive of a tower with slits that enlarged outward, so letting bullets in easily. Three blocks south of the Parque is a central market where leather goods and wickerware are sold alongside the usual edible produce. Like San José's Mercado Central, the market is also a good place for inexpensive meals. Take time to wander around Heredia's pretty central streets and, before sunset, do not miss the outrageous natural light show painting the valley skies, best watched from the top-floor bar of the Hotel Valladolid.

Beyond the town Between Heredia and Barva is **Café Britt**▶▶ plantation and coffee mill (tel: 260-2748, fax: 238-1848, www.coffeetour.com for bookings. *Admission: expensive*). A must on tour group itineraries (tours at 9 and 3 Dec–Apr, or by group reservation; transport from San José), the mill's

The curious beehive fortress is a striking landmark on the main square

BUSES TO HEREDIA
Bus connections between Heredia and San José are frequent and easy: from Avenida 7 & 9 Calle 1 in San José, buses leave every five minutes from 5am to 11pm, and from Avenida 2 Calle 12 every ten minutes from 4:40am to 11pm. In Heredia the San José buses leave from Avenida 4 Calle Central, one block south of the Parque Central. Fares are inexpensive.

HIBISCUS
The large pink, orange or blood-red flowers that grace the hedges and gardens of the Central Valley are those of *Hibiscus rosa-sinensis* or, as it is known locally, the *amapola*. Athough a common sight in Costa Rica, it originated from tropical Asia, which has a similar climate. Horticulturalists have developed more than 5,000 varieties of this flower.

COSTA RICA IN MICRCOCOSM
In Santo Domingo de Heredia, INBioparque (tel: 507-8107, fax: 507-8271. *Open* 7.30–4. *Admission: moderate* including self-guiding tour) conserves biodiversity and provides an educational resource. The park has ecosystems representative of all the types found in Costa Rica: Central Valley forest, humid forest, tropical dry forest and wetland. There are 51 bird species and 583 native plant species, together with mammals and reptiles, and a butterfly garden.

presentation includes costumed actors. Caffeine addicts can indulge in tasting the various roasts and buy stocks at factory prices. On a lower key and certainly less visited is the **Museo de Cultura Popular▶▶** (tel: 260-1619, www.ilam.org/cr/museoculturapopular *Open* Mon–Fri 8–4, Sat–Sun 10–5. *Admission: inexpensive*), located in a northeastern suburb of Heredia and well signposted from the main road. At the back of a garden, an attractive mid-19th-century adobe farmhouse displays an eclectic collection, including an ancient gramophone (the caretaker will crank it up for you to play pre-World War II hits).

Barva and upward A nice stop south of Heredia is Santo Domingo de Heredia, home of the new INBioparque (see panel), but **Barva de Heredia▶▶**, to the north, has more character. The village is protected as a national monument because of its well-preserved central square, flanked by adobe houses with a white church set among palm trees. Peaceful Barva's easy access to the capital have attracted a colony of artists and craftspeople. North of here the road forks. To the right it winds up through pine-clad hills to **San José de la Montaña▶▶**, where mountain lodges offer outdoor activities and bird-watching or trips to Volcán Barva (see page 78). The left fork leads to Volcán Poás (see page 79) and north through the Cordillera Central to Puerto Viejo de Sarapiquí (see page 79 and Drive, pages 84–85).

Earthquakes and volcanic eruptions have wrought havoc on much of Costa Rica's architectural heritage, but some remnants exist, hidden in far-flung towns or engulfed by San José's low-rise concrete jungle. Each surviving style reflects a momentous stage in the nation's history.

TO EVERY HOUSE A STORY

One of Los Yoses's strangest mansions is Casa Matute, an elaborate 1920s construction purchased in 1935 by a Venezuelan, Matute Gomez, who was fleeing political persecution following the fall of his dictator brother. He moved in with his daughters and, it is said, a minor fortune in gold coins fresh from the Venezuelan treasury. Flamboyant parties and eccentric conduct were the rule until 1951, when Matute mysteriously disappeared to Panama, where he died in obscurity. The sole remaining resident was his daughter Isola, who lived alone in the enormous house until her death in 1990. Her heirs were her housekeeper and chauffeur, and the house has now become a buzzing nightspot.

Casa Verde, one of San José's many century-old houses to be converted into a hotel

Costa Rica was transformed in the mid-19th century as a result of the expanding coffee trade. New horizons, money and status brought a blossoming of architectural styles, above all in San José. In many cases they were inspired by European designs, in others they appropriated the more climatically suitable Caribbean colonial style. For several decades the capital enjoyed this new-found prosperity and cultural refinement, becoming the third city in the world to have public lighting and, later, art-deco cinemas. During the 1950s, Costa Rica's population boomed to a million, double that of the 1930s, and there followed a catastrophic period of aping North American norms. Up went cheap, functional concrete blocks and down came the elegant façades of the immediate past. Today the majority of Costa Rican towns are indistinguishable from one another, although each has notable exceptions to the mediocre rule.

From *ranchos* to adobe In the Península de Nicoya and southern Costa Rica, *ranchos* are common. These originated in the indigenous culture, but are built today not only for tourists' interest but often also as well-ventilated sitting spaces attached to stuffier modern homes. Traditional *rancho* floors were of beaten earth or pounded logs, from which split-bamboo walls rose to a palm-leaf roof, so allowing air to circulate freely while keeping rain at bay.

The main architectural innovation of the Spanish Conquest was adobe building. Walls were built of mud inserted into a wooden or bamboo framework, then limewashed in bright hues. Sloping tiled roofs often extended to shelter shady verandas that ran the full length of the (usually L-shaped) houses. Picturesque examples survive in the Central Valley (Escazú, Heredia and, above all, Barva de Heredia) as well as in the Guanacastecan towns of Liberia and Nicoya, where the *puertas del sol* were developed (see panel on page 44).

Clapboard Although concrete and corrugated iron have made inroads into urban Costa Rica, they have not eradicated the widespread use of clapboard in rural areas for simple farms or generously proportioned mansions, embellished with intricate fretwork eaves and sometimes raised on piles. This "Caribbean Victorian" architectural form reached fantastic heights at the turn of the 20th

century under the proprietorial eye of wealthy coffee barons and hacienda owners, and was extended in the New Orleans-style frame-houses of the United Fruit Company, still visible in Golfito. San José's aristocratic Barrio Amón has preserved some wonderful early examples, many of which have been transformed into exclusive hotels. Casa Verde (c1910) belonged to the wealthy owner of a cattle ranch near Limón, and the 100-percent mahogany Hotel Santo Tomás (1910) was once the home of a coffee planter's family. Hotel Alóki combines a Moorish layout (internal courtyard with fountain) with European detailing, while two adjacent residences followed the turn-of-the-20th-century fashion for Moorish style to the last arch and stained-glass panel. In the 1920s, wealthy residences spread to an inner suburban ring, from Los Yoses to Paseo Colón, preserved today as numerous hotels.

Solid appeal Commercial architecture of the period adopted the European neo-classical style with a vengeance. Pillars, porches, pediments and balustrades bristled over façades, while decorative stonework adorned banks, colleges, hospitals, churches and government buildings. San José's Correo (post office), built by an English company in 1914, typically blends neo-classicism with ornate flourishes. Interesting exceptions include the Escuela Metálica, a prefabricated import of cast-iron plates from Belgium, and San José's crown jewel, the Teatro Nacional, a combination of a neo-classical exterior and sumptuous neo-baroque interior styled on the Paris Opera. Since World War II, innovative architecture has been abandoned in the public domain but, in recent years, Costa Rica's tourist industry has inspired some lively architectural innovation, with eco-lodges such as Lapa Rios displaying an inspired integration of indigenous style, environmental sensitivity, and rough-hewn luxury, while hotels such as Villa Caletas interpret the notion of opulence in richly imaginative ways.

Spanish colonial in San José contrasts with the 1990s

CARIBBEAN GENESIS
Early Afro-Caribbean settlers of the Talamanca coast were turtle fishermen, whose temporary huts, built for shelter during their fishing season, were the precursors of typical homes in the region today. They were made of planks cut from the rawa palm, raised on piles and thatched with a common swamp palm. The palm would be cut only after the new moon when it was insect-free. Thatch has since been replaced by zinc roofs—a great mistake as zinc is hot and ugly while thatch, if properly made, provides good insulation for years as well as looking better.

Jacó is easy to reach by car for a budget escape from the capital

PETROGLYPHS
So far 53 petroglyphs (carved stone slabs) have been unearthed on the causeways and around the mounds of Guayabo, and most are displayed in San José's museums. One petroglyph exhibited in the undergrowth of Guayabo's main trail shows a crude bas-relief carving of a jaguar and a crocodile, both of which lived in the area until relatively recently. For the Talamanca Indians, the crocodile/alligator symbolized Sibu, their god, and the jaguar (an animal considered to have supernatural attributes), a shaman.

▶ **Jacó** 88B2

This hot coastal resort offers a cheerful atmosphere within easy reach of the capital (109km/68 miles away), so it makes a popular Tico destination. Budget *cabinas* first sprang up to cater to surfers who came for the almost constant waves, but Jacó has since developed facilities for the leisure-seeking crowd, with shops, restaurants and hotels all located along an uninspiring low-rise strip backing the long curve of the bay. Sonesta and Ramada hotels have recently signed on to major developments here. Water sports, fishing and river-rafting activities are extensive, but swimmers should be careful as the currents here can be unpredictable.

Just north of Jacó, once tranquil Playa Herradura now boasts a major hotel, a gated, walled-in housing development (supposedly popular with San Jose's aristocratic class), and a new marina which has taken over Flamingo's position as Costa Rica's premier marina. However, the beach itself remains low-key and accessible. High above the coast here is one of Costa Rica's most inspiring luxury hotels, Villa Caletas, definitely worth the precipitous 3km (2-mile) ascent for a drink or fine lunch with a spellbinding view. Farther north still, at Punta Leona, a string of exquisite beaches backed by rain forest has unfortunately been transformed into an inaccessible, private, gated and guarded resort community with no public facilities. South of Jacó, Playa Hermosa offers more challenging surf and a string of low- and mid-price beachfront hotels and *cabinas* primarily catering to the wave-riding set.

▶▶▶ **Monumento Nacional Guayabo** 89E3

Open: daily 8–3.30. Admission: moderate
Part of Costa Rica's largest archeological site has been sensitively excavated at the heart of pristine natural surroundings, and combines easy nature trails through primary and secondary forest with a unique close-up view of the country's indigenous past. Although the site itself is in no way comparable to Inca or Mesoamerican monuments, its circular mounds, stone causeways, walls, aqueducts, water tank, tombs and petroglyphs (see panel) offer a clear picture of a sophisticated pre-Columbian structure. It is thought to have been occupied from 1000BC until AD1400.

Mysteries Since 1968 an estimated 10 percent (2ha/5 acres) of the total area has been excavated by the University of Costa Rica. Although it is known that Guayabo's apogee was AD300 to 700, a question mark remains over why it was abandoned before the Spanish Conquest: disease and war are two hypotheses. Construction techniques reflect both South American and Mesoamerican influences, but interpretation of many of the uncovered petroglyphs remains incomplete. What is certain is that Guayabo was ruled by a *cacique* (chief) who exercised power over a large region, and that the inhabitants were specialists in a variety of trades.

Trails The 1.2km (0.7-mile) self-guiding Los Montículos trail winds through luxuriant rain forest where turquoise morpho butterflies, toucans, loriots and oropendolas may cross your path as you climb to a look-out point over the archeological site. From here the path continues down through the site before circling back to the entrance. A second trail, Los Cantarillos, leads from the amphitheater at

the entrance, down through rain forest to the Río Lajitas. A small visitor information point is opposite the entrance, and Spanish-speaking volunteer guides are available.

▶ Orosí   89D2

In the heart of the beautiful coffee-growing **Orosí Valley▶▶** lies this small, much rebuilt town. Its simple church, dating from 1743, is lined with paintings and has two ornate shrines flanking the wooden altar, one with a polychrome statue of St Francis. An adjoining monastery houses the **Museum of Religious Art▶▶** (tel: 533-3051. *Open* Tue–Sun 1–5. *Admission: inexpensive*), which displays an odd assortment of religious statuary, colonial paintings from Mexico, silver, vestments, and even an ancient typewriter. Orosí has two *balnearios* (thermal pools) with grounds: Los Patios *balneario* (tel: 533-3009. *Open* Tue–Sun 7.30–4. *Admission: inexpensive*), south of town, has pools (50°C/122°F), changing rooms, and a bar and restaurant; in the heart of town is Balnearios Termales (tel: 533-2156. *Open* Wed–Mon 7.30–4. *Admission: inexpensive*). For sublime views over the valley, stop at the Mirador de Orosí, on the road to Paraíso.

Coffee plantations punctuated by flame trees clad the slopes of the Orosí Valley

101

VALLEY FLAMES
A recurring sight in the Orosí Valley is the fiery orange glow of the flamboyant or flame tree (*Delonix regia*), creating a luminous contrast with the undulating slopes of dark-green coffee bushes. One of the world's most strikingly beautiful trees, this native of Madagascar resembles a delicate flame-orange umbrella, and its dense clusters of flowers bloom from early spring until late summer. The fernlike foliage later gives way to long brown seed pods— hence the Greek name *Delonix*, meaning "long claw." The common Costa Rican name for this tree is *malinche*.

The charming Franciscan church of Orosí is Costa Rica's oldest still in use

Lankester Gardens:
floral surprises

BENEATH THE SURFACE
The turquoise waters of Manuel Antonio are particularly transparent during the dry season. Anybody with a snorkel and mask will be mesmerized by the life around the coral reefs that line the coast and islands between the park and Quepos. Green turtles also discovered these beaches long ago, and pre-Columbian inhabitants developed a sophisticated system of wooden traps in rocky inlets, where, at low tide, the turtles would be left high and dry. These are still visible at either end of Playa Blanca.

▶ **Paraíso**   89D2

"Paradise" is a surprising name for this nondescript little town 9km (5.5 miles) southeast of Cartago, but it was allegedly coined by exhausted Spaniards after they had struggled up from the Caribbean coast to reach cooler climates. Today Paraíso serves only as a stop-over for visitors before or after a trip to the **Jardín Botánico Carlos H Lankester (Lankester Gardens)**▶▶▶ (tel: 552-3247, fax: 552-3151, www.jardinbotanicolankester.org *Open* daily 8.30–4.30, visits on the hour. *Admission: inexpensive*). Signposted from the main road northwest of town, these botanic gardens were founded in the 1950s by Charles Lankester, an English coffee planter, and are now managed by the University of Costa Rica. Often referred to as orchid gardens, the 10.5ha (26-acre) area in fact supports a wealth of tropical plants, from bamboo to bromeliads, ornamental plants, aloe, palms and amaryllis, as well as a wilder part of regenerated rain forest at the back. February to May is the best time to see the 800 species of orchids in bloom.

▶▶▶ **Parque Nacional Manuel Antonio**   88C1

Open: Tue–Sun 7–4. Admission: moderate

Manuel Antonio's modest 683ha (1,688 acres) combine white-sand beaches backed by lush tropical forest with white-faced monkeys, sloths, grunting howler monkeys, iguanas and the poisonous manzanilla tree. Above all it is the spectacularly jagged coastline and exquisite sheltered waters that have made its reputation. These attractions are also the park's downfall, as human overload has caused considerable damage. Quotas limit visitor numbers, but the lack of buffer zones around the park inspires little confidence. Some of the parkland is still privately owned and has been exploited by clandestine tree-cutting. Worse still, the surfeit of hotels near by has built right up to the river you cross to access the park. (At low tide it's a walk, at high tide you can wade across or pay a small fee for a boat ride.)

True paradise On a brighter note, the beautiful coastline starts with the blissful sweep of Playa Espadilla Sur and continues beyond the densely forested headland of Punta Catedral to the magnificent **Playa Blanca**▶▶▶, also known as Playa Manuel Antonio or Playa Tres. Picnic tables, showers and troops of tame (to the point of being irritating) white-faced monkeys add to this beach's popularity. From here, trails lead uphill past Playas Gemelas and the "sloth trail" to end steeply at another sheltered but rockier cove, Puerto Escondido, best visited at low tide. Those lucky enough to visit the park by boat will see the curiously eroded cliff, Punta Serrucho, that divides this bay from the final beach, Playa Playita.

Rare specimens Visitors who have come for the wildlife should not be put off by the beach-party atmosphere around bars and hotels. Waterbirds, including tri-colored herons, willets and Amazon kingfishers, feed beside the tidal pools and mangrove creeks, and the tiny offshore islands are refuges for common terns, magnificent frigate birds and brown pelicans. Tracts of primary forest shelter bully trees, cow trees, Santa Marías, silk cottons and the increasingly rare black locust tree. Monkeys are numerous (including the endemic but endangered squirrel monkey), as are agoutis and iguanas, and three-toed sloths are usually easy to see. To help spot these and other animals, bilingual guides with telescopes can be hired at the entrance. As you wander the trails, watch for coatis crossing, and listen for orange-collared manakins in the undergrowth—the males snap their wings as they gather to display.

▶ Parque Nacional Tapantí–Macizo de la Muerte

89D2

Open: daily 8–4. Admission: moderate
Promoted from wildlife refuge to national park status in 1992 and expanded in 1999, Tapantí offers the dubious attraction of having the greatest amount of rain and cloud cover in the country (800cm/315in annual rainfall). The well-maintained dirt tracks of this 58,500ha (144,557-acre) park straddling the northern Talamanca Mountains are popular with mountain bikers, and there are swimming areas in the cool rivers. With altitudes rising from 1,220 to 2,440m (4,000 to 8,000ft), bird and plant life is varied, but cloud forest dominates and butterflies are abundant. The entrance is along a poor road 8km (5 miles) southeast of Orosí.

TOMBOLO
The wedge-shaped headland of Punta Catedral, connected by a thin neck to Playa Espadilla Sur, was once an island. Sand gradually built up in the intervening channel over a period of hundreds of thousands of years, until finally a *tombolo*, or sand bridge, was formed. Grass, shrubs and eventually trees took root to form the present luxuriant picture. A pleasant 1.4km (0.8-mile) trail encircles the entire headland.

Manuel Antonio offers sublime scenery both on land and underwater

FIREWORKS FOR KENNEDY

The first recorded eruption of Irazú was in 1723, but more vivid in Tico memory is 19 March, 1963, the day President John F. Kennedy arrived on an official visit to San José. As he drove past cheering crowds, something more momentous was happening up in the Cordillera Central. The foothills of Irazú began to shake, gas emissions increased, red-hot rocks rained down around the volcano, lava started flowing and tonnes of ash fell gently over the Central Valley. Kennedy complained of stinging eyes and donned dark glasses, but this was only the beginning of two years of continuous volcanic fallout that forced drivers to use headlights during the day and pedestrians to use umbrellas against the ash. It even inspired a secret plan to evacuate San José.

▶▶▶ Parque Nacional Volcán Irazú 89D3

Open: daily 8–3.30. Admission: moderate

The stark lunar landscape of Irazú, studded with a lime-green crater lake, is in spectacular contrast to the access route that twists up through fertile valleys of volcanic soil. This is perhaps Costa Rica's easiest park to visit. The main crater lies only a few minutes' walk from the car park, although the altitude may make you feel lightheaded or short of breath. Go early to avoid crowds and cloud.

Thunder The name of this 3,431m (11,257ft) subconical volcano derives from an indigenous word meaning "thunder and earthquake mountain," and ash showers continue to worry residents of nearby Cartago. Documented since 1563, Irazú's activity means that access to the craters is restricted, but the principal lake—an almost perfect circle with steeply inclined walls—and the smaller Diego de La Haya crater are visually accessible, though visitors are not allowed to hike near the craters. Drive up to the upper car park and you may have rare views of both oceans and, with a telescope, of Lake Nicaragua. Be careful when walking over the lava shingle, and pay attention to warning signs—Irazú's fumaroles are capricious. Concern was rekindled in December 1993 when Irazú reawoke, and many vulcanologists feel another major eruption is imminent. Hence all cars are parked to facilitate a fast exit in the event of eruption.

Flora and fauna Surrounding vegetation is premontane and montane wet forest, partly lichen-draped, interspersed with open grass- and scrublands. Birds are scarce owing to deforestation and volcanic activity, but include clay-colored robins, mountain robins, owls, hummingbirds and volcano juncos. Rabbits, foxes, armadillos, porcupines, coyotes and tiger cats can also be spotted.

▶▶ Puntarenas 88A3

While Puntarenas' position on a narrow spit of land thrusting into the Golfo de Nicoya makes it ideal for ferry traffic to the Nicoya Peninsula, with water taxis now connecting Montezuma with Herradura to the south, and the Friendship Bridge over the Tempisque River speeding motor traffic into central Nicoya to the north, ferry traffic is down, and today Puntarenas is to some extent living on past glories. However, its proximity to San José has always been a draw, and so hotels in every price range abound, and open-air bars and restaurants line the breezy Paseo de los Turistas. A single road leads into the entrance to the spit, gradually fanning out into five main avenues terminating at the lighthouse. Swimming is reasonable on the Pacific side, but avoid the fetid lagoon.

Faded glory The port was founded in the 18th century and rose to prominence in the 19th century when it served as the main route for coffee exports. The Atlantic Railway to Limón put an end to that, along with

Along the breezy waterfront, Puntarenas has polished up its attractions

the new port that opened at Caldera in 1981, but in an ironic twist, the new Tico Train Tour to Caldera, which carries visitors from San José, may help to revive Puntarenas as a stop on the tourist itinerary. The train runs Saturdays and Sundays, and excursions (tel: 233-3300, americatravel@ msn.com *Admission: expensive*). Puntarenas' charm lies in the evidence of its cosmopolitan past—the large Chinese population, decorative clapboard houses, a tumbledown waterside village, salty sailors' cantinas and a market. The town's history can be traced at the Museo Historico Marino (tel: 661-5036. *Open* Tue–Sun 9.45–12, 1–5.15) in a former prison on Avenida Central. New to town is the Parque Marino del Pacifíco (tel: 661-5272, fax: 661-0633, parquemarino@ cinpe.una.ac.cr *Open* Tue–Sun 9–5. *Admission: moderate*) covering all aspects of Costa Rican marine life. The new park is easy to spot near the entrance to town.

Cruising Puntarenas is the starting point for yacht or cruiser tours of the islands in the Golfo de Nicoya, although in all cases transport can be arranged from San José. Calypso Tours (tel/fax: 256-8585, www.calypsotours. com) fishes and snorkels around Islas Tortugas and visits the Private Punta Coral. Bay Island Cruises (tel: 258-3566, fax: 258-1189, www.bayisland cruises.com) takes passengers to snorkel at Islas Tortugas. Surfers head to Boca Barranca, a perfect left break south of town.

Tuna fishing in the Pacific off Puntarenas, still a busy fishing port

CHINESE IMPORTS
In the early 1900s Puntarenas had a population of some 2,000 Chinese, who flocked there to work on the docks. Although many have moved to the capital, the port still has an active Associación China, founded in 1909 by the main families. Their superb old meeting house, its ornate interior worthy of a Chinese Buddhist temple, sadly disappeared in the 1940s, though a photo remains on display at the museum. The building on Avenida 1, dating from 1949, has a strangely anachronistic atmosphere, with flags and banners dedicated to Taiwan's Nationalist Party.

One of the pleasures of this country is its fabulous range of exotic fruit, piled high in the markets, sliced open at street stands, liquefied into a refresco *or dangling from a tree. Some will be immediately familiar, but the appeal of others may need explanation.*

Pejibaye (top) is grown extensively by indigenous peoples

THE COCONUT
Quintessential fruit of tropical beaches, the coconut is exceptionally multifunctional. The fresh white flesh and milk are often used as blending ingredients, particularly on the Caribbean coast, and young coconuts (*pipa*) are sold on stands (look for signs) in all coastal regions as refreshing drinks. The green casing is hacked off to open the nut, at the same time creating a convenient "spoon" to scoop out the flesh. Both the milk (which resembles water when fresh) and the flesh are highly nutritious. Coconut oil, made by heating the white flesh, is traditionally used as a sunscreen and skin softener.

Breadfruit (*fruta de pan*) The large, seedless fruit of the breadfruit tree was introduced to the Caribbean by England's Captain Bligh (1754–1817), who brought it to Jamaica from Tahiti. It is found above all on the Caribbean coast, where it is eaten fried, roasted or boiled, and is an excellent source of vitamins A, B and C.

Cashew apple (*marañon*) Yes, the kidney-shaped nut also has a fruit from which it grows. This bright scarlet, pear-shaped fruit has delectable soft, sharp-tasting flesh whose strong perfume makes it popular for jams and drinks. Watch out for the nut that grows from the fruit: this is edible only once roasted; otherwise it is poisonous.

Guava (*guayaba*) The guava is cultivated throughout the tropics for its thin-skinned, lemon-like fruits, whose aromatic pink pulp is rich in vitamins A and C, iron and calcium. It can be consumed raw, cooked into jams and jellies or served as a juice. Guava leaves are also used to make tea as a treatment for amoebic dysentery.

Mango (*mango/manga*) Seen in the city square of Alajuela, arid Guanacaste, and throughout the tropics, the "king of fruits" is ubiquitous. Maturing fruit dangle prolifically from the tree from March to October—but be careful, some people are allergic to the sap and skin. The male mango (*mango*) is greener, smaller and harder than the more generous, yellow female (*manga*), which contains a fibrous orange pulp. Green *mangos* are used for chutneys, preserves and pies, and Ticos also eat this male variety sprinkled with lemon and salt.

Mombin (*jocote*) When Spaniards first set eyes on this, they called it a plum. In fact this dark-green- to red-skinned juicy fruit has a spicy taste and is consumed in large quantities from August to October. A wild, yellow-skinned cousin called the hogplum is popular with tapirs.

Mountain apple (*manzana de agua*) Like the breadfruit, the mountain or Malay apple was introduced from Tahiti to the Caribbean by Captain Bligh in 1793. The crisp white flesh of this small, oval, pink-ish fruit tastes similar to that of apples and is eaten raw or stewed into jams. A distant, equally

A young trader arranges large, ripe pineapples at the farmer's market in San Ramón

delicious cousin, the **rose apple** (*manzana rosa*), has the bonus of being rose-perfumed.

Palm fruit (*pejibaye*) This is the Tico fruit *par excellence* and is considered sacred by the Guaymi Indians. Like small coconuts, *pejibayes* grow in clusters among the fronds of the *pejibaye* palm tree. *Palmito*, or palm heart, is extracted from the base of the same tree. The glossy orange fruit is only eaten cooked and is often blended with mayonnaise to soften its dry texture, whose taste is a cross between chestnut and pumpkin.

Papaya/pawpaw (*papaya*) Forty-five varieties grow all over the tropics, but the papaya is indigenous to Central America. Yellow-, green- or orange-skinned, the elongated fruits grow in clusters at the top of a hollow trunk beneath a spray of leaves. The taste of the slightly bland though wonderfully smooth orange flesh is heightened by a squeeze of lime or lemon juice.

Soursop (*guanábana*) The hardly inspiring English name of this prickly, kidney-shaped fruit bears no relation to its subtly perfumed white pulp, from which a sweet-sour juice is extracted to make *refrescos* or ice cream. It is a relative of the custard-apple, also found in Costa Rica.

Starfruit (*carambola*) The starfruit's shiny, pale-yellow skin conceals a very juicy white flesh.

CHIVERRE

The notoriously sweet Tico tooth meets its match when Easter arrives and mounds of large green-and-white-striped fruits appear on roadsides and in markets. The *chiverre* is a member of the pumpkin family that somewhat resembles a squash. For centuries Ticos have transformed the *chiverre* into a sweet jam by mixing its dried pulp with a block of brown sugar, *tapa dulce*. The resulting stringy texture and sugary taste is an essential ingredient in pies made for the Easter feast.

107

Papayas, mangoes, bananas, plantains and cashew apples (by the vendor's hand)

Stilt-houses lining the estuary date from Quepos's less sophisticated past

▶▶▶ Quepos 88C1

Quepos's origins as a major banana-exporting port are apparent in the neat little plantation villages lining the access road. These are now surrounded by more lucrative oil palms, whose advent ended the port's importance. However, Quepos has a new *raison d'être*, namely as a base for visitors to Manuel Antonio National Park (see pages 102–103). From the picturesque town, a road winds 6.5km (4 miles) along the cliff to reach Playa Espadilla Norte and the park entrance. This stretch (known as Manuel Antonio) is the focus for burgeoning hotel and restaurant developments, many with fabulous ocean views, some with private beaches, and nearly all exclusive. Budget visitors should either stick to downtown Quepos or take a bus directly to the *cabinas* and budget hotels that are clustered near the park entrance.

The choice Apart from some bars, discos, souvenir shops, restaurants and a casino, the attractions of downtown Quepos lie in its sleepy, tropical port atmosphere. Lynch Travel (tel: 777-1170, www.lynchtravel.com) features horseback trips to nearby waterfalls and scenic viewpoints. For whitewater rafting on the Parrita, Naranjo and Savegre rivers, contact Amigos del Río (tel: 777-0082). Iguana Tours (tel: 777-2052, www.iguanatours.com) organizes whitewater runs and kayaking trips. Fishing enthusiasts can book charters with Costa Rican Dreams (tel: 777-0593) or Sportfishing Wahoo (tel: 777-0832). Swimmers should be wary of dangerous riptides at Playa Espadilla Norte.

Action! Tour companies in Quepos and Manuel Antonio offer a range of outdoor activities in addition to those listed above. One fast-growing, perhaps questionable new action sport is ATV riding. Climb into an all-terrain vehicle and tear through the countryside with King Tours (tel: 643-2441, www.kingtours.com) who also offer canopy touring, rafting and other mainstream activities. Canopy tours are also offered by Canopy Safari (tel: 771-0100, www.canopysafari.com), Titi Canopy Tour (tel: 777-3130, www.titicanopytours.com) and Gaia Link Tours (tel: 431-2939, www.gaialinktours.com). Another new action sport is canyoning, or canyoneering, which involves rappelling down cliffs and waterfalls. The young in mind and body can try this at Pacific Ecotours (tel: 777-3030) or Canyoning Tours (tel/fax: 777-1924, fattan@racsa.co.cr). Parasail with Gold Coast Parasail (tel: 777-2746) at Manuel Antonio, or learn to fly an ultra-light aircraft through Sky Raiders Tours at Blue Fin Sportfishing (tel: 777-2222, www.bluefinsportfishing.com).

►► Parque Nacional Carara 88B2
Open: daily 8–4. Admission: moderate
This national park is one of Costa Rica's last habitats for scarlet macaws (see panel). The rich biodiversity of Carara is owed to its transitional position between the dry northern forests and the humid tropical forests of the south. Its rivers and lagoon are inhabited by crocodiles, roseate spoonbills, boat-billed herons, blue-winged teals, howler and white-faced monkeys, deer and peccaries. Two trails lead through the park: a short 800m (875yd) trail starts at the main entrance, about 3km (2 miles) south of the Río Tárcoles bridge, and a 4km (2.5-mile) trail starts about 500m (550yd) past the bridge. Black-hooded antshrikes, long-tailed hermit humming-birds and armadillos are quite often encountered, and you may see nesting pairs of macaws in hollows up large trees. Wear repellent: the mosquitoes are voracious.

Alternatives If you are interested in crocodiles, stop at the Tárcoles river bridge: you can usually spot a few sunning themselves on the banks. Crocodile tours, usually pricey, can be booked through Crocodile Mantour (tel: 637-0426, www.crocodilemantour.com), or Jungle Crocodile Safari (tel: 236-6473, www.junglecrocodilesafari.com). A turn-off 4km (2.5 miles) past the bridge leads to Villa Lapas Sky Way and Canopy Tour (tel: 637-0232, www.villalapas.com), Jardin Pura Vida (tel: 200-5040, stannard@racsa.co.cr) for hiking and views, Siempre Verde Eco-Farm (tel: 353-2193) for eco-tours, and Bijagual Waterfall Tours (tel: 661-8263) for hikes and horseback rides to a spectacular waterfall.

SCARLET MACAWS
The brilliant blue, yellow and red plumage of this tropical bird has been its downfall. Christopher Columbus was the first to bring a scarlet macaw to Europe, and baby macaws now fetch up to $1,250 on the black market. Poaching and destruction of their habitat have made them an endangered species. Scarlet macaws can be seen on Costa Rica's Pacific coast, in Parque Nacional Corcovado, and at Parque Nacional Carara which is a nesting ground for more than 100 pairs, best seen at dusk in the mangrove swamps at the mouth of the Río Grande de Tárcoles.

109

Scarlet macaws fetch high prices—an attractive incentive for poachers

▶▶▶ San José   89D3

See pages 116–127.

▶ San Ramón   88B3

A visit to the agricultural community of San Ramón is best made on Saturday mornings, when you can see the *feria del agricultor* (farmers' market) in full swing. Fruit, vegetables and cattle are haggled over by local *campesinos* (farmers). On a weekday, the San Ramón museum (tel: 437-9851. *Open* Mon–Fri 8–12, 1–5. *Admission: inexpensive*), on the main square, displays a reproduction *campesino* home from the turn of the 20th century, while photographs and panels recount local history. The history of Costa Rica's 1948 civil war is told at the nearby Centro Cultural e Histórico José Figueres Ferrer (tel: 447-2178, fax: 447-2321, www.centro-josefigueres.org). The surrounding mountainous region is particularly beautiful; 18km (11 miles) to the north lies a private reserve, the **Los Angeles Cloud Forest▶ ▶** (tel: 461-0300, fax: 461-0302, www.villablanca-costarica.com *Open* daily. *Admission: expensive*), owned by former president Rodrigo Carazo. The 800ha (1,980 acres) of cloud forest are crossed by an easy 1.5km (1-mile) trail (guides are available). Next to the reserve is the charming Villa Blanca hotel, under the same ownership, which organizes treks on horseback.

▶ Santa Ana   88C3

The location of this once dusty rural town, on the highway 14km (9 miles) west of San José, has given it a new identity as a satellite of the capital, much preferred by expatriates. Yet the old rural spirit prevails. Roadside vendors announce Santa Ana's particular product—braided strings of onions, also seen hanging from the eaves of houses—while roasted onions are served in local restaurants. The central area still boasts some picturesque old buildings in adobe and clapboard, wreathed in crimson bougainvillea.

BASEBALLS, BY HAND
In addition to its proximity to whitewater, CATIE and the Guayabo National Monument, Turrialba is home to Rawlings de Costa Rica, S.A., a factory on the outskirts of town whose workers make by hand all of the baseballs used in US Major League Baseball. The business has been in Costa Rica since 1989 when political instability drove it out of Haiti. A factory tour takes around three hours; no organized tours were being offered as of spring 2007, but if you ask around in Turrialba, you'll probably find someone willing to take you to the factory for an informal tour.

▶ Sarchí 88C3

Once a sleepy little village, Sarchí is now a commercial crafts hub, invaded daily by tour buses. A new Mercado de Artesanía combines restaurants, bars and craft shops, and there is also a co-operative, but Fabrica Joaquín Chaveri (tel: 454-4411) remains the commercial leader of Sarchí. Small workshops surround the garden at the back, where oxcarts are laboriously painted, and the front shop displays a huge range of furniture, bowls, platters, boxes and parrot-headed walking canes made from tropical hardwoods. This is the place to buy your folding cowhide rocking chair, a traditional feature of many verandas throughout the country. Sarchí's main square has a twin-towered church (1949), set in a garden where even the benches, like the local bus stops and rubbish bins, are painted in Sarchí floral style. The entrance to **Parque Nacional Juan Castro Blanco▶** is reached from Bajos del Toro, a pretty little town nearby.

▶ Turrialba 89E3

This small town was once devoted to agriculture, but a prosperous new era has opened up with the development of kayaking and intense whitewater rafting on the nearby Río Pacuare, considered to be one of Costa Rica's top destinations. There are reasonable places to stay in the town, and more luxurious establishments in the scenic surroundings. Look closely at the trees in the central square, where sloths laze the day away. CATIE, founded in 1942, is a pioneering station specializing in agronomical research. It experiments with tropical crops over an area of nearly 1,000ha (2,470 acres). The extensive laboratories, library, experimental plots and greenhouses can be visited on a full five-hour guided tour or 2-hour tour of the botanical garden (tel/fax: 556-2700, www.catie.ac.cr *Admission: expensive*. Advanced booking essential). The Parque Nacional Volcán Turrialba centers on the 3,340m (10,955ft) volcano—volcanic activity can occasionally be seen. Reaching the park is best with a tour group from San José, or by staying at Volcán Turrialba Lodge (tel: 273-4335, www.volcanturrialbalodge.com) in the valley between the Turrialba and Irazú volcanoes.

OXCART GENESIS
Sarchí's painted souvenir oxcarts, resplendent with floral motifs, are not an old tradition. Although wooden oxcarts were introduced from Nicaragua in the mid-1800s to haul coffee beans, it was not until 1903 that an inspired *campesina* decided to decorate the wheels. Soon after, metal axles and sectioned wheels led to even more elaborate designs while preserving the original star-shaped motif. Around 1915, painting spread to the body of the cart and hues evolved from grays and greens to today's standard orange. When motorized transport took over in the 1960s, Sarchí's oxcart painters turned to the tourist trade, though some carts are still in use in San Antonio de Escazú.

111

Oxcart, Sarchí: a breakaway design abandons the floral tradition

Opposite: the ruined church, Ujarrás

MYSTICAL HISTORY
The church at Ujarrás was pre-dated by a venerated shrine dedicated to Our Lady of Ransom. In 1565, according to legend, Mary appeared from inside a tree trunk to an Indian fishing in the Río Reventazón. Spurred into action, the Indian carried the trunk back to Ujarrás, but as he proceeded, it became heavier and heavier until finally, on his arrival, it could not even be lifted by a gang of helpers. Local Franciscan fathers interpreted this as a sign to build a shrine. When the incident of the pirates took place a century later, it was assumed that the Virgin had saved the day, as they advanced no farther than Turrialba.

▶▶ Ujarrás   88C4

The abandoned village of Ujarrás nestles in the Orosí Valley at the base of steep cultivated slopes running down to the Cachí reservoir. In 1883 a flood wiped out the village, and today there is little here except a swimming pool and a few restaurants. However, in the middle of chayote plantations stands the star of Ujarrás, the evocative ruins of **Nuestra Señora de La Limpia Concepción (Church of the Immaculate Conception)**, built between 1681 and 1693 to commemorate the retreat of the pirates Morgan and Mansfield, who threatened to sack Costa Rica. A century later the church was destroyed by an earthquake, and today the old stone walls stand in a carefully tended garden of flowering shrubs.

About 3km (2 miles) northeast is the Cachí dam and nearby Charrara recreation area (closed Monday), with pools, a restaurant, trails and rowing boats. Farther toward Orosí stands the unique **Casa del Soñador (Dreamer's House)**, a whimsical one-man work by the late folk-sculptor Macedonio Quesada, now occupied by his son, Hermes. Woodcarvings are still made by Hermes, who will show you around the simple house, faced with bas-reliefs and sprouting carved figures at every corner.

▶▶ Zarcero   88C3

This mountain village of ruddy-cheeked inhabitants boasts the work of another of Costa Rica's idiosyncratic sculptors (see Ujarrás, above). This artist uses topiary as his medium. The astonishing garden fronts a pastel-toned church (1895), whose horseshoe steps seem designed to lead the eye to the creations of Evangelisto Blanco, the park gardener. For some 30 years he has trimmed and pruned these cypress bushes, rejecting lucrative offers to apply his talents elsewhere, and as a result Zarcero's Parque Central offers a vegetal gallery of animals and human forms—from faces peeping out of niches to elephants, huge standing figures, a cat riding a motorcycle and even a populated bullring.

Visit the impeccably maintained and highly decorated church, and do not leave Zarcero without sampling its gastronomic offerings: *cajeta* (fudge), candied orange, honey, cheese and wonderfully thick cream. A series of roadside stands just south of town offers all of the above and more.

Delicate designs grace the wood panels of Zarcero's church

Drive

Valley and volcano

See map on pages 88–89.

Make an early start to complete this full one-day circuit, which takes in Cartago and Volcán Irazú before meandering through the enchanting Orosí Valley. Cultural stops are included and, if time allows, a therapeutic soak in a mineral pool.

From San José drive out through San Pedro on the highway to **Cartago▶** (see page 92). Negotiate the confusing streets of this town, stopping to look at **Las Ruinas▶▶▶**, and the remarkable **Basílica de Nuestra Señora de Los Angeles▶▶**, before heading northeast toward Cot. At a major fork, branch left to Potrero Cerrado, then wind up through beautiful agricultural valleys and pine forests to the national park of **Volcán Irazú▶▶▶** (see page 104). On the way back down, stop at the Restaurant Linda Vista for a snack.

Backtrack to Cartago, then drive east to Paraíso, stopping just before it at the **Jardín Botánico Carlos H Lankester▶▶▶** (see page 102). In Paraíso itself, drive through the main square and follow signs to Cachí. This part of the Orosí Valley is blanketed with rich fields of cane, coffee and macadamia, and the road twisting down to the Cachí Reservoir offers plenty of views as well as the gushing Los Novios waterfall. A right turn from the main road leads shortly to **Ujarrás▶▶** (see opposite) and its melancholic ruins (above). If hunger strikes, indulge at a modest little open-air restaurant at the intersection. From here return to the main road and continue round the lake, passing the hydroelectric dam where water flows through channels into a spillway, before winding uphill to the carved Casa del Soñador.

The road continues through stunning, undulating landscapes of coffee plantations, with the foothills of the Cordillera de Talamanca looming up to the south. At **Orosí▶** (see page 101) stop to look at the venerable church and/or relax in the thermal pools. Do not miss the panoramas from the mirador outside town, before heading back through more bucolic landscapes to Paraíso, then Cartago and San José.

Costa Rica's handicrafts may not compare with the range available in Guatemala or Mexico, yet the country continues to play a strategic role as a market-place for artisans from north and south. Indigenous peoples have rediscovered old craft skills, and tropical woods inspire skilled North American carvers.

CRAFT SOURCES
Near San José, Green Turtle Souvenirs (tel: 430-0211, www.greenturtlesouvenirs.com) in San Vicente de Moravia (usually called Moravia) offers a wide choice of arts and crafts. At Bello Horizonte, uphill from Escazú, is Biesanz Woodworks (tel: 289-4337, www.biesanz.com). Jay Morrison's furniture is displayed at his Tierra Extraña showroom in Piedades de Santa Ana (tel: 282-6697). The CASEM crafts co-operative (tel: 645-5190, staelena@sol.racsa.co.cr) in Monteverde sells souvenirs inspired by local nature. Considered by some to be the best in Costa Rica is Toad Hall (tel: 692-8020, www.toadhall-gallery.com) near Nuevo Arenal. See also San José (pages 120–121) and Sarchí (page 111).

114

Folding rocking chairs are easily exported

Since pre-Columbian days when Costa Rica's indigenous peoples extensively traded their stunning pottery, gold ornaments and stone carvings, the standard of handicrafts has taken a downward turn. Gone are the intricately carved metates and the inspired zoomorphic jade and gold pieces. Today you are more likely to see primitive gourds, baskets and weavings. However, the growth of the tourist market has given the necessary impetus not only to the development of new directions but also to a revival of old traditions. Add to this an influx of North American craftspeople, usually inspired by Costa Rica's wide range of tropical woods, plus the crossroads position of Costa Rica on the Latin American map, and the result is a steadily growing crafts industry.

Indigenous traditions Of all Costa Rican traditional handicrafts, it is the pottery of Guaitíl (see page 42) that carries off the prizes. In pre-Columbian days, the pottery of the Chorotegas of the Nicoya Peninsula was acclaimed and commissioned by Zapotecs and Aztecs, and traded to southern Costa Rica and Panama. Today the kilns of Guaitíl are firing again in an impressive revival that spurns modern technology. Similarly, with the help of an enlightened Tico artist, the Boruca Indians have now rejected synthetic dyes and threads and revived traditional techniques with backstrap looms, usually installed in a family kitchen. Like the Talamanca Indians, they continue to make carved gourds and incorporate symbolic designs into fine string baskets (*chácaras*) of natural fibres. Elaborately carved and painted balsa-wood masks made by the Borucas for their Diablitos celebration are sold in craft shops everywhere, while iguana-skin drums are produced by more remote indigenous groups.

Bring on the ox Ubiquitous to the point of over-exposure, the painted oxcart is a distant reflection of old *campesino* traditions transformed into easily packable miniature versions, the ultimate Tico souvenir. These decorative objects are hand-painted at Sarchí (see page 111), where visitors can watch craftsmen at work at the pioneering Chaveri workshop, which dates from 1903 and developed for the nascent tourist market in the 1960s. Sarchí has since become *the* crafts town of the country, and this is where visitors can stock up on every imaginable transformation of tropical wood: There is no shortage and the quality is generally high. Although materials come straight from the tropical forest, the high profit margin on these comparatively small objects makes

Animals assume mystical status in Guaitíl's centuries-old forms and designs

them ecologically acceptable compared with large-scale commercial logging. Another typical Tico souvenir is the collapsible leather-and-wood rocking chair, a Spanish inheritance that is easily transportable.

Foreign input Perhaps the most beautifully crafted wooden items come from the workshop of Barry Biesanz. Rosewoods, lacewood, ironwood, purpleheart, tigerwood, balsam of Peru, satinwood and many more of Costa Rica's 1,500 tree species are transformed into combs, bowls and boxes, often combining two or three woods in one perfectly joined piece. In harmony with a strictly conservationist attitude, his expanding Escazú workshop, Biesanz Woodworks, maintains a seedbank, a rare-wood nursery, and whenever possible uses fallen or dead trees. A similar approach is expounded by Jay Morrison and his company, Tierra Extraña, through their reafforestation project. Morrison produces extraordinarily crafted furniture made from native Costa Rican woods, and like Biesanz allows their textures, grains and tones to influence his designs.

New directions Whether adapting indigenous beeswax whistles (*ocarinas*) into clay and adding an animal head or two, or importing Mexican silver from Taxco, clothes and textiles from Guatemala, ceramic-bead necklaces from Colombia, embroidered panels from Panama or llama-wool jackets from Ecuador, Costa Rica is re-establishing itself as Latin America's handicrafts crossroads. Parallel to this, a renewed interest in and intelligent promotion of indigenous crafts, plus the dynamism of talented expatriates, may take future Costa Rican crafts beyond banana-paper, the latest novelty.

WHAT'S IN A GOURD?
If you spot a short-trunked tree with long spreading branches and green, volleyball-size spheres hanging from them, you are looking at a calabash tree. Gourds and maracas are made by hollowing out calabash fruits, then letting them dry for several days. The hard shells can be incised or beautifully polished, and odd shapes can be created by binding the fruits as they dry. Their usual function is as a container for food or water, a custom of the Afro-Caribbeans as well as the indigenous people of Talamanca.

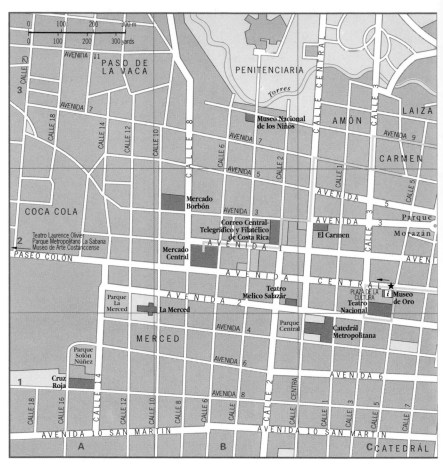

San José

Nestling at 1,149m (3,770ft) in the Meseta Central (Central Plateau), the capital of Costa Rica is a crossroads between the country's natural sights. In addition to being the hub of the nation's political, economic and cultural life, San José also maintains a well-oiled tourist infrastructure, offering just enough to keep visitors busy for a few days before they head out to more distant forests, volcanoes and beaches. The small scale of the central area (310,000 inhabitants), its easy grid layout, mild spring-like climate and lively cultural life create a pleasant introduction to the country, although belching buses, impossibly heavy traffic and crowded streets are a disincentive to a long stay. It is relatively safe compared with other Latin American capitals, but pickpockets, drug abuse and muggers are on the increase even here. Whatever its drawbacks, San José retains a distinctly provincial, small-town feel—where else does a president drive his own car and flag down passing motorists when he runs out of fuel?

New look Although founded in 1737, San José only replaced Cartago as Costa Rica's capital in 1823, following a short civil war. Its socio-economic zenith was reached toward the

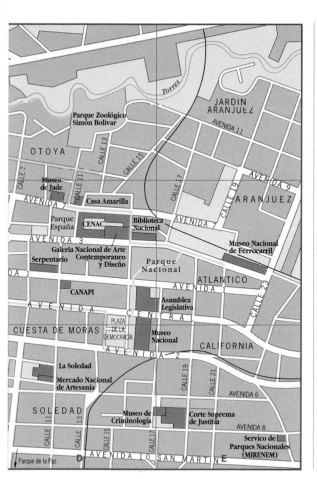

Left: central San José

SAFETY

The days of San José being a safe city are over, and although the level of risk is far below that of adjoining countries, tourists are considered easy targets. Beware of certain areas—the Coca-Cola bus station being number one, closely followed by central streets south of Avenida 2 and around Parque Central. Conmen and conwomen (often masquerading as prostitutes to trap unsuspecting male visitors) abound, so be wary of any nocturnal street contact, however harmless it may seem. Also watch out for the *chapuline*s, teenage gangs who organize distractions, all the better to rob their chosen victims.

117

Below: San José sprawls some 10sq km (4sq miles) across the central plateau
Left: lottery-ticket seller

BARRIOS

San José is divided into *barrios*, or localities, and, as with any large city, some *barrios* are worth seeing, while others are best avoided. Barrios Amon and Otoya, north of the central area, should be explored for their historic buildings. Los Yoses and Escalante, to the east, are residential zones with little to offer visitors, while San Pedro, farther east, is home to the University of Costa Rica and so sports numerous lively nightspots. The north-western area, the Zona Roja, shelters the lowlife—prostitutes, drunks and generally dubious types—and should be avoided, especially at night. The same goes for much of the city's southern half.

San José street life is lively, and food and drinks are easily available

end of the 19th century, when the coffee trade was booming: most of the capital's more impressive public buildings date from this period, as do the surviving pockets of plantation owners' homes. Earthquakes, property developers and a population explosion have taken their toll, leading to the replacement of numerous old architectural gems with characterless concrete edifices. Government buildings range from the elegant old Legislative Assembly, immediately north of the Museo Nacional, to aberrations such as the tower-block headquarters of the ICT (tourist institute) or the uninspiring law-courts complex southeast of the central area. As a welcome contrast, the heart of town is dotted with verdant squares, and the old airport at La Sabana has been transformed into a large park from which the silhouettes of surrounding hills are easily visible. This vista, too, is part of San José's small-town appeal, which suits the scale of so diminutive a country.

Central zone Most points of interest are located within a dozen or so blocks bordered to the north by Barrio Amón (Avenida 7–9), to the south by Avenida 6, to the west by Calle 16 (with its infamous Coca-Cola bus station), and to the east by Calle 19. Avenida Central bisects the city east–west, with odd-numbered avenues lying north of Central and even-numbered avenues lying south. For several central blocks it becomes a pedestrian street. West of La Merced Church it is renamed Paseo Colón, a prestigious business quarter whose quiet side-streets feature some splendid small hotels. Beyond here lie La Sabana and the embassies of Rohrmoser. A few blocks east of the Museo Nacional, Avenida Central skirts the prosperous residential area of Los Yoses before entering San Pedro, another grand suburb and also the site of San José's university.

Churches There are no outstanding churches left in San José, although a few neo-classical examples have had facelifts following the 1991 earthquake. The Catedral Metropolitana (Avenida 2/Calle Central) and adjoining archbishop's palace date from the founding of San José in the early 18th century, but were virtually destroyed by the 1821 earthquake and not rebuilt until 1871. It was visited by Pope John Paull II during his visit in 1983 and recently underwent a light facelift. Looking equally pristine is La Soledad (Avenida

La Merced, fronted by one of the mystery spheres from southern Costa Rica. Made of granite and accurate to 18mm (0.7in), the pre-Columbian spheres baffle archeologists to this day

4/Calle 11), an eclectic 1909 construction with two symmetrical towers flanking a central atrium. The small plaza in front once hosted seasonal fairs but has now been supplanted by the adjoining square in front of the overbearing ICT tower block. La Merced, unmistakable in its strategic location where one-way traffic careers round to Avenida 2 from Paseo Colón, is in a mixed neo-Gothic/neo-classical style and was undergoing extensive renovations in the spring of 2007.

Culture Tickets to cultural events are astonishingly cheap thanks to government sponsorship. San José boasts some 25 theaters, and, if your Spanish is up to it, an outing to a show should be on your agenda. Otherwise, English-language plays are regularly staged at the Teatro Laurence Olivier. Josefinos are justly proud of their National Symphony Orchestra: you may catch it in full melodic swing at the Teatro Nacional or on tour in a provincial capital. Plentiful cinemas offer the full gamut of Hollywood productions, often screened in San José even before they reach Europe, while independent foreign films can be seen at the University Cinemateca in San Pedro or the Sala Garbo off Paseo Colón. And don't miss the dance and theatrical performances staged at the CENAC complex (see Galería Nacional de Arte Contemporaneo y Diseño, page 120).

TOURIST INFORMATION
The ICT (Instituto Costarricense de Turismo) has a public office next to the Museo de Oro beneath the Plaza de La Cultura (tel: 222-1090 ext. 277. *Open* Mon–Fri 9–1, 2–5), and another in the central Costa Rica Post Office building on Calle 2, Avenida 1/3 (tel: 258-8762. *Open* Mon–Fri 8–4). An office can also be found at the Juan Santamaria International Airport (tel: 443-1535, 443-2883. *Open* Mon–Fri 9–5). Offices outside San José are at the border crossings of Peñas Blancas (tel: 677-0138, fax: 677-0138. *Open* Mon–Fri 8–8) and Paso Canoas (tel: 732-2035. *Open* 7am–10pm). ICT officials do not always speak English, but their offices are well-supplied with brochures promoting everything from hotels to hang-gliding. The website, www.visitcostarica.com, is an excellent place to start trip-planning and includes toll-free telephone information in English at 866-COSTA RICA.

The local English-language weekly *Tico Times* has a useful website (www.ticotimes.net), and their print edition contains listings of cultural and other events. Other informative websites include: www.costaricapages.com and www.costaricaguides.com.

JADE

Costa Rican jade is actually jadeite, as opposed to the denser nephrite jade used in Asia. Jade has been unearthed only in graves in Guanacaste and on the Atlantic side, some items carved according to Olmec or Maya traditions but the majority made in a distinctive Costa Rican style. From about 300BC to AD500, jade was considered the most valuable material for ritual objects used by priests and shamans, as it attracted and absorbed energy as well as being associated with agricultural fertility. Carving techniques varied from elaborate string-sawing and carving in the round (on the Atlantic side) to carving into the curved surface of a polished jade piece (Guanacaste's tradition).

A finely carved and etched jade piece, c300BC, from the Península de Nicoya, on display at the Museo del Jade

▶ Galería Nacional de Arte Contemporaneo y Diseño   117D2

Avenida 3/Calle 15, tel: 257-7202, fax: 257-8702, www.madc.ac.cr Open: daily 10.30–5.30. Admission: inexpensive; Mon free

In 1994 an old liquor distillery was successfully renovated to create a dynamic cultural complex **(CENAC)**, sprawling between the Parque España and the Parque Nacional. In its southeastern corner stands this impressive museum—the National Gallery of Contemporary Art and Design, which displays a permanent collection of Latin American art and temporary exhibitions of international artists and designers. Check the performing arts schedule and explore the whole complex, which dates from the late 19th century.

▶ Mercado Central   116B2

Avenida Central/Calle 6

This, the Central Market, is the place for a close encounter with Josefinos (the people of San José)—a far cry from the muted calm of the hotel circuit. Hues, smells and bustle are typically Latin American, and the goods range from live chickens to medicinal herbs—the latter all have labels detailing their respective uses and are sold by many vendors. A few vendors target the tourist trade with leather goods, hammocks or pottery, and the surrounding streets are teeming with impromptu salesmen. The covered market area is also the best place in San José to sample traditional Tico food at rock-bottom prices. One drawback is the pickpockets, who take advantage of the market crowds.

▶▶▶ Museo del Jade   117D2

Instituto Nacional de Seguros, Avenida 7/Calle 9, tel: 287-6034, fax: 255-3456. Open: Mon–Fri 8.30–3.30. Admission: inexpensive

The odd location of the Jade Museum, hidden away on the 11th floor of the social security building, belies its immense interest. Jade is not the only exhibit here: the entire display gives a fascinating account of Costa Rica's pre-Columbian civilizations and their links with Mesoamerica and South America. Besides the extensive collection of superbly crafted jade pieces, there are exquisite gold pieces, mainly produced by the Diquís, numerous well-preserved or restored examples of anthropomorphic and zoomorphic pottery and a fabulous array of *metates*, used for grinding grain. These elaborately carved three- or four-legged andesite stool-like objects are unique to Costa Rica, and held great sculptural and symbolic significance. Some date from as early as 500BC. The last room holds fertility symbols, from phallic sculptures to terracotta models of copulating couples and pregnant women.

▶▶▶ Museo Nacional   117D1

Avenida 2/Calle 17, tel: 257-1433, fax: 233-7427, www.museocostarica.go.cr Open: Tue–Sun 9–4.30. Admission: inexpensive

Housed in the imposing Bellavista fortress (1887), whose corner tower is still pockmarked with bullet holes from the 1948 civil war, the National Museum presents a sweeping overview of Costa Rica's history. It incorporates a lovely breezy garden courtyard with fine views over San José and

121

Nuestra Señora de la Cueva (left) and San Roque (below), both at the Museo Nacional

the mountains of Escazú. Follow the collection in a counterclockwise direction, starting on the south side of the courtyard and ending at the entrance overlooking the Plaza de la Democrácia. Pre-Columbian exhibits include petroglyphs from Orosí and Guanacaste, imaginative *metates* including flying-panel versions, staff heads, gold ornaments, carved funerary stones and several stone spheres from the Palmar region (see pages 156–157). Colonial furniture of the 17th century is followed by the Sala Historica, where panels and captions in Spanish and English, often highly critical, outline the socio-economic effects of colonialism. Photos and documents end with the Nobel Peace Prize certificate awarded to President Oscar Arias in 1987.

▶ **Museo de Formas, Espacios, y Sonidos** *117E2*
Avenida 3/Calle 19, tel: 223-4173, 256-1281, fax: 222-9462, mufes@racsa.co.cr Open Mon–Fri 9.30–3. Admission: inexpensive
Housed in the original Atlantic Railway terminal (1908), the new Museum of Forms, Spaces and Sounds is devoted to exhibiting elements that you can touch and hear—the opening exhibit featured tools and other items from ancient cultures in one room, and musical instruments displayed in the other, with a tactile path on the floor to help those with disabilities find their way around. The museum places special emphasis on creating exhibits which are accessible to visitors with disabilities, especially children, but it welcomes everyone. Railway history is not entirely forgotten: a collection of old railroad cars remains on the nearby tracks, open for inspection.

The Center

PEACEFUL PASTIMES

A popular Josefino escape route from urban stress leads to Parque de la Paz, unfortunately bisected by the ring road on the southeastern edge of the city. Established by the Arias regime in 1988 after the president had won the Nobel Peace Prize, it boasts three artificial lakes and a large roller-skating rink as well as jogging paths. The most striking sight is the Sunday morning mass work-out, when hundreds of capital dwellers gather here for a large-scale aerobics class.

Gold pendant of a harpy eagle, Museo de Oro

IF, IF, IF...

"If San Salvador and Guatemala City were hosed down, all the shacks cleared and the people rehoused in tidy bungalows, the buildings painted, the stray dogs collared and fed, the children given shoes, the refuse picked up in the parks, the soldiers pensioned off—there is no army in Costa Rica—and all the political prisoners released, those cities would, I think, begin to look a little like San José." Paul Theroux, *The Old Patagonian Express* (1979).

▶ Museo Nacional de los Niños　　116B3

Avenida 9/Calle 4, tel: 258-4929, fax: 223-3470, www.museocr.com
Open: Tue–Fri 8–4.30, Sat–Sun 9.30–5 Admission: inexpensive
This addition to San José's museum circuit, opened in 1994, is aimed solely at children, with didactic and interactive displays covering children's rights, the universe, living creatures, health, communication, city life, Costa Rican history and numerous scientific exhibits. The striking, fortress-like setting on the north side of town is actually a former prison.

▶▶▶ Museo de Oro　　116C2

Beneath the Plaza de La Cultura, entrance on Calle 5,
tel: 243-4202, fax: 243-4220, www.museosdelbancocentral.org
Open: daily 9.30–5. Admission: moderate
The Gold Museum's spectacular display is one of the highlights of Costa Rica, and certainly of San José. Pre-Columbian gold, nothing more, nothing less, is the subject, whether hammered breastplates with fine *repoussé* work, *tumbaga* (an alloy of copper and gold), or intricately sculpted ornaments cast by the lost-wax method. The latter technique was probably introduced to Costa Rica from Venezuela and Colombia around AD400 and obviously fired the imagination of the craftsmen, who created miniature versions of armadillos, alligators, frogs, parrots (symbol of intelligence) and butterflies (the Bribrí symbol of femininity). Explanatory panels in Spanish and English give background information about alloys, craft methods and the function and significance of decorative designs, and the entire collection is dramatically spotlit in its shadowy setting. An ironic climax comes in the form of some glass-bead necklaces astutely exchanged by the Spaniards in 1502 for local gold ornaments. The same underground complex, an innovative 1975 design belonging to the Banco Nacional, houses temporary art exhibitions and the Museo Numismatica. The ICT tourist information office is situated at the entrance.

▶ Parque Metropolitano La Sabana　　off 116A2

San José's largest city park offers a temporary bucolic escape from the frenzy of central traffic and crowds. Josefino joggers, aspiring soccer stars and local families share the shady lawns and lake, all of which were landscaped from the former airport. The imposing terminal building at the eastern end now houses the **Museo de Arte Costaricense▶** (tel: 222-7155, fax: 222-7247, www.crc.co.cr/cultural/musarco. *Open* Tue–Sun 10–5. *Admission: moderate*). Permanent and temporary exhibits here are firmly national in scope and of variable quality, and the Salón Dorado occasionally presents free chamber music concerts. Don't miss the lofty ground-floor café with views through the trees. At the western end of the park is the national stadium, also used for international rock concerts, beyond which lies the spacious suburb of Rohrmoser, popular with embassies and diplomats. A gymnasium, free tennis courts and an Olympic swimming pool (not always open) occupy the southeastern corner of the park.

▶ **Parque Morazán** 116C2

Avenida 3/Calle 6–9

These flourishing gardens covering four city blocks include two oddities—the domed and colonnaded Templo de la Musica (Music Temple), which has a distinctly French 18th-century style, and the Escuela Metálica, made of bolted metal plates, which was shipped in pieces from Belgium in 1890 before being assembled to house 1,000 students.

▶ **Parque Zoológico Simón Bolívar** 117D3

Avenida 11/Calle 7 & 9, Barrio Amón, tel: 233-6701, fax: 223-1817
Open: Mon–Fri 8–3.30, Sat–Sun 9–4.30. Admission: inexpensive
You can see live specimens here that you may not have seen in the wild: wildcats, coatimundis, reptiles, tapirs, monkeys, sloths and birds, from Africa and Asia as well as native species. The zoo has been recently renovated, but given Costa Rica's abundant wildlife, one has to ask: Why bother with the zoo?

Escuela Metálica: Not only the style but also the entire building came from Europe

LET THERE BE OPERA

The construction of the Teatro Nacional was paid for by a special coffee tax that the 19th-century coffee barons imposed on themselves. The incentive came when the Italian opera singer Adelina Patti was touring Guatemala but was unable to extend her visit to Costa Rica because it had no appropriate concert hall. Not wanting to be left out of the *fin de siècle* swing, the plantation owners decided to tax every bag of coffee exported from Costa Rica. Within a short time they were able to call upon European architects, muralists and decorators to fashion this remarkable construction.

▶ Plaza de La Cultura 116C2

This busy central square just behind the Teatro Nacional is home to the Museo de Oro and the tourist information office, both beneath the Banco Central. Restructuring of the plaza was financed by McDonald's, of burger fame, which garishly presides over the northern flank. Peruvian musicians frequent the precinct, and vendors do a fast trade in assorted trinkets, while pigeons flock around children scattering breadcrumbs. The plaza and the adjacent Gran Hotel terrace café together provide San José's best people-watching spot.

The streets immediately to the northeast include a few establishments that comprise part of San José's red-light district, although much of this sordid scenery seems to have moved elsewhere in recent years. A number of casinos and internet cafés abound, as do several grand old establishments like the restaurant El Balcon de Europa, still in its original location (since 1903) at Calle 9 and Avenida Central, not far from the notorious Hotel & Casino Del Rey (see page 127).

▶▶▶ Teatro Nacional 116C2

Avenida 2/Calle 3 & 5, tel: 221-9417, www.teatronacional.go.cr
Open: weekdays 10–noon, 2–6. Admission: inexpensive

This ornately decorated 1890s building reflects the heyday of San José, when coffee barons and bankers flocked to see

A lyrical Muse at the Teatro Nacional

opera and concerts in a gilded interior worthy of, and styled on, the Opéra de Paris. The neo-classical exterior is less impressive than the interior, and it is not helped by an uninspired revamping of the square outside. Inside, much of the dazzling decoration was badly damaged by the 1991 earthquake, but a \$880,000 restoration has actually improved on the original. Still intact, however, are the Carrara marble statues and grand staircase, gold-leaf mouldings and the original ceiling mural, *Alegoría*, depicting coffee harvesters reaping the profitable crop that paid for the building (see panel on this page). Try to go to a free Sunday morning concert (11am) to soak up the old-world atmosphere. A coffee shop to the left of the building's foyer holds art exhibitions and offers the visitor a quiet alternative to the nearby, bustling Plaza de la Cultura and the crowded, lively café terrace belonging to the imposing Gran Hotel de Costa Rica.

Marimba players in central San José

Walk

Old San José

See map on pages 116–117.

This walk takes in some of the city's finest museums, several downtown sights and outstanding old buildings in Barrio Amón before returning to the central area. Allow three to four hours, which includes time for brief tours of the Gold and Jade museums, a shop and coffee stop at the Hotel Don Carlos.

From the **Teatro Nacional**▶▶▶ drop into the **Museo de Oro**▶▶▶ before walking east down the pedestrian boulevard of Avenida Central to the **Plaza de La Democrácia**, with its crafts market, and the vast **Museo Nacional**▶▶▶. Circle the square and re-cross Avenida Central on to Calle 15, passing the **Asamblea Legislativa (Legislative Assembly) building** and coming to the **Parque Nacional**, a lovely square where **Monumento Nacional** is a bronze homage to the nation's spirited rejection of William Walker (see page 32). A short detour east along Avenida 3 brings you to the old **Atlantic Railway terminus**, now the **Museo de Formas, Espacios, y Sonidos**▶. Return to Calle 15. North of

the Parque Nacional looms **Biblioteca Nacional**; to the west, explore **Galería Nacional de Arte Contemporaneo y Diseño**▶▶. Turn left (downhill) on Avenida 7. You'll pass the Mexican Embassy on your right, and then **Parque España** on your left. The **Museo del Jade**▶▶▶ is on the upper floors of the modern block in front of you. Turn right on Calle 11, which winds past the neobaroque **Casa Amarilla (Yellow House)**, now the Ministry of Foreign Affairs. At Avenida 9, turn right. A block down (at the corner of Calle 13) is a park with a chunk of the Berlin Wall (a gift from Germany) set on a pedestal. Return along Avenida 9, passing decorative clapboard residences, some now converted into hotels: most notable are the mint-green **Casa Verde** (corner of Calle 7) and the **Don Carlos** (Calle 9, between Avenidas 7 and 9), which has a café, and lively mural of the city. Continue down Avenida 9 to Calle 3. Turn left, then left again on to Avenida 7 for a quick detour to the Caribbean-style **Alliance Française**. Backtrack past the **Hotel Santo Tomás**, converted from a 1900s coffee baron's residence. Walk straight on to Calle Central, and turn left to find **Iglesia del Carmen**. Cross the square on your right to Calle 2, pass the **Correo Central** (post office)—a remarkable building dating from 1914. Turn left on Avenida 1 and walk two blocks to the **Mercado Central**▶ on your left.

BEAT THE BILL

Some hotels add surcharges to phone calls. To avoid paying these, buy a CHIP card for a pro paid amount of *colones*. To use, insert the card into the phone (CHIP pay-phones are ubiquitous) and follow instructions in Spanish or English. Alternatively, buy a Servicio 197 card to make local calls on touch-tone pay-phones, and a Servicio 199 card for international calls. Email is far cheaper, and internet cafés can be found in almost every town.

Practical details

Getting around The central grid system is easy, but street numbers soon disappear as you enter the outer districts. There, addresses are given with reference to a nearby landmark—which could be the American Embassy or Pizza Hut. Each block is counted as 100m , so *"125 metros al oeste y 200 metros al norte de la Cruz Roja"* means roughly one-and-a-quarter blocks west and two blocks north of the Red Cross.

The central zone can easily be covered on foot. Buses run from suburbs such as Los Yoses and San Francisco, which are quieter places to stay. Destinations are marked on the front, and fares are paid to the driver. Taxis are cheap, but make sure *la maria* (meter) is functioning. If not, negotiate a fare.

Buses to outlying towns leave from designated stops—contact the tourist office for details

Shopping San José has a wide range of shopping, although Sarchí (see page 111) is acknowledged to be the country's main crafts town. **Galería Namu** (Avenida 7/Calle 5 y 7, tel: 256-3412, www.galerianamu.com) houses one of the best collections of Boruca masks and other carvings, jade pieces, and framed artwork by local artists. It's one of the best places in Costa Rica for Indigenous arts and crafts and works directly with many of the artists and tribes. **Angie Theologos** in San Pedro (tel: 225-6565) designs custom-made jackets, waistcoats, and so on, from Guatemalan and Panamanian fabrics. **Boutique Annemarie** (Calle 9/ Avenida 7–9) in the Hotel Don Carlos has more than 100,000 handicrafts and art pieces at some of the best prices in the city. The 25 or so shops in the **Las Garzas** handicraft market in Moravia (tel: 236-0037. *Open* daily 9–6) sell a range of wood, ceramic and metal works. Books in English can be found at **7th Street Books** (Avenida 1 & Central/Calle 7, tel: 256-8251, fax: 258-3302) and at **Libreria Lehmann**, a few steps away (tel: 223-1212, fax: 233-6270). Department stores such as **La Gloria** (Avenida Central/Calle 4 & 6) can be useful, as can the myriad discount shops along the pedestrian Avenida Central, but if you are looking for high fashion, investigate the shopping malls on the road to Escazú (Multiplaza being Costa Rica's largest) in San Pedro or El Pueblo in Barrio Tournón.

Nightlife Cautious visitors to San José could check out El Pueblo in Barrio Tournón, a tourist-oriented complex that offers a Spanish pueblo-style maze of bars, restaurants and nightclubs aimed at a mature clientele. For a livelier, hipper scene, stroll San Pedro's strip, just south of the university of Costa Rica. Current hot spots here include **Omar Khayyam** (tel: 253-8455), **Pizza Caccio** (tel: 224-3261) and the **Jazz Café** (tel: 253-8933). One of the hottest dance clubs of the moment, **Déjà Vu** (Calle 2 & Avenida 14/16, tel: 223-3758), brings a trendy gay/straight crowd who come to enjoy the top DJ's spinning house, salsa, and techno. The lively, four-level **Risa's Bar** (Calle 1 between Avenidas Central & 1, tel: 223-2803) is another restored beauty, with two floors of disco, half a dozen bars and a restaurant. Also in San Pedro, and popular with politicos, poets and the like, **La Villa** (tel: 225-9612), a converted Victorian mansion 200m (220yd) east and 150m (165yd) north of the church. Long-standing and still popular is **El Cuartel de la Boca del Monte** (Avenida 1/Calle 21 & 23, tel: 221-0327), a relaxed bar/restaurant with background rock, live music on Mondays, good bocas and great cocktails. Small and intimate with occasional live music, **The Shakespeare** (100m/110yd south of Pizza Hut, Paseo Colón, tel: 257-1288) is plastered with old movie posters, and is popular with the intelligentsia after a show at the nearby Laurence Olivier Theater or a film at Sala Garbo. Casinos offer lively distraction—the **Gran Hotel de Costa Rica** off Plaza de la Cultura sports a busy one. Adults who have any desire to see the gaudy underbelly of Costa Rican nightlife may want to taxi over and take a peek into the Blue Marlin bar at the **Hotel & Casino Del Rey**, where dozens of Costa Rica's professional sex workers gather nightly to do business. It is not a dangerous place, but it is like nothing else in Costa Rica. For expat hangouts, try **Nashville South** (Calle 5/Avenida 1-3, tel: 221-7374) off of Parque Morozán, or the **Tropix** bar (tel: 222-3232) at the Hotel Dunn Inn.

Time for a snack before the bus leaves

TOP OF THE BILL
Costa Rica boasts plenty of home-grown bands working in just about every musical genre. In this dance-crazed country, Cantoamerica tops the dance band bill, and the reggae band called Mekatelyu is currently very hot. Also chart-topping and room-bopping are the salsa legends Brillianticos and the cumbia and disco-style Kalua and Calle 8. Rockers dig the Inconsciente Colectivo and Gandhi, who have been playing the circuit for years. At spots like the Jazz Café you'll find groups such as Editus, winner of two grammys (with Ruben Blades) in 1999 and 2003, as well as El Sexteto de Jazz Latino, Marfil and Manuel Obregon y Mal Pais. World music fans dig Amoun Sulu, while Walter Ferguson offers folk/protest music from all over Latin America. For popsters, there's Por Partes, and the soul/r&b set follows Squad.

Crafts are sold daily on Plaza de la Cultura and Plaza de la Democrácia

The Caribbean

NIC

5

Punta Castilla

Isla
Machura

Barra del Colorado

Isla
Calero

Trinidad

Isla
Brava

San Juan

Colorado

Chirripó

Refugio Nacional
de Fauna Silvestre
Barra del Colorado

119m
Cerro
Tortuguero
Zona Protectora
Tortuguero

Tortuguero

Sardinal

Boca Río Sucio

4

H E R E D I A

Muelle

Puerto Viejo
de Sarapiquí

La Selva

Tigre

Zona Protectora
La Selva

Sucio

Sarapiquí

Encina

Suerte

Canta Gallo

Llanura de Tortuguero

Parque
Nacional
Tortuguero

San Pedro

Cariari

Tortuguero

Esperanza

Sierpe

Parismina

Rara
Avis

Las Horquetas

Griega

Teresa

Río Frío

Rita

Roxana

Zancudo

Jiménez

Villafranca

Río Jiménez

Parismina

Parque
Nacional
Braulio
Carrillo

3

Santa Clara

Llanura de Santa Clara

Guápiles

Jiménez

Guácimo

L I M Ó N

Pacuare

Canal de Tortuguero

Parismina

2047m
Cerro
Honduras

Sucio

Cordillera Central

Rainforest
Aerial Tram

Jardín Botánico
Las Cusingas

Zona Protectora
Acuíferos Guácimo
y Pococí

Pocora

Germania

Cairo

Manila

Cuatro
Millas

Florida

Siquirres

Batán

Matina

Estrada

Larga
Distancia

Zurquí

Parque
Nacional
Volcán
Irazú

3432m
Volcán
Irazú

Parque Nacional
Volcán Turrialba

3328m
Volcán Turrialba

Zona
Protectora
Río Pacuare

Barbilla

Bristol

Stratford

Liverpool

Portet

Moín

San Isidro

Santa
Cruz

Lajas

Peralta

Parque Nacional
Barbilla

Río Blanco

Banano

Tres Ríos

ZP Cerro
La Carpintera

Llano
Grande

Cot

Monumento
Nacional Guayabo

1617m
Cerro
Tigre

Asunción

Pacayas

Turrialba

Cartago

San Rafael

Juan Viñas

Pavones

Tucurrique

Zona
Protectora
Río Banao

Tobosi

Tejar

Paraíso

Llanas

Cachí

La Suiza

Tuís

2251m
Cerro Matama

Fila de Matama

Orosi

Pejibaye

Platanillo

Chirripó
Abajo

Zona Protectora
Río Navarro y
Río Sombrero

Empalme

Tapantí

Parque Nacional
Tapantí - Macizo
de la Muerte

Zona Protectora
Cuenca Río Tuis

Chirripó de Atlántico

Estrella Vall

Jardín

San Marcos
Tarrazú

Cañon

Tres de Junio

C A R T A G O

2378m
Cerro
Tsuitebeta

Reserv
Hito

Santa María
de Dota

Copey

Salsipuedes

Cordillera de Talamanca

S A N
J O S É

1

Fila Pangolín

San Gerardo
de Dota

3491m
Cerro
La Muerte

3394m
Cerro
Cuerci

Siberia

Parque
Nacional
Chirripó

Teliré

Valle d

2435m
Cerro
Punibeta

San Jos
Cabéca

Zona
Protectora
Cerro Nara

Savegre

Fila Zapotales

Santo Tomás

División

Piedra

Herradura

3819m
Cerro Chirripó

Parque

Internacional

Fila Dúrika

Savegre Abajo

Río
Nuevo

San Gerardo de Rivas

La Ese
Rivas

Chirripó del Pacífico

La Amistad

A

B

C

THE CARIBBEAN For centuries the province of Limón was geographically and culturally isolated, its Afro-Caribbean population even banned from journeying into the Central Valley until after the 1948 civil war. Communications with the rest of the country improved with the completion of the Limón highway in 1987, but it has taken longer for reliable phones to reach Puerto Viejo and beyond. Climatic conditions are extreme, with almost constant high humidity and rain interspersed with brilliant sun and clear light. Go to Limón and you will enter a completely different atmosphere and culture, far closer in spirit to the islands of the Caribbean than to Costa Rica's Tico regions.

HIT THE HAMMOCK Tourism is increasingly important in this region. Although much of the low-lying terrain is blanketed with monotonous plantations, Limón is also a naturalist's fantasyland. High on tourist itineraries is Tortuguero, an area crisscrossed by canals and rivers, including the bird-filled estuaries of the Ríos Pacuare and Parismina. It attracts hundreds of bird species, and its beaches are nesting grounds for turtles. More marshes and lagoons are found around Barra del Colorado, Río Estrella and Manzanillo, the latter another site popular with turtles.

Rising to the west is the daunting Cordillera de Talamanca, whose foothills are home to the Reserva Biológica Hitoy Cerere and indigenous reserves. However, the region's greatest attraction lies along its shores, in a string of seductive white beaches edged with coral reefs in true Caribbean tradition. Fling yourself into a hammock at Puerto Viejo or Cahuita, sip a fresh coconut, and let a sybaritic holiday mood take over.

THE FACTS Limón is, after Guanacaste, Costa Rica's least densely populated province, with only 9 percent of the country's total population. Average temperatures are the highest in the country, oscillating between 33°C (91°F) during the day and 20°C (68°F) at night; rainfall is also very high and it seems to fall by the bucketetload in Tortuguero. The best months are March and October, when hot, sunny days produce luminous seas and skies.

HAMMOCKS Hammocks are sometimes thought to have been introduced from the tropical islands of the Caribbean, but they are native to Costa Rica too. Cabécar Indians high in the remote sierra use hammocks made from the coarse fibre of the sago palm. Every traditional hut has at least two that are used for resting, for visitors or for children during the day.

131

Pages 128–129: temperatures on the Caribbean coast can top 32°C (90°F), making Cahuita's waves a welcome relief

Costa Rica's jungle train ground to a halt in 1990 owing to continuous landslides and lack of funds for repairs. Gone are the days of the seven-hour run from San José to Puerto Limón, but the railway's effect on the country's development can still be felt.

WORKING FOR THE COMPANY

"There was plenty of work in Andromeda. The Company needed to open a great swath through the mountains, breaking rocks on the riverbanks, filling and levelling and building bridges to carry a train through the marshy virgin forest, good for the cultivation of bananas, and in the process revive some of the plantations abandoned years earlier when the river had carried away the old railroad."
Carlos Luís Fallas,
In the Shadow of the Banana Tree (1941).

Right: remains of the railway line near Siquirres
Below: locomotive imported from Philadelphia in 1939

Construction of the Atlantic Railway took 20 years and was to transform Costa Rica's economy, demography and society. Before the railway was completed, in 1890, the nation's burgeoning coffee exports were transported by a long and costly route from the port of Puntarenas, right around Cape Horn, and from there to Europe. It soon became obvious that if Costa Rica was to prosper, a port had to be developed on the Atlantic coast, with easy access from the Central Valley's coffee plantations.

Hacking In 1870, the daunting contract went to Minor Cooper Keith, a young, worldly wise American who, within a few decades, rose from being a Texas pig farmer to one of Costa Rica's richest men and husband to the president's daughter. His first major task was to hack the 193km (120-mile) route from Cartago to Limón through rugged mountains, precipitous gorges and dense jungle, in extreme climatic conditions.

The workers brought in from Italy and China for the job were devastated by diseases such as yellow fever and malaria, and also by dysentery. About 4,000 died on the first 32km (20-mile) stretch alone, so Keith turned to the West Indies for sturdier workers who were better accustomed to the hot, humid climate.

Debts and profits Meanwhile, Keith was juggling with the vast £5 million debt that had been contracted with British banks to finance the operation. His astute negotiations brought gratitude from the Costa Rican government in the form of huge tracts of land and the railway concession itself. This pushed Keith and Costa Rica on to the next economic catalyst: bananas. Conveniently situated alongside the railway track, his new plantations flourished, and when the Atlantic Railway was finally operational, bananas were in the freight alongside coffee. Keith was responsible for forming the notorious United Fruit Company.

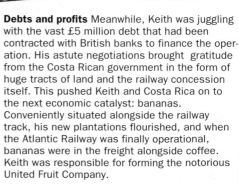

▶ Barra del Colorado
130B5

In the far northeast, this small town is famous for fishing off the coast and in the adjoining wildlife refuge. It can be reached only by plane or by boat, the latter from the north via the Río San Juan, from Puerto Lindo in the west, or from Moín and Tortuguero to the south. The refuge covers 92,000ha (227,300 acres) of channels, lagoons, islands, marshes and hills crossed by three rivers. Annual rainfall of nearly 610cm (240in) floods much of the low-lying land, causing rivers to change course, and nurturing a large mosquito population. Temperatures and humidity are always high, with rain letting up significantly only in March. Those willing to confront these extremes will enjoy great bird-watching and fishing, catered to by several lodges.

▶ Bribrí
131D1

The tiny town of Bribrí forms the entrance to an Indian reserve that spreads along the Panamanian border southwest of Puerto Viejo. A handful of restaurants, shops, a bank and an incongruous new courthouse make up the facilities. Heading southwest from Cahuita and Puerto Viejo, a right turn at the intersection in front of the school takes you 1.6km (1 mile) to Uatsi (also called Volio), a scattered community that is known for its crafts. Follow the sign across a suspension bridge for one outlet, a cluster of thatched stilt houses displaying gourds and baskets.

Back at the school intersection, the opposite direction leads through beautiful mountains opening up southeast across the Río Sixaola. This is Panama, easily accessible by boat for local inhabitants who go there to shop. After entering the confines of the Bribrí reserve the gravel road reaches Shiroles, 18km (11 miles) from Bribrí. There is a good family restaurant here, Se Yamida, which also rents out rooms. *En route* are hamlets and rural scenes of farmers leading cattle and women carrying baskets of vegetables on their heads. At Suretka is the innovative Centro Cultural Namsöl, run by the non-governmental organization CODEBRIWAK (tel: 226-4945, fax: 286-3216, suretka@soliracsa.co.cr) to defend indigenous rights (see panel).

Bribrí's central restaurant and bus stop are the social focal point for local indigenous communities

INDIGENOUS AWAKENING
The impressively equipped CODEBRIWAK is the sign of an increasing indigenous consciousness. Initially an informal committee, it is now a recognized association of the two main Talamancan Indian groups, the Bribrí and the Cabécar, who number some 7,000 altogether. Their health needs are addressed by a single clinic in Bribrí, and until recently there was no socio-cultural education to keep their traditions alive. The activities of this place, built in traditional style, at least supply the latter. They have now joined with ATEC in Puerto Viejo and other indigenous groups to fight plans for exploratory oil drilling off the Talamancan coast.

The Caribbean

▶ Cahuita   131D2

Funky, hip and sometimes dangerous, Cahuita is the main beach resort on the Caribbean coast. Lush vegetation, white sandy beaches fringed with coconut palms and a lively tourist infrastructure have long made it popular with backpackers. It lies 43km (27 miles) southeast of Puerto Limón on a curved bay ending at Punta Cahuita (Cahuita Point), where you can still see flourishing examples of the sangregao tree, or *cawi*, from which the area probably derived its name (see panel). In June the trees' enormous boughs burst into a mass of yellow flowers. This promontory forms the **Parque Nacional Cahuita▶▶▶**, a 1,067ha (2,637-acre) park designed to protect more than 22,000ha (54,360 acres) of marine habitat, including extensive coral reefs.

Bearings Approaching Cahuita, there are three left turnings from the coastal road that runs south from Puerto Limón. All three are virtually unmarked, bumpy little dirt roads, and easy to miss, especially at night. The roads are also scarred with potholes, so in this rain-soaked part of the country proceed with caution. The last of the three roads runs straight into central Cahuita, but all join up with the village's main street, which runs parallel to the beach. At the northern end, edging the beautiful black-sand beach of Playa Negra, are the more prestigious hotels and private residences, all set in lush, tropical gardens, while at the heart of the village, where the beach mixes rocky stretches with sand, is the main concentration of budget *cabinas*, often run by friendly local families. Playa Cahuita, the jungle-backed white beach at the southeastern end, is part of the national park.

Rasta rules Life in Cahuita is typified by hot Caribbean nocturnal rhythms and long, slow, steamy days punctuated by sudden downpours. Bars, restaurants and tourist shops are plentiful, reggae music is everywhere, the English-speaking Afro-Caribbeans are outgoing and Rastafarian style is part of Cahuita's image. However, this happy scene also includes a major problem—drugs—which has led to petty thefts and muggings. Occasionally the crime has been more serious. A tourist was murdered in 1994, and another two in 2000. As a result, local tourism temporarily fell significantly. No one is denying that the town does suffer from drug-related crime, a problem that stems from the fact that the under-policed Caribbean coastline has emerged as a transshipment point for US-bound drugs from South America. Only a handful of Guardia Rural officers patrol a coastal area stretching over 50km (31 miles). New measures such as police roadblocks, vehicle spot checks and citizen patrols have been put in place, and the situation has

Playa Negra has safe swimming, black sand, hammocks and a string of cabinas

improved. Nevertheless, you should be extra alert when you are here, particularly after dark, and take precautions.

Telephones and tours In recent years most of the hotels and restaurants have been connected to private phone lines. Cahuita Tours (tel: 755-0101/0000, fax: 755-0082, www.cahuitatours.com), on the main street, has a public phone, cashes traveler's checks, organizes snorkel and glass-bottom boat tours of the reef, rents bikes, and runs tours to Tortuguero, Panama, and the Bribrí reserve. Not far away, Willie's Tours (tel: 843-4700, www.willies-costarica-tours.com) offers a wide variety of tours from snorkeling, fishing, rafting on the Río Pacuare, Bocas del Toro, Tortuguero and Manzanillo trips, visits to Indigenous reserves and overnight visits with shamans.

National park From the ranger station at Playa Cahuita (*Open 8–4. Admission: inexpensive*), a 6.5km (4-mile) trail leads round the headland to Puerto Vargas, a lovely beach that has a campsite near the second park entrance. Winding in and out of the jungle and across Río Perezoso (Sloth River), the trail takes in a string of secluded beaches alive with fiddler and land crabs, where snorkelers can have close encounters with more than 120 species of tropical fish. Inland, a wealth of palms and dense vegetation shelters raccoons, howler and white-faced monkeys, opossums, sloths, agoutis, armadillos and porcupines, and the birdlife includes tricolored herons, magnificent frigate birds and green kingfishers. Unfortunately, the 1991 earthquake caused extensive damage, toppling trees and destroying parts of the 600ha (1,480-acre) coral reef, already suffering from agricultural pollutants, sedimentation and illegal fishing activities.

BREADFRUIT TREE 135

A typical tree of this region is the breadfruit (*Artocarpus incisus*), a descendant of southeast Asia's jackfruit. It was introduced to the West Indies from the Pacific in 1793 by England's Captain Bligh. From Jamaica, this tree came with early settlers to the province of Limón, and it now flourishes throughout the coastal region. The 20m (66ft) evergreen has dark-green shiny lobed leaves that can reach 1m (3ft) in length. Its large fruits, covered in a bumpy yellowish skin, contain a fibrous flesh that can be fried, roasted or boiled, and is high in carbohydrates.

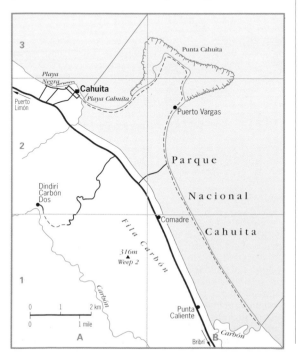

► Manzanillo 131E1

The road south along Costa Rica's Atlantic coast ends just before Panama at the headlands of Punta Manzanillo and Punta Mona (Monkey Point). Just before this lies the village of Manzanillo, not much in itself (except for the wonderful Maxie's Restaurant) but close to a number of imaginative beach hotels and at the heart of the **Refugio Nacional de Vida Silvestre Gandoca Manzanillo (Gandoca-Manzanillo Wildlife Refuge)► ► ►**. Sea, coastline, marshes and tropical rain forest come within its boundaries but, above all, this is where you will find wild, remote beaches with hermit crabs your only companions, except from February to July when leatherback turtles come to lay eggs in the white sand. Coral reefs are only 180m (200yd) from the shore, whose gentle slope and calm waters make it ideal for swimming. In the southeast part of the refuge is the mangrove-lined Gandoca Estuary, home to crocodiles and oysters. There are no facilities in the refuge, which is reached by a 11km (7-mile), paved road from Puerto Viejo. Perhaps the best way to visit is by bicycle, allowing time to watch toucans, parakeets and turkey vultures along the way.

► Puerto Limón 131D2

The decaying capital of the province of Limón is an ethnic melting pot, with a population of Jamaican, Antillais, European, Chinese, Tico and indigenous descent. Many of their forebears came to Puerto Limón (usually shortened to Limón) in the 1870s to work on the railroad and later in the banana plantations of the United Fruit Company. Today, the port has been updated with new docks, and the local economy has been diversified by an electricity plant and large oil refinery, and the now frequent cruise ship stops. In typical tropical port tradition, Puerto Limón has a dual nature: rough and dangerous, and yet exotic and extrovert, characteristics that are most apparent during the carnival week in October. The brightly painted backstreet hovels may appear picturesque, but at all times visitors to Limón should be extra-streetwise, leave rental cars in hotel car parks, and avoid taking nocturnal strolls. In early 2007 a group of elderly cruise ship passengers killed a would-be attacker, which made headlines around the world. Additional police protection was quickly added, although precautions should still be made.

Crumbling glories The central grid of streets abuts a solid sea wall with, at its farthest point, the lovely Parque Vargas, a fading relic of Limón's heyday. Tropical shrubs, huge royal palms and banyans encircle a decaying, ornately stuccoed

Commerce thrives in central Limón

old kiosk, all overlooked by rainbow-hued clapboard hotels and shops. Visitors should keep an eye out for sloths. Nine of the two-toed critters live in the park's trees. From here you can take a breezy walk north beside the sea wall or head three blocks west, along a new pedestrian promenade, to the Mercado Municipal, a vast, decrepit building whose vendors and items for sale spill onto the streets.

Afro-Caribbean culture: a mural in the Parque Vargas, and inspired stucco decoration

A different aspect of Limón's culture can be seen by the railroad, on the western outskirts of town, at Collina China, a hillside cemetery whose horseshoe-shaped Chinese tombs, are decorative reminders of the growing Chinese community.

Out and about Christopher Columbus's first steps on Costa Rican soil were made at **Isla Uvita**▶ ▶, a tiny uninhabited island that is situated about 800m (880yd) east of the port. It can be visited by rental boat. To the northwest of Limón toward Moín is **Playa Bonita**▶, site of Limón's better hotels but polluted by the oil refinery. Less developed is nearby **Playa Portete**▶ ▶, a pretty cove with clear, calm waters that invite swimming and snorkeling. Near the docks at the Paradero de Moín is an attractive tract of wild jungle.

A night in Puerto Limón will set you up to reach the docks at Moín at dawn the next morning, where you can negotiate a ride up the canals to the hamlets of Parismina or Tortuguero, located on the south and north edges of Tortuguero National Park. The three-hour trip up the waterways provides magnificent bird- and animal-watching opportunities, especially if you secure a berth aboard the *Francesca,* operated by guide Modesto Watson (tel/fax: 226-0986, www.tortuguerocanals.com), whose wildlife-spotting skills—abetted by an extraordinarily accurate-sounding howler monkey call—have achieved legendary status.

THE MUGGY STILLNESS
"The sky would suddenly get dark, the clouds thunder, the wind blow loudly, shaking the mountain, the howler monkeys would roar…and a minute later we'd be shoveling yellow mush and shivering from the cold…Then the sun fell on our backs again, drying out our clothes…and again the muggy stillness and the suffocation of the sweat…then water again…then more sun. And that's how it went until noon almost every day." Carlos Luís Fallas, *In the Shadow of the Banana Tree* (1941).

Costa Rica's Afro-Caribbean community is concentrated along the Talamanca coast stretching south from Puerto Limón. After more than a century of geographical and cultural isolation, when Afro-Caribbeans were denied citizenship or any rights, they are now confronting the mitigated benefits of tourism.

138

While fishing and farming still occupy some young Talamancans, many have acquired tastes from visitors—including the passion for surfing

Proud traditions Costa Rican's minority black population, barely 5 percent of the country's total and less than a third of Limón's inhabitants, cling proudly to their traditions and speak English-based Creole at home before learning Spanish in school. For more than a century they have preserved their strong identity, partly because of the lack of any road down their coast and, before the 1949 Constitution, as a result of overt discrimination from the central government. Rastafarian-style beaded hair, a gregarious *carnaval*, Protestant churches, breadfruit and *pan bon* are all part of the lifestyle in this still isolated corner of Central America.

Survival techniques The first Afro-Caribbean immigrants sailed to Costa Rica's shores in the early 19th century from Nicaragua's Miskito Coast and from Panama. Seasonal turtle-hunting and lobster- and crab-fishing drew them here, but some eventually settled down to farm and trade with the Indians. Later that century, a much larger influx from Jamaica and Barbados arrived to construct the Atlantic Railway and subsequently work on the flourishing banana plantations: their natural resilience was recognized and exploited. Others eked out an existence fishing from their dug-out canoes, selling tortoiseshell to European traders in Puerto Limón, or cultivating root crops, breadfruit, mangoes and limes which they had brought from their Caribbean shores. Coconut palms shot up the length of the lush coast, providing essential food and oil, and cacao later became an important crop, although in the 1970s the *monilia* fungus destroyed most cacao plantations.

Today, many educated Afro-Caribbeans have left the province for San José or farther afield in search of more profitable, professional activities. Those who remain have entered the fray of tourism, which has taken off since the coast road was completed in 1979.

Callaloo and rundown Along with Caribbean island agriculture, these newcomers brought with them culinary traditions, animist beliefs

"A trip on a bus took them past tumbledown houses whose porches were filled with black youngsters of all sizes, their naked bellies sporting their navels like misplaced buttons. They waved their arms wildly, greeting the driver. Watching the bus go by was probably one of their favorite diversions and helped them forget the hunger pangs that racked their young bodies. You could see the misery in the houses that were falling apart, in the people dressed in rags, and in the haggard faces of the old folks with their dark stooped bodies."
Julieta Pinto, *The Blue Fish* (1963).

AFRICAN HERITAGE
Before the days of books, radios and TV, which is still rare on the Talamanca coast, local inhabitants would amuse their families by storytelling—a custom that had been passed on down the generations since their ancestors left Africa, but is far from common now. One of the most popular protagonists was Anansi the spider, a narrative vehicle used to explain the mysteries of the world and human actions in whimsical fashion. His activities changed in tune with society: 20th-century versions featured Anansi scheming for the riches of a white landowner.

about nature and life, Creole English and customs adopted from the British colonists. English-language bibles are still used, and the older generation remembers playing cricket, dancing the quadrille and even performing Shakespeare in their coastal villages. The names of respected women are preceded by Miss. Miss Edith in Cahuita, Miss Sam in Puerto Viejo, Miss Junie in Tortuguero and Miss Marva in Manzanillo are the magicians behind local gastronomy, whipping up cassava dishes, callaloo soup or "rundown"—a fish or meat stew with yams, plantains, breadfruit, peppers and spices boiled in rich coconut milk. Johnny cakes (originally "journey cakes"), *pan bon* (from the English word "bun" or possibly from the French for "good bread," *pain bon*), ginger cookies, plantain tarts and *patti* (a spicy meat pie) are washed down with fragrant herbal teas made from wild peppermint, soursop or lime leaves, lemongrass or ginger.

Carnaval! Every 12 October (*El Día de la Raza*, "the People's Day") Limón's Afro-Caribbeans abandon their daily routine and for one memorable week they sway to calypso sounds in a riotous carnival. Unlike the West Indian and Brazilian carnivals that precede Lent, these festivities mark the anniversary of Columbus's first steps on Costa Rican soil, near Puerto Limón. This annual celebration, which started in 1949, reaches a high point when a glittering parade of brightly decorated floats and dance groups staggers along the streets to the irresistible sounds of steel bands, whistles, maracas and even recycled kitchen pans. Dancing, singing, drinking, eating, and smoking grass are the characteristic features of the carnival. In recent years, governmental involvement has made *Carnaval!* safer, if perhaps less exciting. But it is still a wild, popular party, and worth seeing. If you plan to attend, book weeks in advance—that goes for the entire Caribbean coast.

OVER THE BORDER

An increasingly popular destination lies over the Panamanian border near Puerto Viejo, in the beautiful archipelago surrounding Bocas del Toro. Crystalline water, unspoilt beaches, jungle, an English-speaking Afro-Caribbean culture, atmospheric old hotels and above all world-class scuba diving and snorkeling await you in this peaceful backwater. You can get there by taking the bus to the border at Sixaola, then a Panamanian bus to Changuinola, where a 10-minute flight wings you to Bocas. Alternatively continue by bus to the port of Almirante, where there is a inexpensive water-taxi service. Organize your visa in advance in San José. Several tour companies in Cahuita and Puerto Viejo also operate day trips by boat to Panama.

Locals offer basic fishing and snorkeling trips

►►► Puerto Viejo de Limón   *131D1*

Strung along the shore for some distance is the burgeoning beach community of Puerto Viejo, originally a tiny fishing village. Relaxed and friendly, supremely tropical with luxuriant vegetation, croaking nocturnal frogs and scuttling blue land crabs, Puerto Viejo successfully blends low-key Western services with a high-profile Afro-Caribbean culture. Although not as threatening as Cahuita or Puerto Limón, it does have theft problems and a drugs scene, so again, take precautions and be alert.

Slow genesis As with Cahuita, the access road here was not completed until 1979, electricity was not widely available until 1988, and reliable phones are a fairly recent phenomenon. Many of the inhabitants have transformed their village homes into *cabinas*, while an imaginative range of more luxurious hotels, often foreign-owned, spreads 10km (6 miles) eastward along the newly paved road, past blissful Playa Cocles, Playa Chiquita and **Punta Uva**►►► toward **Manzanillo**► (see page 136). Here, tall coconut palms edge white sands scattered with driftwood, and there are coral colonies in the turquoise waters offshore. Surfers ride *La Salsa Brava* at the point, especially from December to April, but there are other more protected areas with gentle slopes offer good swimming and snorkeling, particularly outside those months. Immediately west of Puerto Viejo along the main road is a long black-sand beach, usually safe for swimming and backed by a few hotels.

Local initiative A helpful and efficient source of information here is the office of ATEC (Asociación Talamanqueña de Ecoturismo y Conservación, tel: 750-0398, tel/fax: 750-0191, www.greencoast.com), a non-profitmaking grassroots organization aiming to promote ecologically sound tourism and small, local businesses. This dynamic group plays an essential community role and organizes nature walks, visits to the nearby Kéköldi Indian reserve, rainforest hikes, horse-trekking, snorkeling and fishing trips and Tortuguero tours, all accompanied by local guides and reasonably priced. Their office on the main east–west street of Puerto Viejo, opposite Soda Tamara, provides public phone service, internet access and sells publications related to the Talamanca coastal area.

Several shops around town rent bicycles, the best way to get around, and a couple of blocks inland from the bright green church is the *panadería*, where you can stock up on delicious local pastries for the beach. Along with numerous inexpensive bars and *sodas*, Puerto Viejo now has several good restaurants, including several

highly regarded restaurants serving organic and eclectic cuisine. A few of the hotels toward Punta Uva also feature stylish dining rooms, discos and bars.

Limpid light after the rain at Puerto Viejo

▶▶ Reserva Biológica Hitoy Cerere 130C1

The name of this remote 9,950ha (24,586 acres) reserve derives from Bribrí words meaning respectively "woolly" (referring to moss that blankets the river boulders) and "clear water." Water is the main feature of this under-explored reserve that rises into the Talamanca Mountains from the Valle de la Estrella. Moist rain forest laden with epiphytes, towering trees, ferns, numerous rivers, waterfalls and extremely high humidity greet the few visitors who penetrate it. The 115 (at least) species of bird here include toucans, owls, kingfishers, cuckoos, turkey vultures and the Montezuma oropendola, whose pendulous nests are common sights. Other inhabitants include tapirs, jaguars, sloths, opossums, howler and white-faced monkeys and a large variety of frogs, snakes and butterflies. If possible, visit with a guide, as trails are virtually non-existent. The ranger's station, camping facilities and entrance lie about 10km (6 miles) southwest of Pandora. Access requires four-wheel-drive, though taxis can be hired. Enquire at ATEC for information on guides.

▶ Río Estrella 130C2

After flowing down the foothills of the Matama range, the Estrella River irrigates the banana plantations of the Valle de la Estrella before reaching the ocean near Penshurst, north of Cahuita. The dense network of navigable channels and lagoons is home to more than 280 bird species, above all waterfowl, and there is a private wildlife sanctuary, **Aviarios del Caribe**▶▶ (tel: 750-0725), with lodgings (no children allowed), located right on the estuary. Caymans, crocodiles, sloths and howler monkeys also inhabit the area.

GETTING TO PUERTO VIEJO DE LIMÓN
The paved coastal road from Limón to Sixaola on the Panamanian border is in relatively good shape, but its bridges still suffer from the torrential rains that rarely let up in this region. Bus travel to Puerto Viejo directly from Limón, with nine daily departures and a trip that takes roughly 1½ hours, depending on the number of passengers. This same bus serves Cahuita and Bribrí or Manzanillo. There are also four daily direct buses from San José to Sixaola (leaving from Calle Central/Avenida 11), but these only stop at the turnoff (*el cruce*) to Puerto Viejo on the main road, a 5km (3-mile) hike from the village. Four daily buses link San José directly with Puerto Viejo, a 4½-hour trip.

RAIN, RAIN, RAIN

It never seems to stop raining in Tortuguero, and lodges are all well prepared with rain ponchos and boots. Torrential annual rainfall approaches 610cm (240in), with 85–90 percent humidity during the so-called "dry season" and 95–99 percent in the wet season, making average temperatures of 25°C (77°F) seem far higher. In September and October alone, two of the drier months, rainfall is equivalent to the entire annual rainfall of Cartago or of Santa Rosa National Park. The rain can last for several days on end, though it subsides in March and in the autumn.

Count on a deluge of rain in Tortuguero: lodges are designed for them

▶▶ Tortuguero   *130B4*

Turtles, birds and cruising through jungle-lined waterways are the temptations of Tortuguero, a name that refers to a river, a village, a hill and a national park. Most people come to this isolated region by organized tour from San José, either by bus and boat or directly by small plane, and stay in comfortable lodges along the main canal. However, it is possible to visit Tortuguero on a low-budget tour from Puerto Limón, Cahuita or Puerto Viejo, and stay in simple *cabinas* in the main village. Arriving here independently requires negotiating boat rates at Moín, which may be expensive unless you are in a group.

Water, water... The park covers nearly 19,000ha (46,950 acres) of lagoons, swamps, waterways and rain forest bordering a long, wild, straight beach where three species of turtles come periodically to nest. One main canal runs 69km (43 miles) south of Tortuguero through Parismina to Moín and continues 35km (22 miles) north of the park to Barra del Colorado. It is crisscrossed by numerous rivers, tributaries and minor canals, and all these together create the local community's only transport system. Before the canals were developed in the 1970s, Tortuguero's few residents had to walk down the beach or paddle along circuitous rivers to reach Puerto Limón. Today the canals are the region's lifeline, with dug-out canoes, barges and motorboats hauling livestock, construction materials, fuel, food—and tourists.

Village interest Most points of interest, the airstrip and hotels are located in or near the village of Tortuguero, at the base of a skinny spit of land that creates a secondary waterway. Hotels on this side (Mawamba Lodge, Laguna Lodge and village *cabinas*) have the advantage of direct access to the beach for turtle-watching, though dangerous currents and aggressive sharks make swimming impossible. Village facilities include a handful of souvenir shops and *sodas*, and the Centro Social Turistico La Culebra, which hires out canoes and organizes boat journeys. A guide and ticket are necessary for nocturnal turtle-watching in season: ask at the information kiosk near the football field.

In the heart of the village, the H. Clay Frick Natural History Museum and Visitor Center provides an excellent introduction to green turtles, and has displays on local flora and fauna, related publications and a short video. It is run by the pioneering CCC (Caribbean Conservation Corporation, www.cccturtle.org), founded in 1954 by an American biologist, Dr. Archie Carr, who lobbied for 20 years to have the park and vital turtle protection established. Turtle research continues at a new, full-time station, while the original Casa Verde has been dismantled to build a local school.

Forest The main entrance to the **Parque Nacional Tortuguero** (*Open* daily 8–4. *Admission: moderate*) lies at the southern end of the village. Park rangers are particularly helpful to independent visitors, as most tourist groups arrive with their own guide. Trails lead from here through swamp forest where you may encounter a deadly, 2m (6.5ft) fer-de-lance, white-tailed deer, white-collared peccaries, raccoons, tapirs, anteaters, otters, or three species of monkeys. Glass-frogs, red-eyed tree frogs and Jesus Christ lizards, so-called because they walk on water, are relatively common.

More rain forest can be visited at the **Caño Palma biological station**, a 15-minute boat ride from the village. This Canadian conservation organization offers basic facilities with meals, and informative accompanied hikes through the secondary-growth rain forest (tel: 381-4116, www.coterc.org. *Admission: donation*). Longer treks can be organized with village guides into humid tropical rain forest around the modestly scaled, 311m (1,020ft) Lomas de Sierpe, or to Cerro Tortuguero (119m/390ft), north of the village.

WHITEWATER RAFTING
The torrential Río Pacuare rushes down the slopes of the Cordillera Central before coursing through the swamps of Tortuguero and finally ending in the Caribbean. It attracts large numbers of whitewater enthusiasts, who revel in fast currents and rapids offering Class III and IV rides. Costa Rica Expeditions (tel: 257-0766, fax: 257-1665, www. costaricaexpeditions.com) organizes rafting excursions combined with a stay in a beautiful jungle lodge, a good spot for bird-watching.

The jungle-lined waterways attract flocks of bird-watchers

143

Birds Tortuguero has more than 300 species, including migratory birds from North America. Hawks, falcons, flycatchers and ospreys join great green macaws, curassows, trogons, kingfishers and oropendolas, and numerous waterbirds such as herons, egrets, and cormorants. Any boat trip through the narrow channels, lined with huge clumps of multi-stemmed raffia palms, is accompanied by a melodious soundtrack of jungle cries and rich bird-watching opportunities.

Underwater in Costa Rica means not only exploring the aquamarine depths by scuba diving or snorkeling, but also juggling with giant snook, blue marlin and sailfish from a fishing boat in ecologically correct "catch and release" style. Business is definitely booming out there in the deep blue sea.

144

CORAL ETIQUETTE

Coral is a living organism made up of millions of tiny coral polyps, cup-shaped creatures consisting of a ring of tentacles surrounding a mouth. Many corals resemble plants, but they are in fact carnivorous animals, feeding on plankton that float in the sea and are caught by tentacles charged with stinging cells. These organisms are extremely fragile: a single break can set off a destructive chain reaction that may affect a whole reef. Do not collect coral from the sea-bed, and make sure your diving operator anchors outside the reef.

FISHING PERMITS

Fishing permits are necessary to fish in Costa Rica, and freshwater fishing is subject to strict seasons. Fishing operators will carry out the necessary formalities for deep-sea fishing, but anglers heading for inland rivers need to obtain permits in San José and to be able to present them, together with their passport, to any wildlife rangers. A good source of information about seasons and permits is the San José fishing-tackle shop, Desportes Keko (Calle 20/Avenida 4 & 6, tel: 223-4142, fax: 221-1668).

In a country with more than 900km (560 miles) of coastline, squeezed between two great oceans, marine activities understandably play a large role. Coral reefs once edged most of the coastline, but natural disasters such as earthquakes and the El Niño phenomenon have combined with destruction by humankind to reduce their area drastically. Anglers, on the other hand, find themselves riding the waves of one of the world's best arenas.

Top corals Number-one destination for seasoned scuba divers is the pristine aquatic universe of the remote Isla del Coco, lying off the Pacific coast. Crustaceans and molluscs join 18 species of coral and 200 fish species, including white-tipped sharks, giant hammerhead sharks, tuna, parrotfish, manta rays and crevalle jacks. If your budget does not stretch to such exotic depths, then the next best destination is the Caribbean. Plunge into the waters off Cahuita's national park, and enter a world where 35 species of coral form a backdrop to about 123 types of brilliantly patterned tropical fish, as well as sea urchins, lobsters, turtles, eels and sharks. This reef has, however, suffered from sedimentation caused by banana plantations.

Caribbean Less damaged but also off a less accessible coast are the 485ha (1,200 acres) of coral reef that edge the Gandoca-Manzanillo refuge; the coral colonies off Puerto Viejo also make good snorkeling destinations. In Puerto Viejo, Reef Runner Divers (tel: 750-0480) offers diving and certification courses. Aquamor (tel: 759-9012, Aquamor@sol.racsa.co.cr) runs diving, snorkeling, kayaking and dolphin-watching trips out of Manzanillo, and Cahuita has Cahuita Tours (tel: 755-0101). Fishing is, in contrast, well catered to, at the lodges of Barra del Colorado, where enthusiasts indulge in magnificent tarpon and snook fishing (said to be the world's best), above all from January to June, when these determined creatures start their 193km (120-mile) haul up the Río Colorado to reach Lake Nicaragua. At the beach resorts to the south, this sport becomes a case of catch-a-local-fisherman first, as there are no specialist operators and visitors must organize their own equipment. Small wooden boats are launched by being rolled down the beach on logs, a far cry from the sophisticated, often American-operated vessels of the Pacific.

Pacific highlights On the more developed Pacific coast, scuba diving is much higher on the agenda, with numerous diving shops operating out of large hotels at

145

the main beaches of the Península de Nicoya, and at Bahía Drake, Manuel Antonio, Puntarenas and Dominical. Spectacular tropical fish are guaranteed on this side around the Isla del Caño and also around the protected islands of Manuel Antonio and Marino Ballena, although reefs are limited. This, too, is where deep-sea fishing enjoys year-long popularity thanks to the plentiful snapper, tuna, wahoo, rooster, shark, snook, dorado, sailfish and marlin, though they peak in abundance between May and August. Costa Rica's first fishing operators concentrated on the Golfo de Papagayo, where hefty 50kg (110lb) sailfish indulge in fantastic acrobatics, but countless individuals and agencies now offer their services at other Guanacaste beach resorts, above all around Flamingo, Nosara and Sámara, as well as farther south at Quepos, Golfito and Playa Zancudo.

Fresh water Fishing is not confined to the oceans. *Guapote* (rainbow bass), *bobo* (mullet) and *machacha* (*Brycon guatemalensis*) flourish in Costa Rica's mineral-rich rivers, while mountain streams at higher altitudes, such as those at San Gerardo de Dota, are rich in rainbow trout. Although introduced initially, trout have since bred naturally. The most popular spot for freshwater fishing is Laguna de Arenal, as this is where challenging *guapote* reach up to 6kg (13lb). Gaining in popularity too are the lagoons and rivers of Caño Negro, offering a combination of freshwater fish and huge migrating tarpon and snook straight from the Caribbean.

Top: queen angel fish
Above: Sally Lightfoot crab. Costa Rica offers underwater explorers the opportunity to dive in two different oceans

▶▶▶ REGION HIGHLIGHTS

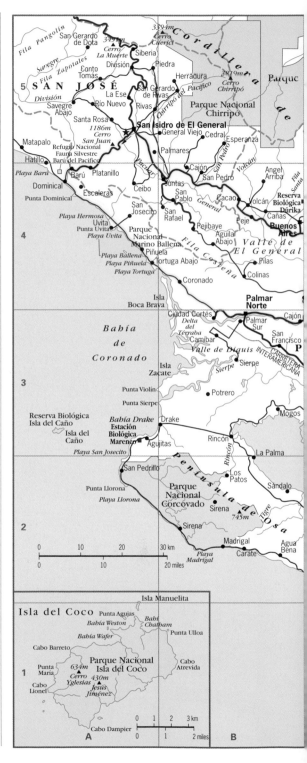

Previous page: Golfito's water village, squeezed between rain forest and the Golfo Dulce

THE BACKPACKING NATURALIST

If you have the luxury of an extended holiday, then opt for at least one back-packing trek into hill country. Always bear in mind the increased strain caused by high altitude and remember to drink plenty of (non-alcoholic) fluids. Naturalists should make the best possible use of the mornings since low cloud and fog often form by midday, making wildlife observation diffi-cult, if not impossible. Arguably the single best piece of advice for a backpacker in Costa Rica is always to stuff your socks into your shoes at night, as scorpions and large spiders have an uncanny way of finding their way into these seemingly safe refuges!

See drive pages 174–175

RANCHO LIFE

As you head south you enter the land of the *rancho* (hut), a typical indigenous construction that is also seen in the Península de Nicoya and in the Bribrí reserve on the Caribbean side. Although every Indian community has its variation, the basic structure consists of wooden poles joined by bamboo and rattan, with a palm-leaf thatch. The thatch can last up to 30 years if a fire is kept lit inside: the wood smoke forms a protective layer that prevents it from rotting during the rainy season. A common feature inside used to be a termite nest, sections of which were spooned onto the fire to produce a fragrant white smoke that kept insects at bay.

A view of the mountain town of San Vito and the surrounding coffee plantations

THE SOUTH Costa Rica's south encompasses some of the wildest, and also poorest, areas of the entire country. It possesses the most extensive of protected areas, the highest mountain, longest river, largest delta, most biologically diverse of the nation's rain forests—and an immense amount of rain. Its western coast borders the cobalt-blue Pacific, but compared with other zones the south remains undeveloped for tourism. Those visitors who do come here revel in the experience.

CONTRASTS RUN DEEP From San José to Paso Canoas on the Panamanian border it is only 354km (220 miles). However, the contrast between the two is enormous, and on the way from one to the other you could take in the biologically vital international park of La Amistad, go through dense and sometimes dangerous jungle in Corcovado, plunge underwater at Marino Ballena, swim with dolphins around the magical Isla del Caño, explore the Wilson Botanical Gardens, or kayak the gentle waters of the beautiful Golfo Dulce. Sybarites and surfers should head for Dominical, a community that is slowly expanding thanks to the near completion of the *costanera sur*, the road down the southwest coast that links Quepos with Palmar Norte, or venture farther south to Playa Zancudo and tiny coves dotted around the gulf northwest of Golfito.

ADVENTURE PACKAGE Jungle, mountain and beachfront lodges are scattered across this region. They are often isolated, usually blighted (or blessed?) by terrible roads, and nearly all claim to be environmentally concerned. Some possess large private reserves, making for convenient bird-watching and hiking. Many lodges offer

package deals from San José, including access by small plane rather than road, so taking the sweat out of the journey. This is ideal for visitors with limited time, but it does mean that you miss out on the sense of adventure and odd encounters that highlight a trip by bumpy road. Telephone systems were not installed in many areas until the late 1990s. A number of hotels and ecotourism stations use Selva Mar (tel: 771-4582, fax: 771-8841, www.exploringcostarica.com) as a central booking agency, while others have agents in local towns.

CIVILIZATION? The main towns in this region are San Isidro, the gateway to the south; Golfito, the old United Fruit Company banana town, now frequented by Ticos for its duty-free status; Palmar Norte/Sur, home to pre-Columbian stone spheres; and, for tourists and gold-panners, the tiny port of Puerto Jiménez. Add to these the prosperous modern coffee town of San Vito and you have the limited selection. Between these scattered outposts lie vast plantations of pineapples, bananas and oil palms and huge tracts of forest, on the slopes of the imposing Talamanca range that forms the southern backbone, on hills towering high above the Pacific, and on the sweltering, low-lying Península de Osa.

WILDERNESS High up in the enormous Reserva de la Biósfera La Amistad (La Amistad Biosphere Reserve), you may encounter only tiny Indian villages and, beyond these, nothing. Wildlife relishes this vast, untouched and unpopulated region, and scientists are moving in to study it, recognizing this as Central America's greatest biological laboratory. Visitors can catch a glimpse of this wealth of wildlife by trekking to the summit of Chirripó, but access to the park of La Amistad itself is still difficult. By contrast, Corcovado has good facilities, and its rival is its former annexe, the national park of Las Esquinas, just north of Golfito.

INDIGENOUS LIFE It is in the south that Costa Rica's largest concentrations of indigenous people live, mostly in loosely defined reserves. Boruca Indians make a living from handicrafts along with subsistence farming, and are quite happy to show off their crafts, although visitors should behave sensitively. Indigenous peoples are regaining confidence in their cultural traditions, which, by design or by default, have been repressed for generations. The Chirripó region is home to the Cabécar, and the Guaymi are scattered between the Coto Brus Valley, the Panamanian border and the Península de Osa.

SOME CAN KILL
"A little further, an iguana is perched on a branch… That same afternoon I see tiny frogs of extraordinary colours—red, green, silver and gold. I have never come across such extraordinary creatures either in the Amazon or in other tropical forests. I later learn that mere contact with some of them can kill you. On the way back I pass a boa constrictor… The boa, unlike other snakes which infest this peninsula (Osa), is not dangerous. A bite from most of them is fatal and it's a permanent cause of concern for the majority of gold-diggers. There are thousands of them, from the small coral snake to the *cascabella muda*, a rattle-snake which can reach three metres." Cizia Zyke, *Oro* (1985).

151

Bushmaster snake

SIR FRANCIS DRAKE
In March 1579, Sir
Francis Drake pulled into
Playa Colorada (at the
northern end of Bahía
Drake) to overhaul his
ship, the *Golden Hind*,
before resuming his
circumnavigation of the
globe. Depending on
one's viewpoint, Drake
was either a pirate or a
great explorer, but the
Costa Rican government
saw fit to erect a plaque
in his memory in Agujitas,
400 years after he
landed there.

SURF CENTRAL
Costa Rica's international
surf debut took place in the
seminal surfing movie
Endless Summer, which
revealed to the world the
exquisitely shaped waves
of Witches Rock in Santa
Rosa National Park. In the
decades since, *Endless
Summer II* and a host of
other surfing movies have
established Costa Rica as
one of the world's premier
surfing destinations. Some
of the country's memorable
breaks—there are dozens
known, and others yet to
be discovered—include
Playas Grande, Tamarindo,
Negra, Avellanes, Malpaís,
Hermosa, Dominical, and
two spots that rank among
the longest, most perfect
left-breaking waves in the
world: Boca Barranca, just
south of Puntarenas, and
Pavones, near the
Panamanian border.

▶▶▶ **Bahía Drake**   *148A3*

This sweeping bay on the Pacific side of the Península de
Osa has become a popular base for trekking into the
Parque Nacional Corcovado (see pages 162–163), and
for bird-watching, horseback-riding, fishing, sailing,
snorkeling, and diving or swimming in transparent
waters off exquisite untouched beaches. This is one of
Costa Rica's jewels, discovered more than 400 years ago
by Sir Francis Drake on his circumnavigation of the globe.
Access to the bay is by plane or a two- to three-hour boat
ride along the Río Sierpe from Sierpe itself, and the nego-
tiation of powerful waves and currents where the river
hits the ocean can be an adrenalin-raising experience.

The small town of Drake lies at the northern end, but it
is around Agujitas at the southern headland that most
lodgings are concentrated, including the pioneering
Drake Bay Wilderness Camp, the luxury Aguila de Osa
Inn and some more affordable places near the tiny
village. Just beyond the point lies **Estación Biológica
Marenco (Marenco Biological Reserve)**, where nearly
500ha (1,235 acres) of rain forest, fringing superb beaches
and the Río Claro, are now devoted to efficiently run
ecotourism. All lodges in this area arrange day-trips to
the Isla del Caño (see page 156), visible on the horizon,
and most have biologist guides who accompany treks
into Corcovado. The only limit to the scope of outdoor
activities is your budget, so come prepared. Wildlife is
omnipresent, from unpleasant *no-see-ums* (sand fleas) on
some of the beaches to scarlet macaws and toucans that
swoop around the lodges (plus the mosquitoes and a
spider or two that enhance your cabin).

▶ **Boruca**   *149C4*

The isolated home of the Boruca Indian community
(see pages 158–159) lies high up in
the dry hills above Palmar Norte.
Access is either from the south
by a rough 8km (5-mile) road
(requiring four-wheel-drive) or
by the marginally more manage-
able road used by buses, which
branches off the Interamerican
Highway at Brujo. This sprawling
village is the source of most of the
Borucan baskets and weavings
sold around the country, and local
women will happily demonstrate
their craft, particularly if you
buy something. Men carve
spears, gourds and balsa-wood
masks, when not tending their
corn and beans. A small thatched
building houses the **Museo
Comunitario Indígena de Boruca**
(tel: 721-2533. *Open* any time.
Admission: inexpensive) and also
sells some handicrafts. There is
one very basic *cabina* and daily
bus connections with Buenos
Aires, which has a bus link with
San Isidro (see page 170).

▶▶ Dominical *148A4*

This tropical beachside community, long a haven for low-budget surfers, seems poised for development now that the *costanera sur* (coast road) from Quepos is to be paved and telephones are no longer scarce. Foreigners have bought up tracts of hillside in an enchanting area called Escaleras, which rises abruptly—with breathtaking views—from the coast, south of town. In Dominical itself, new hotels are popping up, as are real-estate agencies—a sure sign of hustles to come—but Dominical still offers a relaxed setting at the mouth of the lazy Río Barú, with decent, mainly low-budget facilities, a couple of low-key nightclubs and a few small hotels scattered some distance south. Once the road from Quepos is paved, Dominical may emerge as a "hot" Costa Rican destination, for its charms are many: great surf, a beautiful river and fantastic waterfalls, miles of beach, and the rain forest close at hand.

Activities Best for swimming is either the sheltered, though rocky, Playa Dominicalito, 3km (2 miles) south, or, for a small fee, the large pool of the landscaped Río Mar hotel. Meanwhile, surfers slalom the waves on Dominical's main beach. Other activities include diving and snorkeling trips to the Marino Ballena reserve (see page 164), water taxis to Bahía Drake, river kayaking, biking and boogie-boarding, as well as horseback-riding through superb rain forest to the double Nauyaca waterfall and its huge swimming hole (contact Alexandra Jiménez at Don Lulo's, tel: 787-8013, tel/fax: 787-0198). North of the river lies the pioneering Hacienda Barú (tel: 787-0003, fax: 787-0004, www.haciendabaru.com), an American-owned ecotourism station in a wildlife reserve that offers a variety of lodgings and trekking.

BARU DEL PACIFICO

This pioneering operation, recently recognized as a national, not private, reserve known as Refugio Nacional Fauna Silvestre Barú del Pacifico (Barú del Pacifico National Wildlife Reserve), was set up in the early 1970s by Jack and Diane Ewing, who work with partner Steve Stroud. The 320ha (790 acres) of land encompass an immense ecological variety, from primary tropical wet forest to regenerated forest, mangroves, fruit orchards, scrub, beach and cacao plantations. The numerous attractions include night hikes, camping in the jungle and on the beach, tours on horseback, rainforest trekking, and several linked platforms high up in the jungle canopy. An ongoing project is to create an ecological corridor, the "Tapir Trail," linking Corcovado, Barú, and Cerro La Muerte.

153

Dominical—idyllic, but for how much longer?

Typical frame-houses in the Zona Americana

A strange destiny awaited this languishing banana port when in 1990 it was declared a duty-free zone. Ticos now flock here to stock up on their quota of duty-free goods, especially domestic appliances, at the huge warehouses of the Depósito Libre, and as a result the town has been regenerated. Further development is expected with the completion of the colossal Escondida Bay marina, of which construction began in 2007. Golfito occupies an excellent site on a strip of land between sheer forested mountains and the calm waters of an almost enclosed bay opening onto the Golfo Dulce. Much of the surrounding land is protected as a wildlife refuge, where tall hardwoods laden with epiphytes and 146 bird species are encouraged by Golfito's abundant rain. Remember that when it rains in Golfito it can average 69cm (27in) in a single month, October being the worst.

Dual hubs From the air-strip and duty-free complex at the northern end, Golfito's only road enters the sprucer Zona Americana. This was the headquarters of the United Fruit Company, which from 1938 until 1985 (when union troubles led to closure) dominated the area's economy, and where executives lived in elegant frame-houses surrounded by lawns. Many of these have now been converted into guest houses aimed at the big shoppers. South of the Hotel del Cerro, which fronts the old banana company wharf (*muelle bananero*), is Golfito's other persona, the Pueblo Civil. This is the livelier side of town, characterized by a typically decrepit tropical port atmosphere, boatyards, bars and a water village tumbling into the gulf. At the southern end are some stylish hotels and restaurants with gulf views.

DUTY-FREE
Ticos are allowed to invest in $400 worth of duty-free goods twice a year if they first spend 24 hours in Golfito, a law that on some weekends can make the town nightmarish. Specially chartered "shopping" buses descend on the port, *cabinas* fill up and hordes of shopping families, laden with kitchen appliances or TVs, monopolize the taxis. Foreigners can make purchases at the Depósito Libre, but imported items are still heavily taxed and so not necessarily a bargain.

Hire a boat Swinging around the southern end of the bay is the Golfito Península, home to the Sanbar Marina, where foreign yachts dock and sportfishing can be arranged. More practically, water taxis can whizz you across the water to Puerto Jiménez or south to Playa Zancudo and Pavones: contact Zancudo Boat Tours and Taxi Service (tel: 776-0012) for rates and bookings. A cheaper option is the "La Lancha" ferry service, from Puerto Jiménez to Golfito, leaving Puerto Jiménez daily at 6am and Golfito at 11am. The trip takes 90 minutes. Any boat trip may include sightings of dolphins, flying fish or splashing manta rays. For swimmers, clean, palm-fringed Playa Cacao on Golfito's northern headland is the closest beach, accessible by a rough road from the duty-free zone, or by a five-minute boat ride. Several reasonably priced hotels and *cabinas* are here.

Sausage tree

Water babies The coast northwest of Golfito is lined with secluded, jungle-backed beaches and lush, forested headlands, obvious targets for ecotourism projects. The only means of access is by boat, but a 30-minute ride can bring you to paradisaical spots such as Punta Encanto, with its rustic lodge, nature trails, waterfall and sublime sunsets. Next stop up the coast at Playa San Josecito is **Casa de Orquidéa** (contact Land-sea Tours tel: 775-1614, landsea@sol.racsa.co.cr. *Open* Sat–Thu 7–10am. Tours, daily 8.15am. *Admission: inexpensive*), a well-established private botanical garden with an inspiring collection of bromeliads, heliconia, cycads (also called "living fossils"), palms and orchids. Farther on is Playa Cativo, where a decidedly luxurious lodge occupies a 400ha (990-acre) private reserve. Strangest of all, however, is Dolphin Quest, a New Age project run by California maritime spiritualists. If you want to communicate telepathically with dolphins, meditate beneath a waterfall or have your child born on a raft in mid-ocean, this is where to go (tel: 382-8630, fax: 775-0373, www.dolphinquestcostarica.com).

Save the forest A road north from Golfito's duty-free zone leads to Gamba and a remarkable ecotourism project, formerly Las Esquinas, conceived by the Austrian violinist Michael Schnitzler in 1991. It has since raised more than $530,000 to help the Costa Rican government purchase 1,600ha (3,950 acres) of tropical rain forest, now known as the **Parque Nacional Piedras Blancas**▶▶. An attractive rain-forest lodge that obeys every possible precept of ecotourism has been built, as well as a biological research station. Local farmers and former loggers at Gamba have co-operated extensively with the entire project.

SAUSAGES THAT GROW ON TREES
Heard the one about the tree that grows sausages? One of Costa Rica's few specimens stands in a garden of Golfito's Zona Americana. The lofty, wide-spreading tree, *Kigelia africana*, grows sausage-shaped fruits, weighing up to 6kg (13lb) and measuring some 50cm (20in) long, that dangle on cordlike strings from the branches for several months, getting larger and softer with age. These curious fruits are not edible, but are used for external medicinal purposes in Africa.

155

The Golfo Dulce: the hills of the Osa Peninsula shelter the gulf from stormy seas, providing a tranquil port for wandering sailors

▶▶ Isla del Caño   148A3

This magical little island lies 19km (12 miles) west of Bahía Drake and has been protected since 1978 as a biological reserve. Deep turquoise waters and low coral reefs attract divers and snorkelers to explore a rich aquatic world, full of giant conches, limpets, molluscs, lobsters and sea urchins. Polychromatic shoals of tropical fish flit through the rocks while dolphins play in the waves. Diving is best off the northwest corner, but snorkelers can plunge in from the beautiful main beach, also ideal for swimming. Unfortunately, much of the reef has been destroyed by the periodic El Niño phenomenon, in which a mass of abnormally warm water rises to the surface of the Pacific, creating freak weather patterns.

One of the baffling stone spheres peculiar to the Isla del Caño and the Palmar area

MYSTERY SPHERES
The people of Palmar (see opposite page) are justly proud of their mysterious inheritance, and in the early 1980s, when the San José administration tried to sequester two examples (now in Palmar's Colegio) for the capital's Plaza de La Cultura, student demonstrations stopped the scheme. San José's Museo Nacional has other examples on display.

Deep past The 200ha (500-acre) island has produced a wealth of artefacts, giving rise to various theories about its past, one being that it was a pre-Columbian cemetery, although it is known to have been inhabited about 500 years ago. Gold votive offerings, tombs with stone statues and puzzling stone spheres were unearthed in the middle of the island, most of them being taken to San José's museums. Today, only a few minor artefacts are displayed, and even these are disappearing thanks to some light fingers.

Tree milk A one-hour trail to the site leads from the beachfront ranger's hut (*Open 8–4 daily. Admission: moderate*) up the steep slopes to a high plateau thick with shady fig, locust and rubber trees, wild cacao and the cow tree. The cow tree, *Brosimum utile*, is thought to have been planted by Indians for its high-protein white latex, once used as milk for newborn babies and for pregnant women, though this is now prohibited. Although there is little other wildlife, Caño has a wide variety of snakes (boa constrictors, grass snakes, chunk-headed snakes and the poisonous sea snake), as well as an amazing variety of epiphytic plants, above all giant philodendrons, bromeliads and monkey-ladder lianas.

▶▶▶ Isla del Coco   148A1

Only those with generous budgets will reach this legendary paradise island, flung into the Pacific 530km (330 miles) southwest of Costa Rica. Considered a natural ecological laboratory because of its isolation, Coco's rugged topography, virgin rain forest and thundering waterfalls flourish under an annual rainfall of 500 to 760cm (200 to 300in). Some 70 species of plants are said to be endemic, as well as certain birds and insects, but this isolated ecosystem is threatened, bizarrely, by rooting

pigs whose ancestors were introduced in 1793. Access to the island is only by luxury diving tours that periodically explore the surrounding coral reefs, or by private boat.

Red-footed booby

Lusting for booty Part of Coco's fascination lies in its curious history. It was discovered in 1526 by Juan Cabezas and soon appeared on Spanish maritime charts as the Isla del Cocos. During the 17th and 18th centuries it became a haven for pirates and privateers, who used it as a base for forays along the Pacific coast of Spanish America and gave its bays names such as Chatham, Wafer and Weston. Above all it was a hiding place for treasure, including the Lima Booty, a fantastic haul of gold and silver ingots, sheets of gold from church domes and sacred ornaments. English pirate William Davies and Portuguese Benito "Bloody Sword" Bonito added to the island's hoards, titillating imaginations and partly inspiring Robert Louis Stevenson's *Treasure Island*, as well as more than 500 treasure-hunting expeditions over the 19th century. Coco was also the inspiration for *Jurassic Park*'s fictitious Isla Nebular, and aerial views were used in the movie.

FOILED AGAIN
Illustrious visitors to the Isla del Coco have included Franklin D. Roosevelt and Erroll Flynn, their names cut for posterity in rocks on the main landing beaches. A few years ago the South African-born actress Moira Lister invested a minor fortune in seeking the Lima Booty, which she had first heard about as a child from her uncle, who had old charts of the island.

A typical clapboard church in Palmar Sur

▶ **Palmar Norte/Palmar Sur**   148B3
The adjoining villages of Palmar Norte and Palmar Sur lie on either bank of the Río Térraba, in a valley once inhabited by the Diqui Indians. Palmar's only interest lies in the mysterious, almost perfect stone spheres (*esferas*), up to 2m (6.5ft) in diameter, that have been excavated solely in the region of Palmar and on the Isla del Caño. The significance of their function and their fabrication—accurate to within 18mm (0.7in)—continues to puzzle archeologists. Two large versions are displayed on lawns by the road through Palmar Sur, and another more perfect pair may be seen in the grounds of the Colegio in Palmar Norte (see panel opposite).

Three main indigenous groups have retreated to mountainous, inaccessible areas of the country, and the largest concentration is in the Talamanca range. After years of keeping a low profile, Costa Rica's Indians are gaining a new self-assertiveness, which is helping them to counter persistent threats to their land.

158

CHICHA

Chicha, a fermented drink made from corn, *pejibaye*, banana or yucca, is liberally consumed on special occasions by all indigenous groups, men, women and children alike. It is made by parboiling the chosen ingredient, then making a dough to which water is added. This is left to stand for a couple of days before sugar is added and then allowed another day or two's fermentation, during which the alcohol content rises dramatically. Yucca *chicha* has an added attraction: the parboiled tuber is chewed by a young woman who spits it into a calabash before the dough is made. Another typical Indian beverage is cocoa, drunk by the Cabécar, Bribrí and Guaymi.

In his simple workshop, a Boruca Indian works on a carved wooden mask

Descendants of Costa Rica's pre-Columbian Chorotega, Boruca, Guaymi, Maleku, Huetar, Bribrí, Cabécar and Diqui indigenous tribes now number approximately 60,000 people—a sharp decline from the population that inhabited the country when Columbus arrived. After the Indigenous Law was passed in 1977, a concerted effort was made to help protect their traditions, beliefs and land, within the boundaries of 23 reserves. However, a new dynamism has become necessary to defend these areas against commercial operations such as logging, mineral and oil companies, and hydroelectric dams, as well as non-indigenous squatters.

Talamanca groups Bribrí and Cabécar Indians are scattered across a vast, 210,000ha (518,900-acre) area rising from the Valle de Talamanca, near Bribrí, high into the mountains of La Amistad Biosphere Reserve. Belief in a harmonious coexistence with nature is deeply rooted, and medicinal plants and shamans are still part of their culture. Traditionally they live in individual homes far apart from one another, using the virgin forest for hunting, fishing and the shifting cultivation of corn, beans and *pejibaye* (palm fruit), as well as for building materials. Fine string baskets of natural fibres and carved gourds are their main crafts. Reafforestation projects and organic farming methods are now being taught near Shiroles at the Finca Educativa Indigena, the result of co-ordination between more than 20 NGOs and indigenous councils. At the tiny Bribrí Kéköldi reserve, just inland from Puerto Viejo, an experimental project is under way to raise green iguanas, an endangered species.

The Bribrí form Costa Rica's largest indigenous group, and are the more integrated of the two, whereas the Cabécar are less tolerant of outside influences: permits are necessary if you wish to visit any of the latter's remote communities, and these are accessible only on horseback or

on foot. There is, however, growing recognition of the economic potential of tourism, and inroads are slowly being made with carefully controlled, guided groups.

Boruca Boruca and Térraba Indians inhabit a 32,000ha (79,000-acre) reserve around the village of Boruca, high above the Térraba Valley in southern Costa Rica. Descended from the Diquis, the creators of most of the gold ornaments exhibited at San José's Museo de Oro (see page 122), they were given an artificial ethnic unity in 1649, when Franciscan missionaries brought them together under one name. Conversion to Christianity and their relatively accessible location have allowed a greater penetration by the Tico way of life, although a new sense of identity will certainly emerge now that the Boruca language has been introduced at the local school. Apart from cultivating rice, corn and beans, the Boruca are known for their handweaving and for woodcarving, which mostly takes the form of masks for their three-day festival, *Los Diablitos* (the little demons), a re-enactment of the struggle between Indians and Spaniards. In this version, the white man is vanquished.

Guaymi Costa Rica's Guaymi immigrated from Panama in the early 1940s and still maintain close links with their 100,000 or so counterparts there. They are scattered between Coto Brus, north of San Vito, Montezuma, east of Ciudad Neily, and the heart of the Península de Osa. Despite this, traditions remain strong. No other group so closely resembles Amazonian Indians: women wear brilliantly hued, appliquéd dresses and paint their faces for ceremonies, and teeth filing is still carried out. Spanish comes second to their own Guaymi language, and customs are deeply entrenched. In 1995, Costa Rica's first crowning in over 60 years of an Indian *cacique* (chief) took place at the Guaymi village of Montezuma. His role is essentially a moral and spiritual one to complement that of the political leaders, who participate in the community's Development Association.

A typical Bribrí home

SIBU IS GOD
Bribrí and Cabécar Indians believe that Sibu was the creator of all things on earth, and that every object or plant has a supernatural guardian. These protectors allow humans to kill animals and use forest products for subsistence, but otherwise the Bribrí and Cabécar maintain great respect for their natural environment. In the words of a Talamanca shaman: "This land is alive, it is not dead! It lives everywhere in the Talamanca range, in its headwaters... Sibu left this source so it could nourish all the cultures."

Indigenous languages are taught at some schools

The immense sweep of La Amistad contains unique and still untapped biological wealth

TO THE PÁRAMO

The varying altitudes of La Amistad's untouched terrain perfectly illustrate natural graduations in vegetation. Lowland humid tropical forest is characterized by high forests (up to 40m (130ft) tall) wreathed in epiphytes and lianas, and thick with palms, tree ferns and bamboo stands. Next, at about 2,000m (6,560ft), comes the cloud forest, rich in oaks, laurels and shrubs laden with lichen. This is the transition to *pàramo*, a more exposed terrain of stunted, gnarled trees, where temperatures have dropped radically and cold winds blow. At about 3,300m (10,820ft) even these trees thin out, and above that level only grasses survive.

▶▶ Parque Internacional La Amistad   *149C5*

Open: 8–4. Admission: moderate

The vast, often inaccessible area of La Amistad, Costa Rica's largest wilderness area, makes it a boon for scientists and a challenge for hikers. Nearly 200,000ha (495,000 acres) of the Cordillera de Talamanca are incorporated into the park, considered to be one of the world's largest unaltered tropical forests. In 1982 the park and an area around it were declared a Biosphere Reserve by UNESCO, and then named a World Heritage Site. Now co-operation with Panama has joined it to an equivalent area over the border, so making it an international park. La Amistad's great biodiversity (seven life habitats and six transitional zones) comes from its immense variations in altitude, climate and topography. Vegetation changes from very moist forest and rain forest to cloud forest and *pàramo* (high, exposed land with stunted trees) as the territory climbs from 150m (490ft) on the Caribbean side and more than 800m (2,620ft) on the Pacific side to the highest points at Cerro Kámuk (3,593m/11,788ft) and Cerro Dúrika (3,279m/10,758ft).

Natural abundance Wildlife in this large, isolated area is extremely rich and includes endangered species such as the jaguar, cougar, jaguarundi and ocelot, as well as the largest concentration of tapirs in the country and more than 260 species of amphibians and reptiles. Ornithologists revel in some 400 bird species, including the resplendent quetzal, solitary eagles, orange-breasted falcons and sulfur-winged parakeets. Park headquarters are at Progreso, 30km (19 miles) northeast of San Vito, but for the moment there are no public facilities and visitors must rely on services provided by a handful of lodges nearby. (See also Reserva Biológica Dúrika, page 169.) For information, contact the Amistad Biosphere Reserve Office in San Isidro El General (tel: 771-3155, fax: 771-4836, or dial 192 in the country).

▶▶ Parque Nacional Chirripó   *148B5*

Open: 8–4. Admission: moderate

Costa Rica's highest peak rises more than 3,800m (12,460ft) above the Cordillera de Talamanca, at the heart of a 50,500ha (124,800-acre) park that starts at a height of 1,400m (4,600ft). Despite its size, magnificent landscapes and cool mountain environment, few tourists visit Chirripó, although its mountain wildlife is as rich as that of the nearby Parque Internacional La Amistad. Those who do visit encounter striking contrasts between cloud forest and lichen-draped dwarf forest, lakes of glacial origin, rushing rivers and wind-swept *pàramo*—as well as the cold. Chirripó is part of La Amistad Biosphere Reserve and World Heritage Site.

Preparations The base for visiting Chirripó is at the modest mountain village of San Gerardo de Rivas, where park head-quarters are located together with simple lodgings. As the steep, 19km (12-mile) climb to the summit requires a mini-mum of two days, trekkers should book dormitory space in a mountain shelter well in advance. Even those making day-hikes need to book their entrance, as visitor quotas are limited. This should be done through the MINAE office in San Isidro El General (tel: 771-3155). A useful porterage service is offered by villagers who will take your gear on horseback to the huts; guides, horses, sleeping bags and gas stoves can all be rented through lodgings in San Gerardo. Remember that night temperatures on the mountain hover just above freezing point, rains are frequent and you need to take all your own food and water as well as a gas stove (it is illegal to gather firewood here). Be prepared for intense, cold winds and strong sun, and dream of a recuperating soak in the hot springs at nearby Herradura on your return.

Straight up The overnight shelter is 14.5km (9 miles) from the park entrance along a clearly marked though strenuous trail that can take anything from 8 to more than 11 hours. You will need to start the trek before dawn to avoid the after-noon rain. A short distance before the huts are the spectacular Los Crestones, a ridge of sculptural, jagged rocks that stand on a stark, exposed ridge where icy winds reach 64kph (40mph). Numerous hiking trails lead from the huts, including those to the summit (barely two hours away), some beautiful glacial lakes and Cerro Ventisqueros. Alternative routes back to San Gerardo are possible, but make sure you have planned for them.

JAGUAR POWER
Once roaming the forests of the Americas from Oklahoma to Argentina, the jaguar is now a rare sight throughout the continent. Your best chance of seeing one in Costa Rica is at La Amistad. This king of the forest was held in great awe by the indigenous peoples owing to its unique method of killing its prey by crushing the skull with one snap of its jaws. The Mayas' most powerful hieroglyph was a fanged jaguar head, and the animal appeared in all Indian pantheons. Until the advent of the rifle, it was virtually invul-nerable, but today it ranks high on the list of endan-gered species.

San Gerardo de Rivas, the base for Chirripó

161

The South

GOLD FEVER

Fortune-seeking gold diggers (*oreros*) flooded into the park in the early 1980s, and were able to pan undisturbed in rivers high up in remote areas. Their activities created extensive damage by silting up rivers and the central lagoon. Park boundaries are a hazy affair in the thick of the rain forest and patrols are quite insufficient, but in 1986 a concerted effort was made to evict the gold seekers. Many were desperate unemployed farmers, and so the government now allows them to work just outside (theoretically) the park boundaries. You can visit a typical gold-digging settlement at El Tigre, west of Puerto Jiménez.

▶▶▶ Parque Nacional Corcovado   148B2

Open: 8–4. Admission: moderate

Some 54,600ha (135,000 acres) of the steamy Península de Osa are protected as a national park, established in 1975, which offers an abundance of tropical rain forest flora and fauna that is second to none. Annual rainfall exceeds 500cm (200in), nurturing some 500 species of trees (25 percent of Costa Rica's total), numerous mammals and birds and 48 species of frogs and toads. Herds of white-lipped peccaries thunder through the undergrowth, while all four of Costa Rica's monkey species swing from the branches and scarlet macaws wing through the skies. This fascinating destination is well organized for trekkers, who can spend a few hours or several days here.

Ups and downs Corcovado's undulating forest is bordered to the west by a string of deserted, palm-fringed white beaches. A trail follows the entire coastline, with a few inland detours, from Playa San Josecito in the north through Playa Sirena to Playa Madrigal in the south, a tempting proposition for swimming but dangerous owing to currents and sharks. A lesser drawback are the clouds of *no-see-ums* (sand fleas) that infest most of the beaches and are seemingly immune to insect repellents. Inland trails lead past rivers (often full of reptiles) and cooling waterfalls, and basic shelters are conveniently located.

Snake drill Local guides are easily available and will help you understand Corcovado's rich ecosystem as well as its sometimes tricky geography, but make sure you are well prepared with essential trekking gear, and know your snake drill. Thirteen species of poisonous snake inhabit the Península de Osa. Local advice, always delivered in a calm, resigned fashion, is to look at the shape of the head. Poisonous snakes have triangular heads owing to their extra venom-filled glands. They tend to wait

Right: The Corcovado rain forest is particularly rich in wildlife
Inset: palm viper

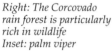

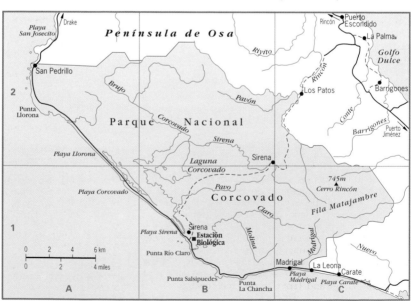

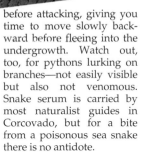

before attacking, giving you time to move slowly backward before fleeing into the undergrowth. Watch out, too, for pythons lurking on branches—not easily visible but also not venomous. Snake serum is carried by most naturalist guides in Corcovado, but for a bite from a poisonous sea snake there is no antidote.

Hit the trail Three entrances lead into the park. San Pedrillo, in the north, is accessible only by boat from Sierpe or from the lodges around Bahía Drake (see page 152). From here there is a circular day-trippers' trail as well as the main beach route, which, at Playa Llorona, branches northeast to limited facilities at Los Planes, or cuts across the middle to the second, eastern entrance, Los Patos, where there is a shelter. The nearby village of La Palma has a few *cabinas*. Another trail leads southwest from Los Patos to the research station at Sirena, where visitor services rise to the sophistication of a dormitory (advance booking necessary) and an airstrip (for charter flights from Puerto Jiménez). This flat area is known for wildlife sightings, and the five-hour beach trail around the point to La Leona, the southern park entrance, combines mangroves with sandy and rocky shores. La Leona is located on the long and wild Playa Madrigal, a 40-minute walk west of Carate.

Carate This small village offers reasonable lodgings, is relatively easily accessible by chartered plane or by daily truck from Puerto Jiménez, and, not least, is the animated social focus for local gold diggers, most of whom work legally outside the park. This is part of a typically Costa Rican compromise that is intended to allow poor farmers to try their luck at panning for gold, while at the same time protecting a sensitive environment. For years the gold diggers have sold their nuggets at the Pulpería Morales, run by a fascinating character who also offers camping facilities. Far more comfortable, however, are the elevated tents of the Corcovado Lodge and Tent Camp in their own rain-forest reserve, a short distance west of Carate.

TICAN ECO-LODGES
In the past decade Costa Rica has proved a haven for (ad)venture capitalists intent on creating ecologically correct resorts. Today, handsome economically viable eco-lodges dot the country from coast to coast.

What makes a hotel "ecologically correct"? There are no rules, but several elements come into play: use of indigenous architectural styles and energy-efficient design; training and employment of local people; benefits to the community; non-interference with wildlife, eg no feeding of monkeys or shining of lights on the turtles' beach; use of recycled or renewable resources. If you're in a hotel with *eco* in the name don't be afraid to enquire about any or all of these issues.

Marino Ballena is best appreciated from a boat or, even better, underwater

WINDOWS ON THE WORLD
Boat trips around Marino Ballena often continue a good distance south to a striking geological phenomenon at Playa Ventanas. This consists of a string of caves (*las ventanas* means "windows") stretching along the rocky shore, including a perfect rock arch that can be entered by boat at low tide. Time your trip carefully to catch another of this park's natural jewels—sunset, a captivating sight in glorious hues behind the foreground of sculptural, rocky pinnacles.

▶▶ Parque Nacional Marino Ballena   *148A4*

Open: at all times. Admission: inexpensive

At first sight there is nothing special about the sparsely vegetated beaches of this park, although they do offer safe swimming. Marino Ballena's main glories lie underwater, in a 5,400ha (13,340-acre) reserve created in 1990 to protect a marine habitat that is one of the last survivors on Costa Rica's Pacific coast. Coral and rock reefs edge the tiny island of Isla Ballena and the main headland of Punta Uvita, which is actually an island joined to the mainland by a rocky tombolo (see panel, page 103). At the point are sponges, sea anemones, corals, molluscs and crabs. To the south, Isla Ballena and Las Tres Hermanas are the tips of a submerged rock arch that extends from Punta Uvita to Punta Piñuela, and are roosting sites for magnificent frigate birds, brown boobies, pelicans and ibises. Back on the shore are the sheltered, gray-sand beaches of Uvita (see page 171) and **Ballena▶▶**, with Hermosa north of the point and **Piñuela▶▶** to the south.

Spot a whale In the water, apart from catfish, flying fish, snappers, Caribbean snook, jewfish and dolphins, you may spot a humpbacked whale. These endangered mammals, measuring up to 15m (50ft), migrate to tropical waters from North America during the winter season, and this area is thought to be their southernmost destination. November to March is their visiting period at Marino Ballena. Boats can be hired through the ranger's station or from fishermen on the beach, but the best way to visit the marine park is through diving places in Dominical (see page 153).

▶ Pavones   *149C2*

This surfers' mecca is reputed by those in the know to have the longest wave in the world, above all during the rainy season. Low-budget lodgings are aimed essentially at surfers' modest needs, though there is also a luxury jungle lodge to the south at Punta Banco. Access from Playa Zancudo to Pavones requires several strenuous hours by four-wheel-drive or, far better, an hour's journey by boat. Such isolation has brought problems. In the 1980s Pavones hit the headlines when it was revealed that it was the site for major international drug-trafficking operations. Although the main protagonist is now imprisoned (see page 24), the repercussions continue in a complex and embittered battle between US landowners, local squatters and the Costa Rican government, which expropriated large portions of the land involved. Late in 1997, the scene around Pavones got even more tense, weapons came into play, and a shoot-out resulted in the deaths of an American landowner and a Costa Rican squatter who had laid claim to the same piece of turf. More recently, these issues have been settled and peace prevails. However, one can reasonably infer that absentee ownership of large tracts of fertile land may not be a good idea in parts of the world that are populated by poor, landless peasants.

A FREE NATIONAL PARK?
Marino Ballena is the only national park in Costa Rica to have no entrance fee. The reason is that many local people and fishermen still live within the park boundaries, between the estuary of the Río Morete at Playa Hermosa and Playa Uvita. By Costa Rican law, you cannot charge some people and not others. So, in this case, tourists are on a much-appreciated freebie. The park was originally set up on the initiative of local inhabitants to protect the area from lobster catchers, who came from farther afield to fish intensively around the coral reefs.

165

▶ Playa Zancudo   *149C2*

About 13km (8 miles) south of Golfito is the Golfo Dulce's main beach development, still a very casual affair. It can be reached in about 1½ hours by car via a gravel road (newly graded in 2000) from Golfito, or in 30 minutes by boat. Playa Zancudo's facilities are scattered along 6.5km (4 miles) of gray-sand beach, on a skinny spit of land created by the mangrove-edged Río Sabalo.

Playa Piñuela, an often deserted beach at Marino Ballena

Surfers and swimmers enjoy the tranquil atmosphere here, using their own hotels for any social action. Zancudo Boat Tours (tel: 776-0012), next door to Cabinas Sol y Mar, provides transport to Golfito and to points of interest north of there, as well as nature tours along the Río Coto, where crocodiles monkeys, otters and birds abound. Some hotels organize boat trips and nature tours for their guests, and fishing trips are available—reserve your place through Roy's Zancudo Lodge (tel: 776-0008, fax: 776-0011, www.royszancudolodge.com) or Golfito Sportfishing (tel: 776-0007, www.costaricafishing. com). In addition to fishing trips, Arena Alta Sportfishing and Adventures (tel: 282-3370, www.costaricasailfish.com) also offers jungle tours and water taxis to Puerto Jiménez.

Enter a tropical rain forest and you observe a system that has remained unchanged for millennia. Camouflage, symbiosis, dependence and mutualism are just some of the games that this multifarious host of trees and plants play in an ongoing battle for survival.

THE CEIBA TREE

On rare occasions the legendary ceiba tree grows to 60m (200ft) making it one of the tallest trees in tropical America. It is also a fast grower, shooting up as much as 4m (13ft) in a year. The tree's structural majesty—a huge, thick trunk with perpendicular branches forming a vast umbrella—made it sacred for the Mayas, who perceived it as the tree of life. Glossy, dark green clusters of leaves produce creamy, white flowers that are eventually replaced by black seed pods. Inside the pods is a white floss used for stuffing cushions and mattresses, which has given the tree its alternative English names—the kapok or silk cotton tree.

The majestic ceiba

Tropical rain forest is one of the 12 life zones to be found in Costa Rica, defined according to elevation, latitude, average annual rainfall and temperatures. It is the archetypal jungle, where tangles of rope-like lianas, huge buttress trunks, gigantic ferns and exuberant bromeliads create a dense, impenetrable universe. Impenetrable is the key word, as 75 percent of the estimated 2,000 species of rain-forest plants and trees remain unknown and unstudied, let alone the thousands of reptiles, mammals, amphibians, insects and birds. In the words of Dr. Donald Perry, inventor of the Rain Forest Aerial Tram (see page 71): "This is the largest genetic reservoir on the planet—a library from the earliest times of evolution."

Three-level structure In any given hectare of tropical rain forest there is a staggering diversity of about 90 tree species—a far cry from the repetitive forests of more temperate North American and European climes. There are also three strata of forest: the main canopy, composed of trees reaching 30 to 40m (100 to 130ft); the sub-canopy, which includes palms 10 to 27m (33 to 87ft) high; and the understory, where familiar houseplants attain gigantic sizes. Capping them all are what are termed "emergents," a handful of species rising to more than 45m (148ft), including the magnificent ceiba (see panel).

Beneath the canopy, sunlight is so rare that seedlings wait years for a gap to appear before starting the sprint to the top. The rate of canopy replacement is estimated at about 1 percent per year. Among the scores of competitors for available light is the fast-growing and hence weak-limbed cecropia, whose ridged trunk resembles bamboo. In a perfect example of co-evolution, or mutualism, the cecropia's partly hollow trunk serves as an ideal nesting site for Azteca ants, which in return defend the tree against encroaching vines or epiphytes that would break the fragile limbs. Cecropia leaves are also the preferred food of three-toed sloths, which seem unperturbed by the giant ants.

Epiphytes Two-thirds of the plant species grow high in the more luminous canopy: the more there are, the more ecologically rich the forest. Generally categorized as epiphytes, they include the bromeliad family, of which 170 species have been recorded in Costa Rica. These self-sufficient, leafy clusters seeded by birds, bats or the wind store water and nutrients which in their turn support an incredible number of insects, frogs and spiders—biologists have identified 250 species living in bromeliad "tanks." A more flamboyant epiphyte is the dazzling orchid

Plants familiar to many visitors as houseplants take on quite different proportions in the rain forests

HARDEST WORKERS
Walking along a trail, you may be bemused to see a line of fresh green leaves moving rapidly in front of you. This is not a rain-forest hallucination, nor a new species. It is a column of the leaf-cutter ants that systematically strip the tropical forest of about 15 percent of its total leaf production. *Atta* workers cut and collect foliage that they transport over distances of up to 200m (220yd) back to their nest. At the nest, home to up to 5 million ants, they carefully clean and chew the leaves before adding them to a sticky mulch deep inside. This nurtures a unique fungus, the leaf-cutter ants' preferred food.

167

family, whose 1,200 species, like bromeliads, use their host tree only for mechanical support. In contrast, a true parasite, the strangler fig, roots itself in its chosen victim, then wraps it in an ever-tightening and all-encompassing grip, finally killing its host.

Undergrowth At ground level, vines, ferns, mosses and philodendrons proliferate, although they are less dense in the shady understory of primary rain forest than in the lighter secondary forest. Woody, twisted lianas drape themselves from tree to tree in the form of chains or ladders. Younger vines resemble ivies, and some, like the passion flower, produce flowers or seeds that are used for food and medicine.

Palm species include the ivory palm, so called because its hard nuts were once used as substitutes for ivory and carved into buttons. Tall, solitary fishtail palms contrast with tree ferns, front-runners in the race for light, and the very common *Welfia georgii,* with its bright-orange young leaves that are devoured by monkeys and agoutis, which then disperse the seeds. Equally common is the *Socratea exorrhiza,* a palm that stands high on a pyramidal root structure and is dubbed the "walking palm." Rain-forest trekkers should watch out for the tree fern with its spiny trunk—it hurts!

The strangler fig spells a slow death for its victims

The shopkeepers of Puerto Jiménez sell machetes to gold panners and bus tickets to visitors

▶▶ **Puerto Jiménez**   149C2

Facing Golfito across the Golfo Dulce is Osa's main town, Puerto Jiménez. This friendly, slow-paced place consists of a handful of streets with essential facilities such as an airstrip, bank, clinic, post office, laundry, hardware shops and general stores, and a reasonable number of *cabinas* and restaurants. A growing community is livening up the town and its environs, and it is an essential stop-over on the route south to Corcovado. It has water sports too.

Organization Puerto Jiménez surrounds a small bay, with the main focal point to the west and the Pueblo Nuevo, airstrip and deserted **Playa Platanares**▶▶ to the east. The two sides are connected by a bridge below the central playing field, and by a backstreet from downtown. All tourist information is located on the main street. At the hub of town is Restaurant Carolina (tel: 735-5185), base for Escondido Trex (tel/fax: 735-5210, www.escondidotrex.com), which offers kayaking, hiking, bird-watching, mountain biking, water sports and camping treks. Four-wheel-drive trucks leave at 6am and 1pm from Restaurante Carolina for Carate (from there it's a hike up the beach to the park), returning around 9am and 4pm. Departures depend on the weather and cost around $8 one way. A second option is to hire a taxi (tel: 735-5222): expect to pay around $60. Other things to do in town and around: Puerto Jiménez gift shop (tel: 735-5267), across from the airstrip, sells local handicrafts. The Herrera Botanical Gardens and Tent Camp (tel: 735-5210), across from Crocodile Bay Resort (www.crocodilebay.com), offers tours of the reserve. Camping is $3, ask at Escondido Trex for information.

To the cape The rough road south to Cabo Matapalo is passable with two-wheel-drive only in the dry season. After crossing farmlands, the road heads into forest with glimpses

ONE TREE DOWN
Few entrepreneurs can claim to have matched the achievement of John and Karen Lewis when constructing their beautiful rain-forest lodge of Lapa Ríos: only one tree was felled. This is typical of an approach that gives ecotourism an active role, in which responsibility is the key concept. Apart from protecting endangered rain forest and obeying strict ecological precepts, the owners of Lapa Ríos (see page 203) have contributed to the building of a community school (previously there was none) and have organized a local chamber of tourism to promote ecotourism, with sustainable development as the main goal.

of the gulf. This beautiful cape has attracted several stylish lodges, all environmentally conscious. The most impressive is the American-owned Lapa Ríos, about 19km (12 miles) south of Puerto Jiménez (see panel opposite), worth a visit for a drink or lunch. The creative Tierra de Los Milagros is New Age in style, and simple lodgings are available.

Heart of the gulf North of Puerto Jiménez, the road reveals the effects of deforestation, counterpointed by several interesting projects and lodges that have been launched. About 25km (16 miles) north of town, the Albergue Ecotouristico Cerro de Oro Lodge (tel: 248-2538, fax: 248-1659) showcases—for groups only, minimum eight persons—a sustainable development project devoted to agriculture and tourism. Cabins ($35 per person including meals) are accessible by horse or tractor, near the eastern border of Corcovado. *En route* to the small town of Dos Brazos, 12km (7 miles) off the main road, the Bosque del Río Tigre (tel: 824-1372, www.osaadventures.com), an eco-lodge and interactive education station run by naturalists, offers rooms for $103 per person including meals, with hiking, swimming, horses and natural history. These are two of several new destinations in this region. It is encouraging that such areas are developing sustainable tourism and agriculture as the economic foundation.

▶▶ **Reserva Biológica Dúrika**   *148B4*

Apartado 9, Buenos Aires, tel/fax: 730-0657, www.durika.org
For those frustrated by the lack of visitor services at Parque Internacional La Amistad (La Amistad International Park; see page 160), this private biological reserve is the solution. It is situated high in the rugged Talamanca Mountains northeast of the village of Buenos Aires, inside La Amistad Biosphere Reserve, and is focused on the self-sufficient farming community of Finca Anael. This was set up in 1991 by a group of idealistic Costa Ricans in search of a back-to-nature existence and, since 1992, has been open to like-minded visitors. Among the reasonably priced facilities are rustic cabins, organic vegetarian meals and a choice of activities: yoga; bird-watching with a naturalist guide to help you spot eagles, parrots, toucans and trogons; hikes to local villages, including the Cabécar Indian community of Ujarrás; and climbing the peak of Cerro Dúrika. Access is by taxi from Buenos Aires, then a one- or two-hour hike or horseback-ride, or trip by four-wheel-drive.

PADDLING AROUND THE GULF
Kayaking in the mellow Golfo Dulce is an unbeatable experience, particularly at sunset, when the coastal rain forest comes alive with roosting birds, dolphins arrive to feed in the calm bays and the gulf glows with photoluminescent microbes. Daytime kayaking along mangrove-fringed estuaries brings sightings of parrots, hawks, eagles, waterbirds and brilliant scarlet macaws, while white-faced and howler monkeys are never far away.

FERRY TO PUERTO JIMÉNEZ
Public passenger boats ply the gulf daily, for approximately $3, leaving Golfito at 11.30am and Puerto Jiménez at 6am, and taking 1½ hours (tel: 775-0472). During the high season, there may be a 4pm departure from Golfito as well. Invest $30 to $40 in a water taxi and the trip takes only 30 minutes—a good deal if you can round up a dozen passengers to share the fare.

169

The carefully conceived lodge of Lapa Ríos

LONGEST RIVERS

The Río Térraba—or Río Grande de Térraba, "the Great Térraba River"—is Costa Rica's longest river. It begins on the southern slopes of the Cordillera de Talamanca, from where it flows 195km (121 miles) westward to end in the Pacific near Sierpe. Next longest is Guanacaste's Río Tempisque (158km/ 98 miles), with Río San Juan (135km/84 miles) and Río Pacuare (133.5km/83 miles), both flowing into the Caribbean, close contenders for third position.

Sierpe, the starting point for trips down crocodile rivers to the Pacific and Bahía Drake

▶ San Isidro de El General   148A5

Theoretically, San Isidro lies in the province of San José, but actually it is the gateway to the south, set in a fertile tropical valley 35km (22 miles) south of the formidable Cerro La Muerte (see page 94). As the road winds down from the pass, it reveals hillsides of orange groves, while beyond San Isidro it enters the **Valle de El General▶▶**. The town of San Isidro itself is a crossroads for people journeying from all directions, including the beach resort of Dominical (see page 153), 32km (20 miles) to the southwest. Of the several bus stations, those serving San José are north of the Parque Central, and the Dominical terminus immediately south. A small museum, **Museo Regional del Sur** (tel: 771-5273. *Open* weekdays 9–noon, 1–5. *Admission free*), in the Complejo Cultural Peréz Zeledón (Avenida 1/Calle 2), has artefacts related to the Talamancan indigenous groups. The community-run biological station, **Centro Biológico Las Quebradas** (tel/fax: 771-4131. *Admission: inexpensive*), 7km (4 miles) from town, offers 2.7km (1.5 miles) of hiking trails through primary rain forest. Camping is allowed.

▶ San Vito   149D3

From the crossroads town of Ciudad Neily a magnificent road twists precipitously north through the **Cordillera Brunqueña▶▶** up to the mountain town of San Vito. This stretch was built, like the Interamerican Highway, by the US in 1945 for strategic purposes related to the Panama Canal. Today the higher slopes are blanketed with coffee plantations and fruit orchards, whose products are marketed at San Vito. You can stock up here with Coto Brus coffee (the name Coto Brus applies to the northern valley), which is one of Costa Rica's finest. San Vito was founded in the 1950s by Italian immigrants, and is now the focal point of a large Italian community. It has integrated and absorbed the Tico spirit to the point of being indistinguishable, but there are a couple of Italian restaurants in the town.

The mountain air, views, good places to stay and proximity to the Wilson Botanical Gardens (see page 176) make it a welcome contrast to the humid, less prosperous towns of the hot plains. The rain forest of Las Tablas lies 35km (22 miles) to the north, while 1.5km (1 mile) south, at Linda Vista, is the **Finca Cantaros▶** (tel: 773-3760,

www.fincacantaros.com), masterminded by Gail Hewson de Gomez, associate director of the Wilson Botanical Gardens. Geared as much to the community as to tourists, it consists of a lakeside park and an excellent roadside handicrafts shop—painted an unmistakable saffron yellow—offering Guaymi and Boruca handicrafts.

▶ Sierpe   148B3

At the end of a vast area of banana plantations south of Palmar Sur lies this small river port and the main jetty for boats to Bahía Drake (see page 152). Sierpe lies at the middle of the extensive and little-visited **Delta del Térraba▶▶**, Costa Rica's largest river basin. The 12,100ha (29,900 acres) of mangrove swamps nurture nearly 400 species of birds and more than 200 of mammals, reptiles and amphibians. This network of channels is used daily by small boats linking tiny villages and farms with the main port of Sierpe. Both the Río Térraba and the Río Sierpe can be navigated for more than 19km (12 miles) upstream. Tours of the delta, which usually include good crocodile sightings, are available through Estero Azul Lodge (tel: 788-1422), and the small, Canadian-owned Hotel Oleaje Sereno (tel: 788-1103, www.hoteloleajesereno.com), near Sierpe's main jetty.

▶ Uvita   148A4

This sleepy coastal village lies in the Parque Nacional Marino Ballena (see page 164). A number of stylish hotels and restaurants have opened in this area, and there are also budget *cabinas*. An alternative to Uvita's marine delights is a family-run biological reserve, **Oro Verde▶▶** (tel: 743-8072, www.costarica-birding-oroverde.com) in the mountain village of San Josecito. This 150ha (370-acre) tract of virgin rain forest with fabulous coastal views has been conserved by a Tico family since the early 1960s, and is now seeing the return of species such as the spider monkey. Howler monkeys, sloths, agoutis and armadillos are also common.

VOLUNTEER PATROLS
Costa Rica's growing consciousness of its natural riches has inspired some private initiatives, not least in Uvita. After lobbying for the national marine park, local inhabitants have now turned to guarding the tropical forests that clad the mountains rising precipitously inland. Three volunteer forest guards are on call 24 hours a day to ward off hunters and to defend the area against fires and logging. This is the achievement of a local association formed specifically to preserve what it can of the Fila Tinomastes, a 4,800ha (11,860-acre) mountainous area of primary and secondary forest.

171

Hand-hewn wooden canoes are still the norm for inhabitants of the Delta del Térraba

Costa Rica's wildlife may be enticing, but it is also disappearing. Certain species are now on the brink of extinction, owing to hunters poachers, or to the disapearance of their natural habitat. Although the government is waking up to this threat and private initiatives are helping, in some cases it may be too late.

GREEN IGUANA

This enormous but herbivorous lizard was once a common sight in Costa Rican lowlands, including the dry tropical forest of Guanacaste. Adults reach 2m (6.5ft), in length and love sunning themselves on riverbanks. Their tender white flesh (they are nick-named "chicken of the tree") is much appreciated on the dinner table, and so the green iguana is one of the nation's endangered species. However, in 1985, a German biologist set up a project to breed iguanas for legalized sale and for reintroduction into the wild. Some 80,000 were released in the first five years, and the rest sold as exotic pets or for food. Cattle farmers may well convert, as iguanas yield ten times more meat per hectare than cattle and relish forested environments.

Buying a wild animal or bird as a pet is now forbidden in Costa Rica. Since the Wildlife Conservation Law of 1992 it has become illegal to keep captive wildlife, especially endangered species, and permits are required for special circumstances. This is one small step toward dealing with the problem of the dramatic loss of bio-diversity, a direct result of deforestation, development and poaching. Another is to create "corridors" linking the national parks, and a greater step would be to extend these throughout Central America to create the projected Paseo Pantera. If realized, this would provide uninterrupted natural forest for larger mammals, which experience genetic decay when isolated within parks. Wildlife breeding stations and a few rehabilitation organizations are the other protagonists in the struggle to preserve numerous extraordinary species.

Big game For decades Costa Rica's wildcats have been hunted for their much prized pelts, and this, combined with their territorial requirements (each adult jaguar needs at least 100sq km (39sq miles) as a hunting ground), has been their downfall. Jaguars used to be common at elevations of up to 900m (2,950ft), but their conspicuous tracks make them easy targets for poachers. Not the most sociable of mammals, they live off peccaries, monkeys, agoutis, deer and alligators.

Pumas, ocelots and margays, in descending order of appetite, are also suffering from the conversion of their natural habitat into plantations or cattle pasture. White-collared peccaries that once roamed in aggressive groups of more than 100 now team up with only 20 to 30 comrades—though this does not stop them from attacking and even devouring humans. With tapirs the situation is different. Their vegetarian diet has given their meat a repu-tation as a delicacy, so they are prized hunting targets.

Three-toed sloth

In the branches Where branches once rustled with activity, today there may be only silence. Costa Rica's only endemic monkey, the gregarious squirrel monkey, is now close to extinction and is only very rarely spotted, in Manuel Antonio National Park and around Golfito. Similarly threatened is the acrobatic spider monkey, which propels itself in the company of two or three comrades through the tallest forest

trees, using its curling tail as a fifth grip.

At the opposite end of the metabolism scale are the sloths, extra-terrestrial-looking creatures that spend their 40-year life spans hanging upside-down from branches, occasionally scooping leaves very slowly into their mouths, and descending to the forest floor once a week to defecate. Both two-toed and three-toed species exist, the former at higher elevations, and both are under threat, mainly through habitat loss or degradation. Even the verdant town squares of Puerto Limón and Alajuela are seeing their resident sloths disappear.

Above, from left: scarlet macaw, ocelot kittens, peccaries, iguana, orange-chinned parakeet, puma. Left: quetzal

173

SANCTUARIES
Private initiatives are valiantly dealing with members of endangered species that have been captured by hunters, confiscated by airport customs controls, or rescued from misguided owners. The late Lily Hagnauer's sanctuary, Las Pumas, located near Cañas (see page 42) is devoted to cats—jaguars, pumas, ocelots and margays—for the most part confiscated from illegal hunters by MIRENEM, the national parks administration. However, once the cats have lived in captivity, it is virtually impossible to release them into the wild. In contrast, Dario Castelfranco's Jardín Gaia (now closed) concentrated on rehabilitating confiscated animals and birds and reintroducing them into their natural habitats.

Airborne Resplendent quetzals, scarlet macaws, harpy eagles, yellow-napped parrots and great curassows are among the numerous bird species that are in danger of extinction within Costa Rica's boundaries. The 16 species of the parrot family range from the tiny barred parakeet to the exuberant scarlet macaw. All are popular on the pet market and need to be protected. The chestnut-mandibled toucan (*Ramphastos swainsonii*), Central America's largest, is also threatened.

Waterlogged Thanks to campaigning, the plight of turtles is well known (see pages 56–57). Less advertised is the predicament of caymans and crocodiles, which are suffering from chemical pollution of their watery habitats and from hunters after their skins. The cayman is a relatively non-aggressive Latin-American crocodilian, measuring up to 1m

American crocodile

(3ft), that lives in lagoons and canals. Its much larger and more dangerous brother, the American crocodile, is literally a prehistoric sight. How much longer will they be around?

Drive

From Pacific to pineapples

See map on pages 148–149

This circuit follows a spectacular stretch of the Pacific coast before turning inland along a river valley and circling north to San Isidro. It requires at least one night *en route* if you want to appreciate the natural offerings and recover from some dire roads. As for most areas of Costa Rica, a four-wheel-drive vehicle is recommended for this drive, especially in the rainy season.

To the beach From San Isidro de El General take the road southwest toward Dominical. This twists up to a pass near the peak of San Juan (1,186m/3,891ft) before descending through a beautiful, often misty valley. Although it is paved all the way, it can be a difficult ride in the rainy season. After the village of Platanillo you can stop at Centro Turistico Nauyaca, a small, private, rain-forest reserve with trails and horseback treks to the impressive Nauyaca Waterfalls. From Barú the road follows the Río Barú down to the coast, where it forks left to the lively beach resort of **Dominical**▶ ▶ (see page 153). To the right, more rain-forest activities and a fuel stop are available near Barú del Pacifico wildlife reserve. If hunger bites, stop at Cabinas

Punta Dominical, located on a promontory ending Dominical's main beach, where surf crashes on both sides. Continue along the *costanera sur* (southern coast road) through lush tropical vegetation, with steep forested hills rising to your left. After 16km (10 miles) you reach **Uvita**▶ (see page 171) and the national marine park of **Marino Ballena**▶ ▶ (see page 164), a must for a swim, snorkel and, if you have time, a boat tour around the offshore reefs and islets.

Spheres and mangroves Farther south, at the thriving beach resorts of Playa Tortuga, a newly paved stretch of road veers inland. After 19km (12 miles) it passes Ciudad Cortés to reach Palmar Norte through altogether flatter, less inspiring landscapes. At **Palmar Norte**▶ (see page 157) don't miss the perfect stone spheres on display. Nature enthusiasts should make a detour from here through seemingly endless banana plantations to tour the mangrove swamps surrounding **Sierpe**▶ (see page 171).

River valley Back at Palmar Norte, follow the road (this is now the freshly paved Interamerican Highway) going east on its circuitous way to Buenos Aires. You immediately enter the broad, majestic Térraba Valley, which for 40km (25 miles) marks the course of the meandering river, its gently sloping hills alternating with sheer rock cliffs on the opposite bank. At the end of the dry season water levels are very low, sometimes nonexistent. Stands selling *pipa fría* (cold, fresh coconut milk), soursops and seasonal avocados dot the roadside in front of tiny farms. Evidence of slash-and-burn methods, used by tropical farmers all over the world, is often painfully visible.

Handicrafts Just before Curré, a dirt road branches off to the left and will take you along a high mountain ridge to **Boruca**▶ (see page

152), but four-wheel-drive is essential. If you make this detour, you can continue north and cut back onto the Interamerican Highway at Brujo. At Curré, stop to buy Borucan handicrafts sold at derisory prices. A short distance farther at Paso Real you pass a turn-off to **La Amistad**▶ ▶ (see page 160) and **San Vito**▶ (see pages 170–171), offering other detours requiring overnight stays. For years this route involved crossing the Térraba by car ferry, but in 1994 a bridge was finally completed.

Canned pineapples From Paso Real the road leaves the stifling lowland temperatures and starts climbing up through a wild, deserted valley, backed in the east by the

The landscape around San Vito, on a detour from the main drive

dramatic Talamanca range. It follows the Río General as far as Brujo, from where it ascends more steeply to reach the high plateau of the Valle de El General around Buenos Aires. This village lies just off the road and offers little other than a food and fuel stop.

Between here and the village of Volcán, huge swathes of tilled terracotta soil alternate with pineapple plantations belonging to the canned fruit company Del Monte. In the distance, splashes of flame trees emerge from the silhouette of the Talamancan foothills. San Isidro de El General is 47km (29 miles) farther on.

Zingiba spectabile,
*also known as shampoo
ginger, at the Wilson
Botanical Gardens.
Indigenous women
are said to have made
shampoo using the
petal-like bracts*

►►► Wilson Botanical Gardens/Jardín Botánico Robert y Catherine Wilson/ Las Cruces   149D3

*Las Cruces, San Vito, tel: 773-4004, fax: 773-3665,
www.esintro.co.cr OTS in San José, tel: 240-6696*
Open: Tue–Sun 8–4. Admission: moderate

This internationally renowned collection of tropical plants extends over 10ha (28 acres) beside a further 145ha (358 acres) of forest reserve in the Brunqueña Mountains. Established in 1963 by Robert and Catherine Wilson, it was transferred to the Organization for Tropical Studies (OTS) for tropical biological research in 1973. Ten years later it was declared part of UNESCO's Reserva de la Biósfera La Amistad (La Amistad Biosphere Reserve) and serves as an important buffer zone to the international park. Day visitors are welcome, and students, researchers and tourists can stay in cozy cabins with private baths, fans and balconies set among the gardens. Overnight stays on site—the 12 available rooms are comfortably appointed—include three meals and a guided walk. Reservations are recommended for both overnight stays and half- or full-day guided walks. Visitors without their own vehicle can travel to the Gardens by taxi from Golfito; expect to pay approximately $40 each way.

Garden of Eden Heavy annual rainfall has helped develop about 7,000 species of tropical plants, including bromeliads, orchids, marantas, heliconias, bamboos, begonias, palms, tree ferns, rhododendrons and cycads, ancient plants that evolved more than 100 million years ago. Paths wind around undulating, superbly landscaped grounds, with detours signposted to wilder areas of rain forest. Greenhouses and an experimental garden can be visited, and an insectarium is planned. Two hours is the minimum time needed for exploring the main garden; longer walks can be taken downhill to the river, where bird-watching opportunities are excellent. Altogether, some 330 avian species have been recorded around Las Cruces, and one researcher reported sighting a third of them in a single day. The numerous flowers also attract more than 3,000 types of butterflies and moths.

PRIMARY AND SECONDARY

The view from the gardens' look-out point west across the valley clearly shows the difference between primary and secondary rain forest. Looking from left to right, to the far left is agricultural land, followed by a patch of forest (in the middle) with even textures and varying hues. This is secondary forest—that is, regrowth following logging. To the right, the primary forest canopy reaches heights of 40m (130ft). Below the canopy, two or more additional levels are formed by trees, palms and ferns.

Travel Facts

Arriving

By air This is the way the majority of visitors arrive in Costa Rica and most flights land at Juan Santamaría Airport (24-hour information, tel: 443-2622), near the capital, San José.

Most international flights transit via Miami, Houston or Dallas. Visitors from Europe will find that MartinAIR, Iberia, British Airways, Continental and American Airlines offer the most convenient connections. The German airline Condor operates a direct Frankfurt to San José service. Count on anything between 16 and 19 hours' to travel from Europe. The Central American Airline Grupo Taca (tel: 223-4314, 800/535-8780), which includes Lacsa (tel: 800/225-2272, flies daily from several Canadian, US, South American and Caribbean cities, often stopping in other Central American locations.

Transatlantic passengers arrive in the evening when exchange offices (*Open Mon–Sat 9–4*) are closed, but there are plenty of unofficial money-changers, and taxis accept US dollars. The airport terminal has car-rental offices and tourist information, and taxis are readily available to whisk you the 18km (11 miles; costing about $17) to the middle of the city. The Alajuela–San José bus passes frequently in front of the airport.

Daniel Oduber Airport, in Liberia, was promoted to international status in 1996, and has constantly expanded since including the completion of a new terminal and the announcement of

The influence of the United States even extends to second-hand clothes shops

another in 2007. Several major US carriers now fly into Oduber.

By sea Apart from private yachts, the only passenger boats to Costa Rica are cruise ships. These stop at Caldera, near Puntarenas on the Pacific coast, or at Moín, near Puerto Limón on the Caribbean: inquire at your local travel agent about itineraries and companies. Freighters sometimes have passenger berths.

By bus Budget visitors can reach Costa Rica by long-distance bus from Managua, in Nicaragua, via Peñas Blancas; from Panama City via Paso Canoas; or from Changuinola on Panama's Caribbean side via Sixaola. These routes can take anything from 9 to 14 hours depending on border delays and road conditions. Services are provided by **Nicabus** (tel: 223-4242); **Ticabus**, Paseo Colón, frente a la Funeraria del Magisterio Nacional (tel: 221-0006); **Tracopa**, Avenida 18/Calle 2 & 4 (tel: 221-4214, www.ticabus.com).

By car Tourists arriving by car must pay a road tax (currently just over $10), buy an insurance stamp ($30 for 3 months) and receive a car entry permit at the border. Cars are also mandatorily fumigated for a small fee. Make sure your insurance covers you as comprehensively as possible.

Customs regulations

Incoming passengers can bring in 200 cigarettes or 500g (17oz) of tobacco, 2L (0.4gal) of alcohol or wine, and up to six rolls of film. There are no restrictions on amounts of currency taken in or out of the country. Sporadic customs checks are made, particularly at land borders.

Travel insurance

Take out a reliable travel insurance policy before leaving home. Most travel agents supply these, which should cover theft, illness and repatriation. If you are considering some of Costa Rica's wilder activities (bungee-jumping, whitewater rafting), read the small print carefully. Check also the benefits attached to your credit card as

some companies offer partial travel insurance cover.

Entry requirements

Check current requirements before departure. A valid passport is required. It is recommended that children travel on their own passport rather than on their parents'. Citizens of the United States, Canada and the United Kingdom do not need visas for stays of up to 90 days. Citizens of Australia and New Zealand are permitted visa-free stays of up to 30 days. For an extension of 30 days, obtain an exit visa through a travel agent at least three working days before your scheduled departure. Alternatively, make a 72-hour exit over the border. When you arrive in Costa Rica, an immigration card is stamped

One of Costa Rica's main draws is her charismatic people

and attached to your passport: keep this document for leaving the country. Visitors arriving by bus or air should be in possession of a return ticket or other ticket out of Costa Rica.

Departing

An airport tax is charged on departure (currently $26). This can be paid in dollars or *colones* at a travel agent when confirming your return ticket, or at the airport check-in. Seats on all international flights must be confirmed with the airline 72 hours before departure. Don't put photographic through the X-ray security machines; they are not film-safe.

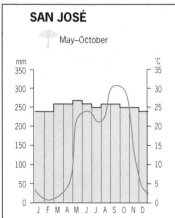

SAN JOSÉ

May–October

Essential facts

Climate

Costa Rica has a hot, dry season (which Ticos call summer) from December to April, and a rainy or "green" season (known as winter), from May to November. Transitional months can bring surprises, and the rainy season is not constantly wet: July invariably brings a temporary abatement and, in general, mornings are clear. There are plenty of micro-climates, too, with temperatures descending as altitudes rise. The climate guide above shows the average daily maximum temperature.

In the dry season, San José and other Central Valley towns enjoy a fresh, breezy, spring-like climate requiring a jacket or sweater in the evenings, while Guanacaste's arid interior endures stifling temperatures. Rain still occurs in high mountainous areas and, above all, in the Caribbean lowlands, where downpours can last for days—or break into brilliant sunshine after a couple of hours. When the green season starts, it is the southern zone around the Golfo Dulce that gets the most rain.

All year round, the sun rises dutifully at about 6am and sets about 12 hours later.

National holidays

- **New Year's Day**
  1 January
- **Feast of St. Joseph** (patron saint of the capital)
  19 March
- **Juan Santamaría Day**
  11 April
- **Easter**
  March/April, from preceding Thursday to Easter Sunday
- **Labor Day**
  1 May
- **Corpus Christi**
  June (movable)
- **St. Peter and St. Paul**
  29 June
- **Guanacaste Day**
  25 July
- **Feast of the Virgin of Los Angeles**
  2 August
- **Assumption** and **Mothers' Day**
  15 August
- **Independence Day**
  15 September
- **Columbus Day** (Limón carnival)
  12 October
- **Immaculate Conception**
  8 December
- **Christmas Eve**
  24 December
- **Christmas Day**
  25 December

When to go

The popular period for holiday-makers is December and January, when hotel rooms tend to fill up. Aim to visit in late March and you will have the advantage of the dry season, and slightly lower hotel rates. If you do not mind downpours, the green season (May to November) offers a more refreshing climate, a wide choice of places to stay and lower prices.

Time differences

Costa Rica time is the same as US Central Standard Time, six hours behind Greenwich Mean Time.

Opening times

Shops generally open Monday to Saturday from 8 or 9 to 6 or 7. Some close for lunch any time between 11.30 and 2. Government offices are theoretically open weekdays from 8am to 4pm but assiduity slows considerably in the afternoon. Banks are open weekdays from 9am to 3pm, with some San José banks opening at 8am.

Addresses

Most residents have a numbered post office box (Apartado, shortened to

Apdo.) for receiving mail. Main towns have a grid layout of avenues cut across by streets. These are numbered starting from the middle, with odd numbers on one side and even numbers on the other (see map of San José on pages 116–117). Addresses are given as intersections between an avenue and a street, or two streets (for example, Avenida 1 & 3/Calle 2 means on Calle 2 between Avenida 1 and Avenida 3). In suburbs and small towns, directions are given in relation to a local landmark.

Money matters

Local currency is the *colón* (*colones* in the plural), written as ¢. It is divided into 100 *centimos*, but these are practically obsolete. Coins range from 1¢ to 100¢, and paper money from 50¢ to 10,000¢. The *colón* is floated against the US dollar, which is the only currency worth bringing. Paper money and traveler's checks can easily be changed at banks with your passport. Most banks have a special counter for foreign exchange (*cambio*): go early to avoid a long wait. San José's Banco Mercantil (Avenida 2/Calle Central) has an outlet specifically for foreign exchange.

Itinerant money-changers abound in the streets of San José near the Banco de Costa Rica (Avenida 2/ Calle 4) but their tricks are many, so use them only if you are desperate. Large hotels change traveler's checks and cash at slightly lower rates than banks.

Credit cards are accepted in almost every hotel and restaurant, and also by car-rental and travel agencies, and by most but not all tour companies and other tourist-related businesses. ATMs for VISA are found at branches of the Banco Popular y Desarollo, and for MasterCard at Credomatic branches, and ATMs can also be found in most towns. For credit card enquiries, or to report loss or theft, contact:

VISA tel: 0800/847-2911

MasterCard and **American Express** both work through Credomatic tel: 0800/827-5382 or (local) 295-9898

US dollars are accepted in most large hotels, but you should change sufficient amounts into *colones* before heading out into the countryside. Many small towns and resorts have no money-exchange facilities.

Tipping

Tourist hotels and restaurants automatically add on a tax and service charge amounting to around 25 percent. Bellboys and chambermaids are tipped anywhere from $.50–$2 a day, while guides at eco-lodges anywhere from $5–$10 a day. Taxi drivers appreciate having their modest fares rounded up, and tour guides generally expect a few dollars' tip.

Tico families take to the beaches between December and April

181

Getting around

By car

Car rental Car-rental agencies are numerous in San José and rates follow the tourist season—rising between December and March. Expect to pay $175 to $490 per week with unlimited mileage, depending on whether you want four-wheel-drive (recommended for the rainy season) and/or air-conditioning. Rates should include comprehensive insurance (not always offered, so check carefully) which accounts for about $10.50 to $14 per day. Special deals crop up during leaner periods, so check the local press (*Tico Times, Costa Rica Today*) on arrival. Cars can also be booked in advance from your home country through international companies, but rates may be marginally higher than in Costa Rica.

Car-rental agencies require a valid driver's license (international licenses are not necessary), passport and a major credit card. Few will rent cars to drivers aged under 25. Before signing the rental agreement, check all existing dents on the car and make sure they are noted on the contract. Any car using Costa Rican roads takes a real beating, so make a trial run and check everything before heading out into the wilds. Ask your car-rental agency for contact numbers in case of breakdown. Flat tires can be repaired at filling stations.

Driving may well be an adventure in itself

Rental cars have special license plates, making them easy targets for break-ins. Never leave them parked with your belongings inside (even in the boot) unless well guarded.

Most car-rental agencies have airport locations. San José car-rental offices include:

- **Avis** Avenida Las Americas/Calle 42 (tel: 293-2222, 800/331-1212)
- **Budget** Paseo Colón/Calle 36 (tel: 436-2000, 800/527-0700)
- **Alamo** Avenida18/Calle 11 & 13 (tel: 242-7733, 800/570-0671
- **Hertz** Paseo Colón/Calle 38 (tel: 221-1818, 800/654-3131)
- **National** La Uruca (tel: 242-7990, 800/328-4567)
- **Prego** Paseo Colón/Calle 36 & 38 (tel: 221-8680)
- **Tricolor** (four-wheel-drive specialists) Paseo Colón/Calle 30 & 32 (tel: 440-3333, 800/949-0234)

Speed limits Speed limits are 100kph (62mph) on highways and 40 to 80kph (25 to 50mph) elsewhere: watch for signs and stick to the limits as radar checks are common. In more remote areas where roads have gravel or dirt surfaces, speeds are automatically reduced to around 20kph (12mph), and in the rainy season roads can become impassable even with four-wheel-drive. Always ask about the feasibility of your desired route.

Driving tips San José's complex one-way systems and traffic jams do not make driving fun. Taxis are cheap, so

keep your car for exploring outside the capital. Once you are on the rural roads, Costa Rican pot-holes, streams, landslides, switchbacks, torrential downpours and unpaved surfaces require constant alertness and make for exasperation as well as exhaustion. Cowboys, stray cattle and bikers are occasional obstacles, and the infamous Cerro La Muerte pass can be shrouded in thick fog, greatly reducing visibility. Road signs become a rarity once you are off the main roads, so learn your Spanish and have a good map for asking directions. Rivers are often better signposted than villages, and make useful landmarks. Driving at night is not recommended, partly for security reasons and partly because of badly marked roads and invisible hazards. Fuel costs are reasonable and filling stations are fairly common. Still, it's best to fill up whenever you see one.

Police Traffic police sometimes attempt to extract on-the-spot fines for speeding or other reasons: this is now illegal and fines should only be paid at police stations, where receipts are issued. Armed *guardia rural* manning roadblocks near the Nicaraguan and Panamanian borders sometimes make spot-checks, so carry your passport and all car documents with you.

Accidents In the case of an accident, do not move anything, vehicles included, until the police have arrived. Call the traffic police (tel: 222-9330) if there is no local police station. Insurance claims need to be filed within five days; this should be done by your car-rental agency. Tow vehicles monitor police radios and so will appear without your asking. Rental cars should always be towed back to the agency.

Public transport
Bus Costa Rica's long-distance bus services radiate from different terminals in San José to towns all over the country. This is a budget way to travel (costing about $1 per hour) and buses will drop you at intermediary points on request. However, it means

you are limited to visiting only major hubs, missing out on less accessible parks, reserves, beaches and ecotourism projects. Connections can be tricky, as private bus companies operate from different parts of town, and may involve a long walk or taxi ride and intermediary waits. Buses can be packed to the gills, but they normally respect their timetables. Luggage is stored in side lockers—no receipts are given, so keep your eye on your bags at stops.

The ICT office in San José has current bus schedules and points of departure. If using San José's Coca-Cola bus station, be especially aware of pick-pockets and watch your luggage.

Tourist bus Several private tourist bus companies offer a fast and comfortable alternative to public buses. **Grayline Fantasy Bus** (tel: 220-2126, www.graylinecostarica.com) offers multiple daily trips in air-conditioned buses for $25 or $38 to myriad locations throughout the country. **Interbus** (tel: 0800/748-8853, 283-5573, fax: 283-7655, www.interbusonline.com) connects all the major destinations for $17 to $38, and also offers multi-trip flexipasses.

A traffic (transito) policeman

Taxi travel is relatively cheap in Costa Rica, especially short, metered journeys in San José

Plane Two companies, **Sansa** (tel: 290-4100, fax; 248-1176, www.flysansa.com) and **NatureAir** (tel: 299-6000, fax: 220-0413, www.NatureAir.com), operate small 4- to 15-seat planes to Barra del Colorado, Tortuguero, Golfito, Puerto Jiménez, Palmar Sur, Quepos, Tambor, Sámara, Nosara¡ Tamarindo, Liberia, and La Fortuna de San Carlos. Luggage is limited to 12kg (26lb) and demand for seats is often great in the high season, so book well in advance. NatureAir is slightly more expensive than Sansa but offers a more reliable service with fewer delayed flights. NatureAir flights leave from the small Tobias Bolaños Airport, 5km (3 miles) from the heart of San José, while Sansa operates from the domestic terminal of Juan Santamaría Airport.

Planes can also be chartered to any airstrip in the country. These average a price of about $225 per hour for a six-seater, which is economical for a group as no destination in Costa Rica is more than an hour's flight away. Check the Yellow Pages under *Taxis aereos* for the numerous air-taxi companies that are located at Tobias Bolaños Airport.

Small planes and helicopters may be chartered from:
- **Aero Bell** tel: 290-0000
- **Paradise Air** tel: 231-0938, fax: 296-1429, www.flywithparadise.com
- **Helicópteros Turísticos Tropical** tel: 296-0460
- **Aero Costa Sol** tel: 440-1444, fax: 441-2671

Rail Following the closure of the Atlantic Railway and the Puntarenas line in 1995, it was the turn of two of the three Central Valley commuter trains to cease operation, leaving only the San José–Heredia service functioning. This, too, stopped running from 1998. Currently (in 2007), the only train running is the weekend only tourist train from San José to Caldera (see Puntarenas, page 104).

Taxi Costa Rican taxis are inexpensive, and taxi drivers are mostly honest, though there are exceptions. By law they should use a meter (*maria*) for town trips, but many don't. In 2007, cabs generally cost 500 *colones* ($1.25) for in-town short trips, and 1,000 *colones* ($2.10) for longer trips. Many try to charge a surcharge for waiting outside hotels: this is illegal and you should refuse to pay it. Payment for any trip over 12km (8 miles) should be negotiated before starting: count on around $42 per day. Metered short trips within San José should be very inexpensive.

Radio taxis operate in San José and are useful for nocturnal excursions, rainstorms or early-morning airport trips:
● **Coopeirazú** tel: 254-3211
● **Coopeguaria** tel: 226-1366
● **Coopetaxi** tel: 235-9966
● **Coopetico** tel: 224-7979

Ferries There are several ferry routes to the Península de Nicoya. The shortest, slowest route, crossing the Río Tempisque, has been put out of business by a new bridge. Puntarenas–Playa Naranjo has five daily car-ferry departures in both directions and Puntarenas–Paquera more than a dozen, with two companies competing for the business.

In the south, the La Lancha passenger ferry runs daily between Golfito and Puerto Jiménez, and water taxis can be hired through Zancudo Boat Tours and Taxi Service (tel: 776-0012).

Student and youth travel
Discounts are available on international flights to Costa Rica if you have an International Student Identity Card (ISIC). Some small hotels are affiliated to the International Youth Hostel Federation: check in your home country or contact the student travel agency OTEC, Calle 3/Avenida 1–3, San José (tel: 256-0633, www.otec.co.cr).

185

Inexpensive restaurants and sodas are a bonus for backpackers who are visiting Costa Rica on a budget

Communication

Media

The daily *La República* and *La Nación* both contain freely expressed news and opinions. The official government mouthpiece is the weekly *La Gazette*. English-speaking visitors can rely on the weekly *Tico Times* (Fridays) for a synopsis of events as well as cultural listings, tourist information and classified ads, sometimes useful for finding lodgings, private car rental or local services. The tourist-oriented *Central America Weekly*, published in Spanish, English and German on Thursdays, is distributed in most hotels.

There are six local TV stations and numerous local radio stations. Canal 19, Master and Supercanal are Costa Rican cable TV stations that transmit 24-hour TV from the United States.

Post offices

San José's elegant old central post office (Correo Central, Avenida 1 & 3/Calle 2, *Open* weekdays 7–6, Sat 7–noon) offers the fastest service for international mail: one to two weeks to North America and Europe, about the same time as the inefficient internal mail service. General delivery can be addressed to you at Lista de Correos, Correo Central, San José. Receiving parcels entails complicated customs procedures and duty, and is therefore best avoided. Packages can be sent abroad reasonably reliably (although avoid sending valuables), but postal rates are high. Courier services such as DHL (Paseo Colón/Calle 34, tel: 210-3838) and Fedex (World Service Center, Paseo Colón, tel: 800/052-1090) have become more prevalent and offices can be found in most large cities.

Internet

Fast, fairly reliable and inexpensive internet access is available all over San José and in many hotels and small towns. A good website on Costa Rica is www.infocostarica.com

Telephones and fax

Costa Rica has the highest number of telephones per capita in Latin America. In San José there are two efficient international phone/fax offices: **Telecom**, Avenida 2/Calle 1 & 3 (fax: 257-2272/2273. *Open* Mon–Thu 7am–10pm, Fri–Sun 7am–midnight) **Radiográfica Costarricense (RACSA)**, Avenida 5/Calle 1 & 3 (tel: 287-0087. *Open* 7am–10pm).

Phone booths (using pre-pay cards) exist in most towns, but often there are many people waiting to use them. Beware of collect call, credit card payphones, which are extremely pricey. Most rural villages have at least one public phone run by a local operator, often in a *pulpería* (grocery shop) and signposted from the road. Some parts of Costa Rica outside the Central Valley have no telephone lines, and radio or cell phones are the only means of communication.

- International calls via operator: 175 for the USA, 116 (for reverse charge calls—*una llamada a cobrar*—or if using an international phone card) for all others
- Telegrams/faxes by phone: 123
- International information: 124
- Costa Rica directory: 113
- International call: prefix 00

All phone numbers in Costa Rica have seven digits; there are no area codes. To call Costa Rica from abroad, dial country code 506 before the number.

Language and pronunciation

English is spoken in all the pricier hotels, but elsewhere basic Spanish is essential. Ticos are extremely courteous and pepper their conversation with little phrases such as *con mucho gusto* (with pleasure) and *con permiso* (with your permission), both worth repeating. They also, notoriously, use diminutives such as *ahorita* (in a while) instead of *ahora* (now). In general, every letter is sounded except **h**, which is silent. Pronounce the letter **a** like *ah*, **e** like *eh* or *ay*, **i** like *ee*, **o** like *oh*, **u** like *oo*, and **y** like *ee* (when a vowel) or *y* (when between vowels or beginning a word). Pronounce **c** like *k*, except before the letters **e** or **i**, when it sounds like *s*. The letter **g** is hard (as in *go*) except before **e** or **i**, when it has a strong *h* sound. The letter groups **gue** and **gui** have a hard *g*, while the **u** is silent, as in *guest* and *guitar*. The letter **j** has an *h* sound. The letters **ll** are pronouced *y*, as in *yet*. The **ñ** sounds like the *ny* in *canyon*. **Qu** sounds like *k* before the letters **e** and **i**, and like *kw* before **a** and **o**. The **r** is rolled, **rr** *moreso*. The letter **v** has a soft *b* sound. Accents show where to stress a word. If there is no accent, stress the second-to-last syllable of words ending in a vowel, **n**, or **s**, and the last syllable of other words.

¡hola!	hello
buenos días	good morning
buenas tardes	good afternoon
buenas noches	good evening/night
adiós	goodbye (definitively), also used for hello
hasta luego	goodbye/see you later
por favor	please
(muchas) gracias	thank you (very much)
perdone	excuse me/sorry
si/non	yes/no
¿cómo está?	how are you?
muy bién, gracias	very well, thank you
no entiendo	I don't understand
¿habla inglés?	do you speak English?
¿dónde está/están...?	where is/are...?
el banco	the bank
el parque central	the main square
la gasolinera/bomba	the filling station
los sanitarios/servicios/baños	the lavatories
la parada de autobuses	the bus stop
a la derecha	to the right
a la izquierda	to the left
todo derecho	straight on
¿hay campo...?	is there space/a seat?
¿cuanto vale esto?	how much is this?
la cuenta, por favor	the bill, please
¿tiene...?	do you have...?
un cuarto sencillo/doble	a single/double room
con dos camas	with two beds
con cama matrimonial	with a double bed
con aire acondicionado	with air-conditioning
con ventilador	with fan
con baño privado	with private bathroom
¿puede hacer un descuento?	can you do a discount?
¿cuando/a qué hora?	when/at what time?
pura vida	"good life," used as a greeting or to mean great, fantastic

Emergencies

Crime and police

In the last decade crime has become a serious problem, especially in San José and Puerto Limón. Tourists should not walk in badly lit side-streets or city parks at night, nor attract attention by flaunting posses-sions. Always be alert, especially in markets and crowded bus stations or on packed buses. Beware of over-friendly approaches from either sex, particularly at night—con men and con women abound. Report any theft or assault to the Recepción de Denuncias at the Judicial Police (OIJ) at Avenida 6/Calle 19 & 21, in the court complex, or call 295-3640. You need to file a report to make an insurance claim, so try to find a

In some situations tourists' cameras may be a temptation: In crowded places always keep a careful eye on your possessions

good Spanish-speaker to accom-pany you.

Some corrupt police may try to extract bribes, particularly traffic police. Only pay fines at police stations and demand a receipt. You can file a complaint at the Ombudsman's office (tel: 0800/258-7474) if you have the officer's name and number. By law you must carry your passport (or a photocopy of it) with you.

Emergency phone numbers

- All emergencies: 911
- Police: 911, 295-3640
- Fire: 118
- Red Cross: 128
- Red Cross ambulance: 128
- Hospital San Juan de Dios: 257-6282
- Traffic police: 222-9330/9245

Embassies and consulates

Canada Oficentio Ejecutívo La Sabana, Edificios, Sabana Sur (tel: 242-4400)
United Kingdom Edificio Centro Colón, Paseo Colón/Calle 38 & 40, San José (tel: 258-2025)
USA Carreteras Pavas, Rohrmoser (tel: 220-3939). US Citizens Services, Mon–Fri, 8–11.30

Lost property

Report the loss of passports, trav-eler's checks, or credit cards to the police immediately, and to your embassy and the issuing bank. It helps to have photocopies of your passport and airline tickets, and a note of traveler's check and credit-card numbers (keep these separate from the originals). Report other losses to a local police station for insurance claims (good Spanish will be needed). If lost items are returned, it is common courtesy to give a token reward to the finder.

Health

Hygiene standards are high and medical services excellent. San José's tap water is drinkable, though elsewhere it is advisable to stick to bottled mineral water—easily avail-able. Many towns post "potable water" signs at the roadside—watch for them. Uncooked fruit and

Standards of hygiene are good, but it's always safer to stick to bottled water

Hazards
If the change in diet causes diarrhoea, drink plenty of (reliable) water. Non-prescription medicines alleviate the symptoms. Malaria may not be a risk (see above), but parts of Guanacaste and Puntarenas in the recent past have had outbreaks of dengue fever, another debilitating disease carried by mosquitoes. Always use a strong repellent with a high level of DEET at dusk, and light anti-mosquito spirals (*espirales*, available at all grocery stores) at night. *Pujarras* (*no-see-ums* or sand fleas) are intensely annoying insects whose itchy bites can become infected if scratched. The humid tropical climate does not help healing, and any infected bite or cut should be cleaned with antiseptic cream. Sulfur powder, also a good insect repellent, helps to dry out and disinfect wounds. Snakebites are not common, but if hiking, ask about venomous species to watch out for.

Two constant hazards are dehydration and sunburn. Bring total sun block from home and stock up on high-protection-factor lotions in San José: they are difficult to find outside major resorts. Always drink lots of water (carry it with you on treks) and other non-alcoholic liquids, wear a hat during the midday hours of strong sunshine, and avoid spending long periods in the sun.

Medical treatment
For minor illnesses, prescription drugs and emergency first aid, pharmacies are generally very competent, but bring from home any medication you usually take, and a copy of the prescription or a doctor's note.

Anything more serious can be treated at a local healthcare building or one of San José's social security hospitals. Costa Rica's public health service is among the world's best, and a profusion of private clinics offer inexpensive dental surgery.

vegetables should be washed, but most restaurants prepare food hygienically.

There are no vaccination requirements for visitors entering Costa Rica, but bus passengers arriving from Nicaragua are sometimes asked to prove antimalarial treatment and/or cholera inoculations (although the latter are now recognized as less effective than being careful over food and water). However, the World Health Organization predicts that cholera will spread again through Central America in coming years, particularly after the devastation wrought by Hurricane Mitch in 1998. Check with your doctor or travel health clinic before being vaccinated, but malaria tablets and yellow fever inoculations are advised, despite claims that malaria has virtually been eliminated. Costa Rica does not pose a high risk of contracting hepatitis, but some adjoining countries do. An inoculation called HAVRIX does not use human blood agents with their associated risk of HIV infection.

Other information

Camping
Campsites with facilities are located inside Santa Rosa, Cahuita, Manuel Antonio, Corcovado and La Amistad national parks. For information contact the Servicio de Parques Nacionales (MIRENEM) in San José, Avenida 8 & 10/Calle 25 (tel: 257-0922 or 192 from within the country). Organized camping trips can be booked at Coast to Coast Adventures (tel: 280-8054, www.ctocadventures.com), or Serendipity Adventures (tel: 877/507-1358 in USA and Canada, or 558-1000 locally, www.serendipity adventures.com).

Clothing
Dressing in layers is the best way of dealing with Costa Rica's constantly changing altitudes and climate. Cotton T-shirts, long-sleeved shirts, trousers and a sweater are the essential basics. A waterproof jacket is needed for higher altitudes and beachwear for the coast. If you plan to trek in rain forest, bring sturdy walking shoes, preferably of canvas with thick rubber soles as they dry out easily, and sprinkle your socks with sulfur powder to deter errant insects. Monteverde's cloud-forest reserves and Tortuguero's lodges all hire or supply rubber boots and rain ponchos. San José's cooler climate requires a jacket or sweater in the evenings. If you are visiting during or near the rainy season, a collapsible umbrella is always useful.

Church of Las Mercedes, Grecia

Electricity
The power supply is 110 volts, 60 cycles AC using flat-pin US plugs. Europeans need to bring adaptors.

Etiquette
Ticos are warm, friendly people who have a clear sense of etiquette. When introduced to someone, shake hands and address them by name if you know it. It is considered impolite to enter someone's house unless you have been invited in, even if the door is wide open—if you are looking for someone, call out *Upe!* first. Avoid wearing beach clothes in towns, and never attempt nude sunbathing.

National Parks
National park entry fees for foreigners range from $4-10, depending on the park. The entry fee goes toward the upkeep of park infrastructure and park employees' wages. For more information contact the Sistema Nacional de Areas de Conservación (tel: 234-0973, www.sinaccr.net)

Photography
Film is expensive, so bring all you can with you. Officially the limit is six rolls. Print film is easily available, but stock up in San José on slide or black-and-white film. Do check expiry dates. Rain and cloud forests need fast film, so take 400 ASA or, better still, 1,000 ASA. Take extra batteries, as these run out fast in warm, humid conditions. Twenty-four-hour processing is available in San José but the quality is poor. Do not allow any exposed or unexposed film through the X-ray machines at Juan Santamaría Airport. Memory cards for digital cameras can be burned to CD in almost any photo shop and internet café for just a few dollars.

Places of worship with Protestant services in English
● Episcopal Church, Zapote (tel: 225-4209)
● Union Church, Moravia (tel: 235-6709)
● International Baptist Church, Escazú (tel: 251-2117, intbapchu@racsa.co.cr)
● Escazú Christian Fellowship, Escazú (tel: 228-9163)

● Unitarian Church, Friends Peace Center, Calle 15/Avenida 6 & 8, San José (tel: 228-1947, scotland@racsa.co.cr)

Roman Catholic Mass in English
● St. Mary's Roman Catholic Chapel, Herradura Hotel, Heredia (tel: 239-0033)

Jewish
● B'Nai Israel (Reform Jewish community), San José (tel: 231-5243)
● Chabad Lubavitch of Costa Rica, Rohrmoser, San José (tel: 296-6565)

Lavatories
Public lavatories are found in bus stations (not the most salubrious), airports, museums, restaurants and most *sodas*. Ask for *servicios*, *sanitarios* or *baños*. Tico plumbing is not elaborate, so used paper is thrown into a wastepaper basket.

Visitors with disabilities
Extreme difficulty of access must be expected, even in towns, where such pavements as do exist are often in bad condition and buildings have no ramps. That said, taxis are inexpensive, internal flights may be an option, and spacious four-wheel-drive vehicles can be rented (at a price).

A few hotels have been designed to accommodate wheelchairs. One such is San José's Hotel Aurora Holiday Inn (tel: 233-7233). Two agencies specializing in tours for visitors with disabilities and can give information on other hotels is Vaya con Silla de Ruedas (tel/fax: 454-2810, www.gowithwheelchairs.com); and the Foundation for Universal Access to Nature in San Isidro, dedicated to removing barriers in the tourist industry (tel/fax: 771-7482, chabote@racsa.co.cr).

Women visitors
Costa Rica is as safe for women as it is for men. Follow normal precautions. Avoid walking on deserted urban streets at night, and be careful about choosing budget hotels in large towns and ports. Some Ticos see *gringas* (foreign women) as easy game, so their gambits should be treated with a large pinch of salt. Otherwise, Costa Rica's extensive tourism infrastructure makes it an unusually relaxing destination for women, alone or in groups.

CONVERSION CHARTS

FROM	TO	MULTIPLY BY
Inches	Centimeters	2.54
Centimeters	Inches	0.3937
Feet	Meters	0.3048
Meters	Feet	3.2810
Yards	Meters	0.9144
Meters	Yards	1.0940
Miles	Kilometers	1.6090
Kilometers	Miles	0.6214
Acres	Hectares	0.4047
Hectares	Acres	2.4710
US Gallons	Liters	3.7854
Liters	US Gallons	0.2642
Ounces	Grams	28.35
Grams	Ounces	0.0353
Pounds	Grams	453.6
Grams	Pounds	0.0022
Pounds	Kilograms	0.4536
Kilograms	Pounds	2.205
Tons	Tonnes	0.9072
Tonnes	Tons	1.102

MEN'S SUITS							
US	36	38	40	42	44	46	48
UK	36	38	40	42	44	46	48
Rest of Europe	46	48	50	52	54	56	58

DRESS SIZES						
US	6	8	10	12	14	16
UK	8	10	12	14	16	18
France	36	38	40	42	44	46
Italy	38	40	42	44	46	48
Rest of Europe	34	36	38	40	42	44

MEN'S SHIRTS						
US	14	14.5	15	15.5	16	16.5 17
UK	14	14.5	15	15.5	16	16.5 17
Rest of Europe	36	37	38	39/40	41	42 43

MEN'S SHOES						
US	8	8.5	9.5	10.5	11.5	12
UK	7	7.5	8.5	9.5	10.5	11
Rest of Europe	41	42	43	44	45	46

WOMEN'S SHOES						
US	6	6.5	7	7.5	8	8.5
UK	4.5	5	5.5	6	6.5	7
Rest of Europe	38	38	39	39	40	41

Tourist services

Outside Costa Rica
● **USA** Dial 866-COSTA RICA to reach English-speaking Instituto Costarricense de Turismo (ICT) representatives, or visit the ICT website: www.visitcostarica.com

Inside Costa Rica
● See Tourist Information panel on page 119 for a listing of ICT offices and information about the ICT.

Selected tour agencies
● **Brunca Tours** San Isidro de General (tel: 771-3100, www.Bruncatours. com). Highly recommended tour company covering the south. Various tours, plus snorkeling, scuba-diving, fishing, rafting, bird-watching, horseback-riding.
● **Coast to Coast Adventures** (tel: 280-8054, www.ctocadventures. com). See the country from Caribbean to Pacific. All travel is on horses, rafts, mountain bikes, and on foot. Custom shorter trips also available.
● **Costa Rica Expeditions** Dept 235, PO Box 025216, Miami, FL 33102-5216 (San José, tel: 257-0766, 222-0333, fax: 257-1665, www. costaricaexpeditions.com). American-owned tour agency. Bird-watching tours to CRE-owned lodges in Monteverde, Tortuguero and Corcovado; rafting trips.

● **Desafio Adventure Center** La Fortuna, Monteverde (La Fortuna tel: 479-9464, Monteverde tel: 645-5874). Pioneers in the La Fortuna area. Multiple river offerings, horseback tours, caving, canyoneering, and tours to indigenous peoples' reserves. Highly recommended.
● **Diving Safaris** (tel: 672-0012, fax: 672-0231, www.costaricadiving. com). Guanacaste-based agency. Diving trips off Playa Ocotal, the Islas Murciélagos, and to Isla del Coco.
● **Expediciones Tropicales** Avenida 11-13, Calle 3 (tel: 257-4171, www. expedicionestropicales.com). Wide variety of tours covering the entire country. Particularly popular for day tours from San José and transportation across the country for reasonable prices.
● **Horizontes** Apdo. 1780, 1002 San José (tel: 222-2022, fax: 255-4513, www.horizontes. com). Reputable tour agency with emphasis on environmental concerns. Nature and adventure tours; tailor-made tours for individuals.
● **Rios Tropicales** (tel: 233-6455, fax: 255-4354, www.riostropicales.com). Rates highly among the country's myriad whitewater operations. Rafting, kayaking and hiking from lodge deep in the Pacuare gorge.

Hotels exuding old-world charm may not be the most comfortable

Hotels & Restaurants

Hotels and Restaurants

HOTELS

Costa Rica's hotels range from basic *cabinas* (literally "cabins" but more often a row of simple, family-owned rooms) to luxury lodges set in vast grounds overlooking the ocean, deep in the rain forest or high in the cloud forest. With a few exceptions, hotels are pleasantly small scale, and in many places will be your base for adventure tours and activities. Outside the main tourist hubs of San José and Manuel Antonio and, to a lesser extent, Guanacaste's and Limón's beach resorts, they are often isolated, requiring private transport or the hotel's own shuttles, charter planes, boats or tractors. Prices per double room or *cabina* are grouped here in three categories:

- **budget** ($) under $35
- **moderate** ($$) $35–75
- **expensive** ($$$) over $75

GUANACASTE

Cañas

Palo Verde Biological Station ($$)
Northern end of Palo Verde National Park
tel: 240-6696 fax: 240-6783
reservas@ns.ots.ac.cr, www.ots.ac.cr
Simple single or double rooms inside the park. Fees include meals and guided tours. Book in advance.

Liberia

Hotel La Siesta ($$)
Calle 4/Avenida 4 & 6
tel: 666-0678 fax: 666-2532
Quiet location in central Liberia. Simple, clean rooms with hot showers and fan or air-conditioning. Small pool, restaurant, laundry service.

Malpaís/Santa Teresa

Cabinas Luz de Luna ($)
tel: 640-0280
Across from the beach, just past the surf shop in Santa Teresa. Small collection of *cabinas* with spacious bedrooms (some with kitchens); decks with hammocks, fans, mosquito nets. Breakfast included.

FlorBlanca Resort ($$$)
tel: 640-0232 fax: 640-0226
www.florblanca.com
On hill at north end of Santa Teresa. Elegant hotel, most popular high-end beach resort in Costa Rica. Ten spacious freestanding suites; Balinese-style outdoor showers amid 3ha (7 acres) of landscaped grounds. Open-air restaurant, surfing, horses, yoga, music, massage; beachfront luxury.

Luz de Vida Resort ($$–$$$)
tel/fax: 640-0319 www.luzdevida-resort.com
Set in forest of banana trees and coconut palms on beach at Santa Teresa. Two-level freestanding *cabinas* with balconies overlooking gardens; interiors have handmade furnishings. Surf good to great.

Milarepa ($$$)
tel: 640-0023 fax: 640-0168
www.milarepahotel.com
Several individually decorated bungalows made of bamboo and teak with antique Indonesian furniture. Beautiful pool area and gourmet restaurant serving Latin-Asian fusion dishes.

The Place ($$)
tel/fax: 640-0001 www.theplacemalpais.com
South of the entry crossroads into town and close to the beach. Handsome bungalows and a contemporary open-air restaurant featuring Latin cuisine.

Montezuma

Hotel Amor de Mar ($–$$)
tel/fax: 642-0262 www.amordemar.com
Easy-going atmosphere in old clapboard house at southern end of village. Simple rooms with shared or private bathrooms, some with hot water, all leading off wooden veranda. Bar/restaurant.

Ylang Ylang Beach Resort ($$$)
tel/fax: 642-0068 elbanano@sol.racsa.co.cr
www.elbanano.com
Landscaped beachfront grounds 3km (2 miles) east of Montezuma. Igloo-style or wooden cabins, all with kitchenette, spring-water showers and terrace. Less expensive rooms. Wholefood restaurant ($) (tel: 642-0638) with new bed-and-breakfast upstairs, run by same people on Montezuma's main crossroads. Formerly called El Saño Banano.

Nosara

Hotel Playa de Nosara ($$)
Apdo. 4 tel: 682-0121
www.nosarabeachhotel.com
Extraordinary Mediterranean-style hotel between Playa Guiones and Playa Nosara. The drawback: a constant, ongoing expansion/renovation. Superb views from pricier rooms with balconies, fans and good bathrooms. Garden, pool, and panoramic restaurant.

Hotel Rancho Suizo Lodge ($$)
tel: 682-0057 fax: 682-0055
www.nosara.com/ranchosuizo
Swiss-run, close to pretty Playa Pelada. Hearty Swiss-style breakfasts included in price. Shady grounds popular with monkeys. Air-conditioning, laundry service, hot tub, and turtle tours in season.

Lagarta Lodge ($$)
Apdo. 18-5233 tel: 682-0035 fax: 682-0135
www.lagarta.com
Small lodge (seven units) on a steep hill overlooking Nosara River and Ostional Preserve; a naturalist's dream. Private reserve, with mangroves and forests, and great views. Rooms are sparse but comfortable.

Villa Mango B&B ($$)
Apto 67-5233 tel: 682-0130
www.villamangocr.com
Just a handful of charming rooms in a cozy villa with sweeping views of Playa Pelada and Playa Guiones. Breakfast included.

Papagayo (Playa Panamá)

Costa Blanca del Pacífico ($$$)
tel: 672-0096
www.costablancadelpacifico.com
Elegant resort with just 28 rooms with ocean views. Two private beaches. Thatched roof bar and restaurant. All inclusive packages.

Four Seasons Resort Costa Rica at Peninsula Papagayo ($$$)
tel: 696-0000, 696-0098 fax: 696-0500
www.fourseasons.com
Luxury resort; 153 rooms including 25 suites. Ocean, bay, garden or forest views from private balconies;

some suites have private pools. Spa, gym, Arnold Palmer-designed golf course, hikes, water sports.

Hotel Giardini di Papagayo ($$$)
tel: 672-0067 fax: 672-0223
www.grupopapapagayo.com
Exclusive resort in Bahía Culebra with lovely surrounding gardens. The beautiful suites with private plunge pools are some of the nicest rooms on Playa Panamá.

Occidental Grand Papagayo ($$$)
POB 48–5000 Guanacaste tel: 672-0193 fax: 672-0041 www.occidentalgrandpapagayo.com
Large luxury hotel on spectacular site overlooking Playa Panamá and Bahía Culebra. Recently remodeled and expanded. Now has 169 rooms, two pools, three restaurants and four bars. Tours, casino. All inclusive packages. Formerly called Costa Smeralda resort.

Parque Nacional Guanacaste

Los Inocentes Lodge ($$)
Apdo. 1370-3000, Heredia tel: 679-9190
fax: 265-4385 www.losinocenteslodge.com
orosina@sol.racsa.co.cr www.arweb.com/orosi
Characteristic old hacienda on cattle ranch with lofty rooms, each with private bathroom across corridor. Verandas with rocking chairs and hammocks for gazing at Volcán Orosí. Some cabins in woods. Pool, restaurant, horseback tours, dynamic young owners.

Parque Nacional Rincón de la Vieja

Rincón de la Vieja Mountain Lodge ($$)
Apdo. 114-5000, Liberia tel: 200-0238
fax: 666-2441 www.rincondelaviejalodge.net
rincon@sol.racsa.co.cr www.guanacaste.co.cr
Wooden lodge in beautiful ranch adjoining national park. Modest rooms with porches and private bathrooms, central eating area for mainly European clientele. Horseback and canopy tours, camping.

Playa del Coco

Flor de Itabo ($$$)
tel: 670-0108 fax: 670-0003
www.flordeitabo.com
Set in gardens on main road leading into resort. Well-equipped rooms with air-conditioning, satellite TV. Facilities include pool and an excellent Italian restaurant. Horseback and fishing tours.

La Puerta del Sol ($$–$$$)
tel: 670-0085
Small Italian-run hotel just 100 yards from the beach. The 10 bright rooms have private living rooms and air conditioning. Italian restaurant.

Playa Flamingo

Flamingo Marina Resort ($$–$$$)
Apdo. 321-1002, San José tel: 231-1858
fax: 290-1858 www.flamingomarina.com
Large resort and marina complex with a variety of comfortable rooms and apartments at varying prices. Pool with swim-up bar and Jacuzzi. Tennis courts. Arranges fishing, diving, biking, golf, snorkelng and various nature tours.

Mariner Inn ($–$$)
tel: 654-4081 fax: 654-4042
mariner@costarica.net
Caters to the fishing set so restaurant/bar can get

rowdy. Rooms pleasant, if small, with ~~~ing, cable TV, fridges, microwaves and ~~~

Sugar Beach Hotel ($$$)
Playa Pan de Azúcar tel: 257-4667~~~
4242 fax: 654-4239 www.sugar.beach.com
Fabulous headland setting with views over rocky offshore islands. Comfortable rooms or bungalows with air-conditioning, fans, porches; hammocks on lovely beach with safe swimming. Excellent, breezy bar/restaurant with stunning sunset views. Transport arranged from Tamarindo Airport or Liberia airport.

Playa Grande

Hotel Las Tortugas ($$$)
Apdo. 164-5051, Santa Cruz tel: 653-0423
fax: 653-0458 www.tamarindo.com/tortugas
Even the pool is turtle-shaped on this turtle-obsessed beach. Reasonable rooms with showers and fan or air-conditioning. Restaurant overlooks beach; turtle-related activities, canoe trips, fishing, scuba diving.

Playa Hermosa

Hotel La Finisterra ($$)
On the hill at the south end of Playa Hermosa
tel: 670-0293 fax: 672-0227
www.finisterra.net
The hilltop locality at Hermosa's south end provides views of Playa Hermosa and the sea. The open-air dining room does Costa-nental food quite well, and breakfast is included in the room charge. Nice bright rooms and a pool.

Hotel Playa Hermosa Bosque del Mar ($$$)
tel: 672-0046
www.hotelplayahermosa.com
Beautiful layout in a howler monkey filled forested area at the southern end of the beach. Extremely comfortable and wonderfully designed rooms including a number of suites with sitting rooms and mini fridges. Beautiful pool area with Jacuzzi. Beachfront restaurant and bar. Many small wonderful touches.

Villas del Sueño ($$–$$$)
tel: 672-0026 fax: 672-0021
www.villadelsueno.com
Not on the beach, but a beautiful spread with Mediterranean style architecture a 100 yards away with lavish tropical gardens and a beautiful pool area. Gourmet restaurant and occasional live entertainment.

Playa Junquillal

La Guacamaya Lodge ($$)
tel: 653-8431 fax: 658-8164
www.guacamayalodge.com
Perched on a hillside off Junquillal's long beach. Excellent bird-watching, tranquil setting, fine moderately priced restaurant, pool, bar. Run by Swiss brother and sister.

Playa Langosta

Barcelo Playa Langosta ($$-$$$)
tel: 653-0363
www.barcelo.com
Large complex of the Spanish resort chain with a number of pools, restaurants, and shops. Access to good surfing, deep sea fishing, and diving. All-inclusive and wedding packages.

s and Restaurants

Cala Luna ($$$)
tel: 653-0214
www.calaluna.com
Stunning collection of 20 luxurious hotel rooms constructed of tropical hardwood and 21 large villas with private pools. Beautiful gardens. Main pool area just off the beach with thatched roof bar.

Sueno del Mar ($$$)
On Playa Langosta just south of Tamarindo
tel/fax: 653-0284 www.sueno-del-mar.com
Decorative, tranquil bed-and-breakfast; one of the great, small hotels in Costa Rica. Pool; wonderful breakfasts. No children under 12.

Playa Negra
Hotel Playa Negra ($$–$$$)
Apdo. 31-5151 Santa Cruz, Guanacaste
tel: 652-9134 fax: 652-9035
www.playanegra.com
A collection of ranch-style *cabinas* surrounding pool, looking out on premier surf breaks, made famous in several movies. Sheltered swimming, horses, fishing, volleyball and a children's pool. The giant rancho in front houses the bar and restaurant.

Playa Ocotal
El Ocotal ($$$)
PO Box 1 Playas del Coco tel: 670-0321/0324
fax: 670-0083 ocotal@centralamerica.com
www.ocotalresort.com
Luxurious hotel in spectacular hilltop location. Well-appointed rooms, suites and bungalows with endless amenities, three pools, Jacuzzis, spa, gym, fishing, scuba diving, sailing, tennis, horseback-riding.

Villa Casa Blanca ($$)
tel: 670-0518 fax: 670-0448
vcblanca@sol.racsa.co.cr
www.ticonet.co.cr/casablanca
Texas-owned, Spanish-style villa with 10 well-decorated, fan-cooled or air-conditioned rooms in garden and pool setting. Several apartments for rent as well.

Playa Sámara
Hotel Giada ($)
tel: 656-0132 fax: 656-0131
www.hotelgiada.net
Italian-owned hotel with cheerful modern rooms, bamboo furniture, balconies, fans. Breakfast.

Guanamar Beach Resort ($$$)
Playa Carrillo tel: 293-4544, 656-0054 fax: 293-2713, 656-0001 hherradu@sol.racsa.co.cr
Large resort hotel geared to anglers. Bungalows with lovely views scattered over terraced slope overlooking beach. Kitsch interior decoration but all possible amenities and activities—including a casino. Popular with Tico politicians.

Hotel Punta Islita ($$$)
Nandayure, San José tel: 296-3817, 656-0472, 231-6122 fax: 231-0715, 656-0471
ptaisl@sol.racsa.co.cr www.puntaislita.co.cr
Exclusive hideaway accessible by charter plane or four-wheel-drive from Sámara. Sensational hilltop location overlooking private beach. Tasteful bungalows and exceptional suites. Beautiful pool/bar; lofty rancho restaurant, reasonably priced with excellent wine list. Colonial-style atmosphere.

Hotel Sámara Beach ($$–$$$)
Apdo. 001, Sâmara tel: 656-0218
fax: 656-0326 www.hotelsamarabeach.com
Two-level hotel overlooking garden and pool. Thatched open-air restaurant and 20 tasteful rooms with baths and bidoto, air conditioning or fan. Great value. Fishing, horses, diving, boat and bicycle rental.

Hotel Villas Playa Sámara ($$$)
tel: 656-0100 fax: 656-0109
www.villasplayasamara.com
Villas (57) each have one to three bedrooms, bath, living room and kitchen, cluster around gardens, pool and quiet beachfront south of town. Hot tub, free windsurfing gear. Restaurant, bar, shop. Snorkeling, waterskiing, diving; horseback and other tours.

Playa Tamarindo
Hotel Capitan Suizo ($$$)
tel: 653-0075 fax: 653-0292 capitansuizo@ticonet.co.cr www.hotelcapitansuizo.com
Beautifully designed, white bungalows, with beds on raised platforms, teak furniture, huge windows and luxurious bathrooms. Less expensive rooms in main block. Large open-air restaurant and bar by pool, close to beach at southern end of Tamarindo.

Hotel Jardín del Eden ($$$)
Apdo. 1094-2050, San Pedro tel: 653-0137
fax: 653-0111 www.jardindeleden.com
Italian-French ownership. Landscaped Mediterranean-style hotel overlooking beach. Two free-form pools, swim-up bar. Restaurant with European cuisine. Small, comfortable rooms, air-conditioning, terrace and pretty bathrooms. Large breakfast included.

Hotel Nahua ($-$$)
tel: 653-0010 fax: 653-1033
www.hotelnahua.com
Chic and friendly small hotel a block off the beach. Variety of rooms surround a gorgeous pool area.

Hotel Pasatiempo ($$–$$$)
tel: 653-0096 fax: 653-0275
www.hotelpasatiempo.com
Up the hill, past the crossroads. Relaxed Tamarindo standard with rooms and bar/restaurant wrapped around roomy pool. The bar is a popular hang-out.

Tamarindo Diria Beach and Gold Resort ($$$)
tel: 653-0032 fax: 653-0208
www.tamarindodiria.com
Pre-Colombian statues surround the gorgeous pool area. This large beachfront resort has had a stunning renovation and is now the best hotel in Tamarindo. The 110 rooms line both sides of the road with some on the beach and some on the hill.

Hotel Zullymar ($$)
tel: 653-0140 fax: 653-0028
zullymar@sol.racsa.co.cr www.tr5.com/zullymar
Expanding locally owned complex with a variety of rooms in different price categories. Good central location. Beachfront restaurant.

Playa Tambor
Playa Tango Mar Beach Resort ($$$)
SJO 684, box 025216, Miami FL 33102 tel: 289-9328, 683 0001 fax: 288-1257, 683-0003
tangomar@sol.racsa.co.cr www.tangomar.com
Nine holes of golf, good surfing, and handsome rooms and villas. Great views, horseback tours, pool and fine dining room; waterfall and pristine beach nearby.

Tambor Tropical ($$$)
tel: 683-0011 683-0013 tambor@aol.com
Five hexagonal two-level cabins handcrafted by owner. Open-plan living/bedroom space, with kitchen area, bathroom, terrace and veranda. Set in coconut palms by pool overlooking beach. Horses, snorkeling, fishing.

Río Tempisque
Hotel Rancho Humo ($$–$$$)
Puerto Humo tel: 255-2463 fax: 255-3573 ecologic@sol.racsa.co.cr
On banks of Tempisque River, not far from Palo Verde, Lomas Barbudal and Barra Honda. Superb views. Thatched cabins with shared bathroom or air-conditioned rooms in main lodge. Restaurant, pool, boat tours, horseback-riding, hiking in private reserve.

THE NORTH
Fortuna de San Carlos
Hotel San Bosco ($$)
tel: 479-9050 fax: 479-9109 www.arenalvolcano.com
The nicest place in La Fortuna itself. Two pools, cable TV, gym, hot tub; comfortable, tasteful rooms.
Montana de Fuego ($$–$$$)
En route from La Fortuna to Arenal tel: 460-1220 fax: 460-1455 www.montanadefuego.com
The nicest—and priciest—hotel on the road from La Fortuna to the volcano, offering nifty wooden bunga-lows featuring enclosed porches with superb volcano views. Restaurant, pool, whirlpool.
Tilajari Resort Hotel ($$$)
Apdo. 81-4400, San Carlos tel: 469-9001 fax: 469-9095 www.tilajari.com
Sprawling resort in a somewhat featureless land-scape, offset by splendid volcano views, flower gardens, fabulous bird-watching, and croc-watching in the San Carlos River. Some suites include kitchens and/or balconies; all open onto lovely gardens.

Guápiles
Hotel Rio Palmas ($)
opposite EARTH college, Pocora tel: 760-0305, 760-0330 fax: 760-0296
A good half-way stop between San José and Limón. Small, clean rooms, most with hot showers and TVs. Adjoining private reserve with trail. Rooms flank a lovely courtyard with a fountain and tropical garden. Good restaurant.

Laguna de Arenal
Hotel Tilawa ($$–$$$)
Nuevo Arenal tel: 695-5050 fax: 695-5766 www.hotel-tilawa.com
At western end of lake, a large colonnaded hotel with windsurfing and kite-boarding station down dirt road. Restaurant, bar, pool, tennis, and generously proportioned rooms, some with kitchenettes. Horses and mountain bikes; boat tours to volcano. Weekly package rates.
La Ceiba Tree Lodge ($–$$)
Apdo. 9, Tilarán tel: 814-4004 fax: 692-8050 ceibldg@racsa.co.cr
Named for ancient ceiba tree in grounds. Four comfortable, bright *cabinas* fronted by porch with hammocks and chairs in spectacular scenic position

high above lake. Extensive, well-tended gardens and organic farm surround the steep access track from lake road. Well signposted from road.
Mystica Lodge ($$)
near Nuevo Arenal tel: 692-1001 fax: 692-1002 www.mysticasanctuary.com
Six comfortable, large rooms, with hot-water bath-rooms, open onto front veranda with lovely lake views and cooling breezes. Good Italian restaurant.

Monteverde/Santa Elena
Cabinas Eddy ($)
100 m sw of the supermarket in Santa Elena tel: 645-6618 www.cabinaseddy.com
Clean rooms with private hot baths. A good option if you are just turning up or everything else is full.
El Establo ($$–$$$)
tel: 645-5110 fax: 645-5041 www.hotelelestablo.com
Beautiful modern resort and spa set in a 60ha (150 acre) farm with 50% protected primary forest beside the reserve. All rooms have views of the Gulf of Nicoya. Has its own canopy tour on its grounds.
El Sapo Dorado ($$$)
between Santa Elena and Monteverde tel: 645-5010 fax: 645-5180 www.sapodorado.com
Well-designed and -appointed cabins in landscaped grounds beside main road. Classical music; vege-tarian cuisine available. Owners and operators of Sendero Tranquilo Reserve; additional forest trails on hotel grounds.
Finca Valverde ($$)
Santa Elena tel: 645-5157 fax: 645-5216 www.monteverde.co.cr
Family-run complex of spacious log cabins in forest off main road. Good bird-watching trails. Bar is popular meeting place for American volunteers.
Hotel Fonda Vela ($$–$$$)
Apdo. 7-0060-1000, San José tel: 645-5125 fax: 645-5119 www.fondavela.com
At base of hill leading to Monteverde Cloud Forest Reserve. Twenty-eight well-designed rooms with porches in landscaped grounds. Restaurant, horse-back-riding and sunset views to Gulf of Nicoya.
Monteverde Lodge & Gardens ($$$)
tel: 257-0766 645-5057 fax: 257-1665 www.costaricaexpeditions.com
Beautifully landscaped property near the Cloud Forest Reserve. Rooms have splendid views, plus solar-heated baths. Hotel restaurant (tasty, but pricey meals); adjacent bar great for comparing notes on bird sightings. Hot tub; hiking trails; tours arranged.
Tree House Hotel ($–$$)
In the center in front of the Catholic Church tel: 645-5751 www.canopydining.net
Seven comfortable rooms with private hot water baths above one of the most popular restaurants in the heart of Santa Elena. Cable.

Parque Nacional Volcán Poás
Poás Volcano Lodge ($$–$$$)
tel: 482-2194 fax: 482-2513 www.poasvolcanolodge.com
Elegant old manor house near Vara Blanca offering luxurious bed-and-breakfast. Has recently had a face lift to include a new British-built bar, arts and crafts studio, sauna, and new rooms.

Hotels and Restaurants

Puerto Viejo de Sarapiquí

Gavilán Sarapiquí River Lodge ($$)
Apdo. 445-2010, San José
tel: 776-6743, 234-9507 fax: 253-6556
www.gavilanlodge.com
Pleasant log cabins in lovely peaceful grounds by a river. Open-air restaurant, Jacuzzi, small private reserve. Horseback and boat trips, guided hikes.

Posada Andrea Cristina ($)
Apdo. 14, Puerto Viejo tel/fax: 766-6265
www.andreacristina.com
Relaxed, friendly family-run *cabinas* in lush garden just west of village. Simple rooms with showers, fan, terrace, excellent breakfast. Boat tours, horseback-riding. Very good value. Only four rooms and five bungalows so book ahead.

Rara Avis ($$–$$$)
Sarapiquí tel: 253-0844, 256-4993
fax: 764-4187 www.rara-avis.com
Legendary private reserve founded in 1983 (see page 80). Stay at rustic research station, El Plástico, or at more luxurious Waterfall Lodge in comfortable rooms. Access by tractor from Las Horquetas, south of Puerto Viejo. All-inclusive rates.

Selva Verde Lodge ($$$)
Chilamate tel: 766-6800 fax: 766-6011
www.selvaverde.com
A long-established rain-forest lodge, set back from main road, 8km (5 miles) west of Puerto Viejo, with elaborate walkways in superb private reserve, popular with bird-watching groups. Butterfly enclosure, botanic garden, reference library. Open-air restaurant. Well-conceived rooms; some of the bungalows are set in the forest.

Refugio Nacional Caño Negro

Albergue Caño Negro ($$)
Los Chiles tel: manager's bleeper, 225-2500
fax: 461-8442
Superb, isolated setting in private reserve 10km (6 miles) south of Los Chiles and 6km (4 miles) west along rough track. Four-wheel-drive in dry season, tractor in rainy season. Comfortable wooden cabins, overlooking lagoon by Río Frío, sleep five. Open rancho restaurant. Horses, fishing, boat trips, perfect for bird-watchers.

Tilarán

Cabinas El Sueno ($)
Tel: 695-5347
Quiet, low-budget gem. Upstairs rooms surround central fountain. Every room has private bath and hot water, and owners provide toiletries and fruit baskets. The Parque Restaurant downstairs serves excellent seafood.

Volcán Arenal

Arenal Lodge ($$–$$$)
tel: 253-5080 fax: 253-5016 (San José)
tel: 460-1881 fax: 460-6119 (on site)
www.arenallodge.com
Atmospheric lodge 18km (11 miles) west of La Fortuna up a steep hill. Comfortable, attractive suites and older rooms are all bright and clean with wicker furniture and good bathrooms. New Arenal Hanging Bridges are close by.

Arenal Observatory Lodge ($$–$$$)
tel: 692-2070 fax: 692-2074 (lodge)
tel: 290-7011 fax: 290-8427 (reserve)
www.arenal-observatory.co.cr
About 10km (6 miles) south of main road along rough track requiring four-wheel-drive. Simple, rustic rooms with bunk beds and hot showers, set among pine and eucalyptus trees with fantastic views of the rumbling monster. Buffet-style restaurant, tours.

Arenal Volcano Inn ($$)
6.5km north of La Fortuna
tel: 461-2021 fax: 461-1133
www.arenalvolcanoinn.com
Fifteen comfortable rooms all with clear views of the volcano. Pool and Jacuzzi, busy restaurant and pizzeria, and nice gardens surround the hotel.

Tabacón Grand Spa and Thermal Resort ($$$)
12 km north of La Fortuna
tel: 519-1900
www.tabacon.com
The main focus of this all out luxurious five-star resort is their series of thermal pools and spa set at the base of the volcano with one of the best views possible. Their 114 guestrooms are among the most expensive in the country. A member of the Leading Hotels of the World.

THE CENTER

Alajuela

Hotel Orquídeas Inn ($$–$$$)
about 2km (1.5 miles) northwest of Alajuela
tel: 433-9346 fax: 433-9740
www.orquideasinn.com
Convenient for airport (10 minutes away). Reasonably well-appointed and decorated rooms, some with air-conditioning, some with fans. No children, maybe because of the inn's Marilyn Monroe bar?

Xandari Resort and Spa ($$$)
5 km north of Alajuela tel: 443-2020
www.xandari.com
This luxurious spa has 22 large villas with each a unique design by US architect Sherril Broudy and artist Charlene Broudy. Set amid 16 ha (40 acres) of private gardens and numerous pools, this is one of the top hotels in the country and only a short drive from the airport.

Cerro La Muerte

Savegre Mountain Hotel ($$–$$$)
Apdo. 482, Cartago tel: 740-1028 fax: 740-1027 www.savegre.co.cr
Popular hotel run by the exceptionally friendly family that pioneered the magical valley of San Gerardo de Dota. Clean *cabinas* with hot baths, large dining area for family-style meals, all-inclusive rates. Apple orchards, trout fishing and quetzals.

Trogon Lodge ($$)
Apdo. 10980-1000, San José tel: 293-8181
fax: 239-7657 www.grupomawamba.com
Part of the Mawamba group of lodges. Family-run, comfortable, rustic cabins with heating and hot showers by a river in the beautiful mountain valley of San Gerardo de Dota. Home cooking, trails, quetzals.

Escazú

Hotel Alta ($$$)
Escazú, on the road to Santa Ana
tel: 282-4160 www.thealtahotel.com
Luxurious new boutique hotel in Las Palomas over-
looking the central valley. First class service and
amenities. Just 23 rooms with terracotta balconies
and an Italian tiled pool. Gym. La Luz gourmet
restaurant and a 500-bottle wine cellar.

Hotel Pico Blanco Inn ($$)
Apdo. 900, tel: 228-1908 fax: 289-5189
www.picoblancoinn.com
Sprawling British-owned country inn with fabulous
views high up in San Antonio. Comfortable, white-
washed rooms and good bathrooms. Reasonably
priced restaurant, pool, terraces.

**Tara Resort Hotel, Spa & Conference
Center ($$$)**
San Antonio de Escazú tel: 228-6992
fax: 228-9651
Play at Scarlett O'Hara in this porticoed, Beverly
Hills-style fantasy. Health and spa treatment,
horseback-riding, pool, plush rooms, international
cuisine in restaurant.

Esterillos

Cabinas Flor d'Esterillos ($$)
D'Esterillos Este, Apdo. 41–6300, Parrita
tel: 778-8045 business@racsa.co.cr
Québecois-owned beach hotel in large garden with
pool. Freestanding *cabinas* with high ceilings, nicely
decorated, fans and hot showers. Same rates for
two or four people. Restaurant and relaxed
cocktail bar.

Hotel Monterey del Mar ($$$)
tel: 778-8787 www.montereycr.com
Sprawling beachfront high-end hotel at Esterillos
Este, built on a cattle ranch. Horseback tours of the
ranch, nearby primary forest, mountain trails and the
beach. Ultra-light aircraft school offers flights over
mountains and along the coast.

Heredia

Aparthotel Valladolid ($$–$$$)
*Calle 7/Avenida 7 tel: 260-2905 fax: 260-
2192 valladol@racsa.co.cr*
Spanish ambience. Very comfortable rooms with
cable TV, kitchenette, good showers. Rooftop
Jacuzzi with views over Central Valley, spectacular
sunsets from bar. Adjacent restaurant. Helpful
tour desk arranges all-inclusive three-day tour
packages.

Bougainvillea ($$$)
9 km east of Heredia
tel: 244-1414 www.bougainvillea.co.cr
Set amidst 4ha (10 acres) of tropical gardens and
just 15 minutes from downtown San José. Large art
collection. Pool. Free shuttle service.

Jacó

Hotel Copacabana ($$–$$$)
Apdo. 150, Playa Jacó
tel/fax: 643-3131
www.copacabana.hotel.com
A walk away from central Jacó, with idyllic beachfront locale plus pool. Upstairs sea-facing rooms
best for views and breezes. Sports bar with satellite TV. New wing of ocean-fronted rooms.

Los Sueños Hotel and Golf Club ($$$)
*At Bahía Herradura tel: 637-8886 fax: 637-
8895 www.lossuenosresort.com*
This stunning residential and entertainment
complex is centered on a 200-room hotel, run by
Marriott with a Spanish colonial theme and a
marina with space for roughly 200 yachts. The
beach was used for the scenes of the movie *1492:
Conquest of Paradise*.

Hotel Zabamar ($–$$)
tel: 631-3174
Quiet little two-level hotel just off the main strip;
offers welcome sanctuary from the hustle and
bustle. One minute from the beach. Rooms have
air-conditioning and cable TV. Restaurant/bar
features Mexican food and excellent tequila.
Secure parking.

Villa Caletas ($$$)
Apdo. 12358-1000, San José tel: 257-3653
fax: 222-2059 caletas@ticonet.co.cr
One of Costa Rica's most extraordinary luxury
hotels, perched on hilltop between Tárcoles and
Jacó. Oozes old-world charm and taste, antique
furnishings, superb design, spectacular views.
Comfortable, individual villas, with air-conditioning,
but still no phones or radios; pool melts into
horizon; hosts classical music and jazz recitals.
French-Tico ownership. Fine bar/restaurant ($$).

Playa Hermosa

Hotel Terraza del Pacifico ($$–$$$)
tel: 643-3222 fax: 643-3424
www.terazadelpacifico.com
Two floors of guest rooms encircle pools, the
restaurant/bar faces the beach and the beach
fronts some of Costa Rica's finest waves. Excellent
surfing with stadium lights for night surfing. Air-
conditioning, cable TV and secure parking.
Children's pool, canopy tour; hotel is a popular
wedding venue.

Manuel Antonio

Hotel Arboleda ($$–$$$)
*Apdo. 211-6350, Quepos tel: 777-1056, 777-
1385 fax: 777-0092 www.hotel-arboleda.com*
Hectares of forested grounds spill downhill to
private beach. Wide price range, from budget
rooms with shared bath to comfortable beachfront
cabins. Tours, pool, two restaurants, horseback-
riding, fishing.

Hotel Casitas Eclipse ($$$)
tel/fax: 777-1738 fax: 777-0408
www.casitaseclipse.org
Fresh, tastefully decorated Mediterranean-style villas
in lush tropical garden around pool. Ground-floor
air-conditioned suites with kitchenette and good
bathrooms; double rooms upstairs with large
terraces. Restaurant ($$) with 360-degree panoramic
views serves barbecued seafood and meat, and
international cuisine. Gregarious Tico owner.

Hotel Costa Verde ($$–$$$)
tel: 866-767-7958 (US/Canada), 777-0584
fax: 777-0560 www.hotelcostaverde.com
Comprises older building and new building offering an
assortment of rooms, most with splendid views,
some with kitchens and balconies. Hikes on private
trails through rain forest. Three pools, two restaurants, three bars, plenty of monkeys.

199

Hotels and Restaurants

Kekoldi Beach Hotel ($–$$)
4km (2.5 miles) from Quepos on the road to the park tel: 248-0804 www.kekoldi.com
From the same owners of Kekoldi in San José, this hillside complex of villas is just minutes from the beach and park. Comfortable rooms surround a nice pool area with frequent bird and monkey sightings.

Hotel La Mariposa ($$$)
tel: 777-0355 fax: 777-0050 www.lamariposa.com
A bit over-built these days, but still Manuel Antonio's exclusive hotel. Rooms or villas; rates include breakfast and dinner. Furnishings of vivid hues. Open-air bar/restaurant commands Manuel Antonio's best ocean views.

Makanda by the Sea ($$$)
Apdo. 29, Quepos tel: 777-0442 fax: 777-1032 www.makanda.com
Ultra-contemporary tropical-wood villas in extensive jungle overlooking ocean. Ten-minute trail to private beach, lovely pool. All villas and studios are fully equipped for hire. No children under 16. Great restaurant. Californian owner.

Si Como No ($$)
2.5 km (1.5 miles) from Quepos on the road to the reserve tel: 777-0777 fax: 777-1093 www.sicomono.com
Beautiful and distinctive design with many unique amenities including a 46 seat THX theater, stained glass windows, a solar heated Jacuzzi, two pools with swim up wet bars, spa, net café, and butterfly gardens. Very distinctive.

Parque Nacional Volcán Irazú

Hacienda San Miguel ($–$$)
In Rancho Redondo tel: 229-5058
Twelve-room rustic hacienda with a variety of accommodations and a great pool area. Set directly on the continental divide, so you can see species from the Atlantic and Pacific coasts.

Puntarenas

Costa Rica Yacht Club ($–$$)
Cocal tel: 661-0784 fax: 661-2518 www.costaricayachtclub.com
Fan-cooled or air-conditioned rooms and bungalows with phone, hot water. Pool, parking, laundry, restaurant, tours, yacht charters, fishing, marina. Book ahead.

Hotel Portobello ($$)
tel: 661-1322 fax: 661-0036
On estuary near Yacht Club east of town. Charming, atmospheric hotel in lush tropical gardens. Comfortable rooms with bath, TV, phone, and air-conditioning. Good open-air bar/restaurant, pool, parking, mooring.

Quepos

Hotel Plinio ($$)
tel: 777-0055 fax: 777-0558 www.hotelplinio.com
Little gem that's been around for years. Built on a steep hillside; feels like a hand-crafted treehouse, all polished wood and breezy views. Suites are double-level and spacious. Private nature trail leads to hilltop watchtower. Restaurant serves elegant Thai food. Pool, barbecue.

Rancho Casa Grande ($$)
Near the airstrip tel: 777-3130 www.ranchocasagrande.com
Stunning new resort in an isolated setting near the rain forest. Rooms are in villas, bungalows, and suites. Stylish pool with open air restaurant and bar.

Carara National Park

Hotel Villa Lapas ($$$)
tel: 222-5191 fax: 222-3450 www.villalapas.com
Unadulterated nature in private forest reserve adjoining Carara. Lodge with 47 spacious, gabled rooms, excellent bathrooms, fans, safe. Small pool; riverside trail. Open-air restaurant serves international cuisine; bar. A bird-watchers' paradise. All inclusive.

San José

Casa Roland ($$)
tel: 231-6571 fax: 290-5462 www.casa-roland.com
Beautiful boutique hotel with contemporary décor in a restored colonial house. Rooms have private baths and cable. Suites with Jacuzzis. Breakfast included.

Hemingway Inn ($$)
Avenida 9/Calle 9, Interlink 670, PO Box 02-5635, Miami FL 33102 tel/fax: 221-1804 (reservations only) www.hemingwayinn.com
Lovingly converted home in Barrio Amon. Built in 1920s as hacienda; opened as bed-and-breakfast in mid-1990s. Rooms (17) have free internet access, hot tub, cable TV; gourmet restaurant next door.

Hotel Dunn Inn ($$)
Avenida 11/Calle 5 tel: 222-3237, 222-3426 fax: 221-4596 www.hoteldunninn.com
Small hotel in 1900s house. Simple, comfortable rooms. Restaurant, patio bar safety boxes, tours.

Hotel Don Carlos ($$)
Avenida 7 & 9/779 Calle 9, Dept 1686, PO Box 025216, Miami FL 33102 tel: 221-6707 fax: 255-0828 www.doncarloshotel.com
Once the home of a Costa Rican president, conjures old, coffee-baron San José like no other place. Courtyard, lounge and deck; statuary and parrots. Pool, excellent gift shop. Rooms vary in size.

Gran Hotel Costa Rica ($$$)
Avenida 2, Calle Central tel: 221-4000 www.granhotelcr.com
Right in the heart of the city center beside the national theater. Wonderfully restored to its former grandeur. The building is a national historic landmark and where John F. Kennedy stayed during his 1963 visit. 24-hour street café is quite popular. Casino and conference facilities.

Hotel Grano de Oro ($$$)
Avenida 2 & 4/Calle 30 tel: 255-3322 fax: 221-2782 www.hotelgranodeoro.com
Charming luxury hotel in renovated 1920s mansion full of plants and vintage photos. Excellent conservatory restaurant spilling into small garden. Roof-top Jacuzzi. Tasteful rooms and three suites, all no-smoking. Efficient, friendly staff. Book well ahead.

Kekoldi ($$)
Avenida 9, Calle 5-7 tel: 248-0804 www.kekoldi.com
Charming boutique hotel in an art deco building with a private garden in Barrio Amon. Ten elegant rooms with cable, wifi, safes, and private hot water baths.

Occidental Torremolinos ($$$)
Avenida. 5, Calle 40 tel: 222-5266
fax: 255-3167 www.occidentalhotels.com
In a quiet location near Parque La Sabana and a five minute walk from downtown. The 84 rooms are getting a bit worn, but are still first class with all modern amenities. Popular with business travelers.

Hotel Rosa del Paseo ($$–$$$)
tel: 257-3258 fax: 223-2776
www.rosadelpaseo.com
Former coffee baron's mansion on Paseo Colón near west end of town (toward airport), now an inviting small hotel. Private baths, TV, phones.

San Ramón

Villa Blanca ($$$)
tel: 228-4603 fax: 228-4004
www.villablanca-costarica.com
Well-appointed rooms with balconies in charming *casona*; bathrooms, fridge, fireplace, desks. Buffet-style meals, hiking and horseback-riding.

THE CARIBBEAN

Barra del Colorado

Río Colorado Lodge ($$$)
tel: 232-4063, 800/243-9777 fax: 231-5987
www.riocoloradolodge.com
Founded for serious fishermen by Archie Fields. Sophisticated boats, experienced guides. Labyrinthine walkways, zoo, gardens. Lively atmosphere; hearty meals.

Silver King Lodge ($$$)
tel: 381-1403 www.silverkinglodge.com
Luxurious accommodations, world-class food, and a nice pool area make staying at one of the world's best Tarpon fishing lodges that much easier. Top of the line rods, reels, and boats.

Cahuita

Atlantic Surf ($)
50m (50 yards) from park entrance
tel: 755 0116
Simple cabins with mosquito nets, fans, private baths, and hammock laden porches just steps from the national park.

Atlántida Lodge ($$)
tel: 755-0115 fax: 755-0213
Comfortable, rustic rooms with insect screens in peaceful garden near Playa Negra. Large pool, boutique, laundry, breakfasts, bar, tours, parking, internet access.

Aviarios del Caribe ($$–$$$)
tel: 750-0775 fax: 750-0725
www.ogphoto.com/aviarios
Fantastic private reserve, great hiking trails through private wildlife sanctuary, bird-watching river trips, and pet sloth Buttercup in dining room.

Magellan Inn ($$)
Apdo. 1132, Puerto Limón tel/fax: 755-0035
Intimate, stylish hotel at northern end of Cahuita. Elegant rooms with fans, patio, real American hot showers. Gardens with pool, full bar, restaurant.

Puerto Limón

Hotel Matama ($$–$$$)
Playa Bonita tel: 795-1123, 795-1409
Well-appointed, if slightly run-down, air-conditioned rooms across from scenic beach north of town. Garden, pool, international restaurant, tours.

Park Hotel ($–$$)
Avenida 3/Calles 1 & 3 tel: 798-0555
fax: 758-4364
On the waterfront a few blocks from the middle of town. Breezy, with spacious sea-view dining room. Seaside rooms—which are cooler, prettier, and have balconies, breezes and/or air-conditioning—are worth the extra expense.

Puerto Viejo

Almendras y Corales (Almonds & Coral Lodge Tent Camp) ($$)
Punta Uva/Manzanillo tel: 272-2024
fax: 272-2220 www.almondsandcorals.com
Astonishing tent lodge in jungle with walkways to wild beach. Raised, screened platforms, basic comforts, shared showers. Back-to-nature experience. Restaurant.

Hotel Buganvillea Resort ($$)
Punta Cocles
tel: 750-2012 www.buganvillearesort.com
Twelve cozy rooms with air conditioning, satellite TV, set in a heavily forested area a few blocks from the beach. Pool with sauna and solarium. A number of tours and packages are available.

Cabinas Almendros ($$)
50m (50 yards) north of the bus stop
tel: 750-0235 flchwg@racsa.co.cr
Modern, comfortable rooms with air conditioning and cable at moderate prices. A good find in Puerto Viejo although lacking any real character.

Casa Verde ($–$$)
tel: 750-0015 fax: 750-0047
www.cabinascasaverde.com
Popular German-run *cabinas* in middle of village. Hardwood rooms, porches with hammocks, hot water, ceiling fans, lush gardens.

Playa Chiquita Lodge ($$)
tel: 750-0062 fax: 750-0408
www.playachiquitalodge.com
Ten tranquil *cabinas* in dense vegetation; 50m (55 yard) trail to beach. All rooms have hot shower, screens, fan, veranda. Open-air restaurant. Snorkeling, fishing, jungle tours. Houses for rent.

Shawandha Lodge ($$$)
tel: 750-0018 fax: 750-0037
www.shawandhalodge.com
Ten exquisitely designed wooden bungalows in jungle setting across from Playa Chiquita; restaurant serves well-prepared international/French cuisine. Tours, hiking, surfing, horseback-riding, snorkeling.

Tortuguero

Mawamba ($$$)
tel: 293-8181 fax: 239-7697
www.grupomawamba.com
Located 800m (87 yards) north of village; grounds back onto beach. Well-maintained cabins, large dining room, luxuriant gardens, pool. Pleasant staff; good guide service. Two- or three-day packages from San José.

Miss Junie ($$)
tel: 710-0523
New *cabinas* on the main path through the village. Private showers, fans, but small rooms. Adjoining restaurant.

Hotels and Restaurants

Tortuga Lodge and Gardens ($$$)
tel: 257-0766, 222-0333 fax: 257-1665
www.expeditions.co.cr
Across the canal from Tortuguero's airstrip, north
of the national park. Complete package tours,
including flight from San José. Wonderful cabinas,
dining room and deck, new pool, expert guides,
varied tours.

THE SOUTH

Bahía Drake

Cabinas Jinetes de Osa ($$–$$$)
*tel: 800/317-0333, 371-1598, 236-5637,
396-4405 www.drakebayhotel.com*
Eleven-unit lodge (six with shared bath) provides
diving packages, lessons, PADI certification
courses. Price includes three meals. Excellent
location over beach and close to river.

Drake Bay Wilderness Camp ($$–$$$)
tel: 770-8012 fax: 221-4948
www.drakebay.com
Twenty cabins in lush jungly headland at southern
end of Bahía Drake. Canoes, kayaks, fishing,
horses, scuba diving. Bar/restaurant.

Marenco Beach and Rainforest Resort ($$)
tel: 258-1919 fax: 255-1346
www.marencolodge.com
Tico-owned 1,500ha (3,700-acre) reserve bordering
Corcovado. Comfortable wooden cabins in pristine
jungle with ocean views. Good restaurant. Friendly
staff. Guided hikes to Corcovado; beach, snorkeling, boat trips. All-inclusive packages from San
José via Sierpe.

Dominical

Cuna del Angel ($$$)
9km (55 miles) south of Domincal
tel: 222-0704 www.cunadelangel.com
Beautiful German-owned boutique hotel and spa with
lots of unique touches such as mosaic tiles, sculptures, and architectural designs based on Boruca
tradtions. Idyllic beachfront and rain forest setting.

Hacienda Barú ($$)
tel: 787-0003 fax: 787-0057
www.haciendabaru.com
Near beach north of Dominical in reserve (see panel
page 153). Six family cabins, with kitchenette, living
room, bathroom, veranda. Great forest and beach
tours, canopy tours, camping.

Hotel Diu Wak ($$–$$$)
tel: 787-0087 fax: 787-0089 www.diuwak.com
On beach crossroads in garden with hot tub. Clean,
simple *cabinas* with decent bathrooms, fans, porch.
Family suites also available.

Villas Escaleras ($$$)
Las Escaleras tel: 787-0031
www.villas-escaleras.com
Appears like a mirage in stunning, isolated spot overlooking Pacific, 400m (1,310ft) above Dominical.
Californian owners have accomplished building miracles. Very comfortable, tasteful rooms, cabins.
Private pools for various villas. Four-wheel-drive
recommended.

Villas Río Mar ($$$)
Playa Dominical tel: 787-0052 fax: 787-0054
www.villasriomar.com
Ambitious Dutch-owned hotel in beautifully

landscaped grounds up the river from town. Forty
well-appointed thatched bungalows with generous
curtained verandas but undersized bedrooms.
Large pool and swim-up bar, rancho restaurant,
tennis, gym, bicycle hire.

Golfito

Complejo Turistico Samoa del Sur ($$)
tel: 775-0233 fax:775-0573
www.samoadelsur.com
Sky-high ranchos in a waterfront spot. Newly styled
and offering clean, spacious rooms with cable TV
and air-conditioning. Marina, yacht club, restau-
rant/bar with handicraft museum, souvenir shop,
pool table. Sportfishing, kayaking, bicycle rentals.

Esquinas Rainforest Lodge ($$$)
La Gamba tel: 775-0901
www.esquinaslodge.com
Exceptional ecotourism project in depths of rain
forest, now a national park (see page 155). Ten
comfortable, rustic cabins in gardens with pool. Well-
designed restaurant, all-inclusive rates. Trails and
numerous excursions.

Hotel El Gran Ceibo ($)
tel: 775-0403 fax: 775-2303
www.hotel-elgranceibo.com
Good low-budget spot on the water at the edge of
town. Comfortable rooms, air-conditioning, cable TV,
pool. Tour office in the restaurant/bar next door.

Playa Nicuesa Lodge ($$$)
25 minutes north of Golfito
tel: 735-5237 www.nicuesalodge.com
Set between the gulf and rain forest on the border
of Playas Blanca National park. Just four fantastic
cabins and four rooms. Very eco-friendly and laid-
back. Gourmet meals based on local ingredients
and seafood. If you can get a room you won't go
wrong.

Parque Internacional La Amistad

Finca Anael ($)
Reserva Biológica Dúrika tel: 730-0657
www.durika.org
Rustic cabins high in remote Talamanca Mountains.
Exceptional ecological farm project (see page 169),
all-inclusive prices from Buenos Aires, good value.
Reservations necessary.

La Amistad Lodge ($$$)
Reserva Las Tablas tel: 290-2251
fax: 232-1913 amistad@sol.racsa.co.cr
www.laamistad.com
Lovely old home in private reserve bordering La
Amistad. Comfortable rooms, sitting area, family
atmosphere. Guided hiking, bird-watching and
horses. Four-day packages from San José.

Parque Nacional Chirripó

Posada del Descanso ($)
San Gerardo de Rivas tel/fax: 771-7962
Budget lodgings with shared bathroom, hearty
meals, horses, guides available.

Parque Nacional Corcovado

Corcovado Tent Lodge Camp ($$$)
*Playa Madrigal. Contact: Costa Rica Expeditions,
San José tel: 257-0766, 222-0333*
fax: 257-1665 costarica@expeditions.co.cr
www.expeditions.co.cr

Screened tents on raised platforms in jungle clearing overlooking beach near park entrance. Facilities include shared bathrooms, restaurant, boat trips, guided hikes. An adventure experience. Two- or three-day packages by charter plane.

Luna Lodge ($$–$$$)
Near Carate tel: 380-5036 www.lunalodge.com
Eight thatched roof bungalows with private terraces deep within primary rain forest. Lavish spa and wellness center with yoga, tai-chi, and many new age activities and workshops. Will arrange nearly any type of tour or activity on the Osa peninsula.

Pavones

Casa Siempre Domingo ($$)
tel: 820-4709 tel/fax: 775-0631
A small inn south of town, up a hillside, with four guest rooms. Pricier than basic in-town *cabinas* catering to the surf crowd. Breezy, great views, satellite TV; price includes breakfast and dinner. No credit cards.

Tiskita Lodge ($$$)
Bahía Pavones tel: 296-8125
fax: 296-8133 tiskita@sol.racsa.co.cr
www.tiskita-lodge.co.cr
Last stop in the deep south, located on Punta Banco south of Pavones. Packages from San José by charter plane. Ten rustic cabins overlooking unspoilt beach, experimental fruit farm, private reserve with trails, great bird-watching.

Playa Zancudo

Cabinas Los Cocos ($$)
tel/fax: 776-0012 www.loscocos.com
In town, but secluded location just off the beach. Two new units, and a pair of banana plantation houses moved here and reborn as bungalows with large verandah, bedrooms and kitchens. Boogie boards, kayaks, and boat taxi and tours available.

Cabinas Sol y Mar ($–$$$)
Apdo. 87, Golfito tel: 776-0014
fax: 776-0015 www.zancudo.com/sol_cab
Well-designed German-owned hotel on beach. Four comfortable rooms with fans, hot showers, screens, verandas. Good restaurant, boat tours, safe swimming. Two-bedroom house for rent; camping.

Puerto Jiménez

Bosque del Cabo ($$$)
Cabo Matapalo tel/fax: 735-5206
www.bosquedelcabo.com
Tranquil spot above the cape in private reserve, with trails and lawns rolling down to the sea. Six cabins, garden showers, screens, large deck, hammocks. Full board, horses, kayaking, fishing, bird-watching.

Cabinas Puerto Jiménez ($–$$)
tel: 735-5090, 735-5152
www.cabinasjimenez.com
The rooms and bungalows were remodeled in 2004. Each has air-conditioning, private hot water baths, and art from local artists. Some have private balconies overlooking the gulf. Pleasant sculpted tropical gardens.

Lapa Ríos ($$$)
Apdo. 100, Puerto Jiménez Box 025216, SJO-706 Miami, FL 33102 tel: 735-5130 fax: 735-5179 www.laparios.com

Fourteen thatched bungalows with garden showers, screened walls. Extensive rain-forest reserve with trails, restaurant, look-out point, nature tours, boat trips. A tropical paradise (see panel page 168).

Playa Preciosa Lodge ($$)
Playa Platanares, c/o Souvenir Corcovado Shop tel/fax: 735-5165, 735-5062 fax: 735-5043
www.playa-preciosa-lodge.de
Twelve cleverly designed thatched cabins with good bathrooms, porches with hammocks. Isolated beachfront location 6km (4 miles) from town, extensive gardens, orchards, fresh spring water, look-out point, restaurant, horses, kayaking, scuba diving.

San Isidro de El General

Hotel Country Club del Sur ($$)
tel: 771-3033 fax: 771-0527
Large hotel complex on Interamerican Highway just south of San Isidro. Family-oriented sports facilities, pool, restaurant, bar. Well-appointed rooms, wheelchair accessible.

San Vito

Hotel El Ceibo ($–$$)
tel: 773-3025 fax: 773-5025
Large, modern hotel with popular restaurant by central crossroads. Nice, well-furnished rooms with hot showers at back of main block overlooking forest. Cheaper *cabinas* have cold water. Good restaurant.

Sierpe

Hotel Oleaje Serena ($$)
Sierpe de Osa tel: 786-7580 fax: 786-7111
oleajeserena@racsa.co.cr
Canadian-owned hotel beside embarkation point on Río Sierpe. Ten rooms with hot showers and fan or air-conditioning. Open-air restaurant. Tours to Isla del Caño, Corcovado, and mangrove swamps.

Rio Sierpe Lodge ($$$)
tel: 384-5595 fax: 786-6291
www.riosierpelodge.com
About 24km (15 miles) downstream from Sierpe village, with 17 rooms. Specializes in fishing and diving trips; charter packages include guides, gear, boats. Trails into rain forest, tours, restaurant with recreation area, library.

Uvita

Hotel Posada Playa Tortuga ($$–$$$)
tel: 384-5489
Excellent small hotel with 10 secluded rooms (seven more to come) in a colonial-style building. Just 75m (80 yards) from superb beach; 500m (550 yards) from the highway. DVD players, air-conditioning, balconies with hot tubs, pool, gourmet restaurant, internet café.

Hotels Villas Gaia ($$)
tel: 244-0316, www.villasgaia.com
Perhaps the best resort between Manuel Antonio and the Osa Peninsula, particularly since the coastal road has been paved. Twelve cozy *casitas* each sleeping up to four people. Set in tropical surroundings with a private jungle trail leading to Playa Tortuga. Hill top swimming pool with great ocean views.

203

RESTAURANTS

Outside San José, most of the better restaurants are attached to mid-range or luxury hotels, (see pages 194–203). Otherwise, budget *sodas* are the classic haunts of Ticos. Food is good value.

The restaurants recommended below are divided into three price categories:
● budget ($)
● moderate ($$)
● expensive ($$$)

GUANACASTE

Liberia

Pizzeria da Beppe ($)
Avenida Central/Calle 10 tel: 666-0917
A Liberian institution in verdant setting. Great pizza with wide choice of toppings cooked in wood oven.

Playa Tamarindo

La Caracola ($$) *tel: 653-0583*
This resto-bar is one of the trendiest options in town and has daily drink specials and live entertainment.
Fish and Meat ($$)
tel: 653-0535
Asian fusion dishes and often has "all you can eat" sushi nights.

Playa del Coco

Couleur Café ($$)
tel: 670-1696
Refined French and contemporary cuisine in an intimate tropical garden setting.

Playa Hermosa

Ginger ($$$)
On the main road to Playa Panama
Pan-Asian fusion restaurant and tapas bar, the most exciting restaurant at Playa Hermosa.

Playa Ocotal

Father Rooster Bar and Grill ($$)
On the beach
tel: 670-1246 www.fatherrooster.com
Lively and rustic with burgers, sandwiches, seafood, and margaritas and other beachside cocktails.

THE NORTH

Fortuna de San Carlos

La Vaca Muca ($)
tel: 479-9186
Great Tican/neo-Latino food at good prices. Located on the edge of town en route to the volcano.

Monteverde/Santa Elena

Tree House Restaurant ($-$$)
Santa Elena tel: 645-6751
Popular Tico-owned restaurant built around a huge Higuerón tree. *Casados*, Mexican, pizza and salads.

THE CENTER

Escazú

Café de Artistas ($)
South of Plaza Rolex tel: 288-5082
Popular breakfast and lunch spot that's home to a community of artists and hosts live music.
La Luz ($-$$$)
tel: 282-4160
In Hotel Alta on old road to Santa Ana. Refined menu fusing local ingredients in myriad ethnic styles. Reservations recommended.

Manuel Antonio/Quepos

El Gran Escape ($-$$$)
tel: 777-0395 fax: 777-0765
www.elgranescape.net
On waterfront in Quepos. Three meals ranging from *tipico* Tico to all-American; plentiful fresh fish, generous servings, lively bar, and sushi bar around corner (dinner only; closed Thu).

San José

Bakea ($-$$$)
Calle 11 & Avenida 7, Casa 956
tel: 221-1051 www.restaurantebakea.com
Fusion restaurant and coffee house part of the slow food movement. Influences range from French and Mediterranean to Asian and Caribbean.
Restaurant Le Chandelier ($$$)
About 100m (110 yards) southwest of ICE building tel: 225-3980 fax: 253-8984
San José's top restaurant, preferred by politicians and diplomats for its private rooms, art and antiques.
Macchu Picchu ($$)
Avenida 1 & 3/Calle 32
tel: 222-7384
Authentic Peruvian cuisine, with an emphasis on seafood, wonderful *ceviches*, intense hot sauce. Very popular; reservations recommended.
Park Café ($$$)
Sabana Norte
tel: 290-6324 www.richardneat.blogspot.com
Cutting-edge restaurant in a colonial house. Owner Richard Neat is the most celebrated chef to open up in Costa Rica. Tapas only.

THE CARIBBEAN

Cahuita

Miss Edith's ($$)
One of the best Caribbean restaurants in the country. Always busy, in a hidden corner of town. Rondon, curries, chicken and fish.

Manzanillo

Maxie's ($-$$)
tel: 759-9073
The upstairs dining room at Maxie's offers views, sea breezes, and fabulous seafood. Try a lobster.

Puerto Viejo

El Loco Natural ($$)
tel: 750-0263
Eclectic and creative world cuisine with an organic tangent.

THE SOUTH

Dominical

Su Raza ($)
tel: 787-0108
Formerly Soda Laura, and an institution. Fruit salads and local dishes in simple setting at heart of village.

Bold figures denote the main entry of a particular subject.

Index

207

Q
Quaker community 77
Quepos 90, **108–109**
quetzal 49, 68

Index

208

Publisher's Acknowledgements

The Automobile Association would like to thank the following photographers, libraries and associations for their assistance.

CLIVE SAWYER (AA PHOTO LIBRARY) took all the pictures in this book except those listed below.

AA PHOTO LIBRARY 28c, 31b. NICHOLAS SUMNER 13b, 132c, 184. ASSOCIATED PRESS 13a. BRUCE COLEMAN COLLECTION Front cover (top left, top right, bottom right), Back cover. COSTA RICAN EMBASSY 12, 13b. CORBIS 33b. DANITA DELIMONT/ALAMY 173e. DUNLOP 19a, 22b, 43, 45, 46b, 62, 131, 141, 148, 155a, 158b, 166b, 167b, 192, 193. JOHN CANCALOSI/ NATUREPL.COM 151. MARY EVANS PICTURE LIBRARY 25a, 28/9, 32. THE NATIONAL MARITIME MUSEUM 29a, 30, 31a, 31c. NATIONAL MUSEUM OF COSTA RICA 25b, 26b, 27a. NATURE PHO-TOGRAPHERS LTD 16a, 16b, 17a (P R Sterry), 24a (B Burbidge), 48a, 48b, 48c, 49a, 49b, 49c, 49d (P R Sterry), 56a (J Sutherland), 57 (A J Watson), 58a, 58b (P R Sterry), 60a (S C Bisserot), 80 (K Carlson), 82a (A J Cleave), 91a (S C Bisserot), 109 (P R Sterry), 143b, 144/5, 145a, 145b, 157a (P R Sterry), 161a (E A Janes), 163a, 166a (P R Sterry), 172a, 172b (K Carlson), 172c (P R Sterry), 173a (K Carlson), 173c (S C Bisserot), 173d, 173f (E A Janes). TOPHAM PICTUREPOINT 35a, 35b.

The Automobile Association would also like to thank Journey Latin America, 14–16 Devonshire Road, Chiswick, London (tel 020-8747 8315) for their help.

Author's Acknowledgements

The author, Fiona Dunlop, would like to thank the following for assisting her in the preparation of this book: Janina Rovinski at the Costa Rican Embassy, Paris; Alfredo Oporta & Susana Orozco at ICT; inspired driver, Jorge Chacon; equally inspired botanist, René Menjivar; the efficient staff of Horizontes Tours; dedicated environmentalist, Dario Castelfranco; hotel manager *extraordinaire*, Loic Dervieu; sloth-sleuth, Jessica Johnson; and countless well-disposed and helpful inhabitants of Costa Rica.

Photographer's Acknowledgements

The photographer, Clive Sawyer, would like to thank the following for their assistance and help in making the photography of Costa Rica a great experience: Ines Trejos at the Embassy of Costa Rica, London; Fernando Chavarria of Costa Rica Top Tours, San José; Eric Maze, guide, San José; Christian Fassler and Pascale Berchmaear of Switzerland, who helped carry bags, mend cars and navigate through the wilds of Costa Rica.

Contributors

Revision editor: Apostrophe S Limited   Original copy editor: Susi Bailey
Revision Verifier: Nicholas Gill